JIM CROW AND THE WILSON ADMINISTRATION

10-20-12

Dear Ruthann,

I am so happy to present you with a copy of my book. Thank you for everything you do to make Bethany Theological Seminary what it is, and the deeply meaningful experience that it has been for me and that it will continue to be as my seminary experience progresses. Shalom,
Nick

JIM CROW AND THE WILSON ADMINISTRATION

Protesting Federal Segregation in the Early Twentieth Century

NICHOLAS PATLER

UNIVERSITY PRESS OF COLORADO

Published by the University Press of Colorado
5589 Arapahoe Avenue, Suite 206C
Boulder, Colorado 80303

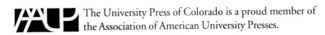 The University Press of Colorado is a proud member of
the Association of American University Presses.

The University Press of Colorado is a cooperative publishing enterprise supported, in part, by Adams
State College, Colorado State University, Fort Lewis College, Mesa State College, Metropolitan State
College of Denver, University of Colorado, University of Northern Colorado, and Western State
College of Colorado.

∞ The paper used in this publication meets the minimum requirements of the American National
Standard for Information Sciences—Permanence of Paper for Printed Library Materials. ANSI Z39.48-
1992

Library of Congress Cataloging-in-Publication Data

Patler, Nicholas.
  Jim Crow and the Wilson administration : protesting federal segregation in the early twentieth
century / Nicholas Patler.
      p. cm.
Includes bibliographical references (p.) and index.
   ISBN-10: 0-87081-760-4 (hardcover : alk. paper)
   ISBN-13: 978-0-87081-864-6 (pbk. : alk. paper)
   1. African Americans in the civil service. 2. African Americans—Segregation. 3. Protest move-
ments—United States—History—20th century. 4. Wilson, Woodrow, 1856–1924—Views on
African Americans. I. Title.
   JK723.A34P38 2004
   323.1196'073'009041—dc22
                                                                                    2003025086

Design by Daniel Pratt

16   15   14   13   12   11   10   09   08   07   10   9   8   7   6   5   4   3   2   1

To the children:
Ashley, Mackenzie, Jalyn, Amber, Morgan, Samuel, Jonah, Cierra, Nathan, Adika, Gabrielle, Katie, Jonathan, Sarah, Caressa, Annie, Darick, Trisha, Jeffrey, Kayla, Christopher, Angel, Kiersten, Brittni, Gavin, April, Andrew, Allison, Jackie, Madison, Cole, Ryan, and baby Izaiah, and to my amazing sister, Shannon

Hope lies in the possibility that our children will learn to love rather than condemn.

Contents

List of Illustrations   *ix*

Preface   *xi*

Acknowledgments   *xiii*

A Note on Usage   *xvii*

Introduction: "Set Apart as Lepers"   *1*

1   The Return of the South   *9*

2   The Color Line Is Drawn in Washington:
The NAACP Prepares for Battle in New York   *54*

3   Jim Crow in the White House   *72*

4   The NAACP Launches Its Campaign Against Jim Crow   *90*

5   "Meeting Foes in Human Form": William Monroe
Trotter, the NIPL, and the Crusade for Freedom   *117*

6   Nerney Goes to Washington, Grimke Takes on Jim Crow   *154*

7   The Finale at Washington: Mr. Trotter and Mr. Wilson   *175*

8   The Struggle Moves On   *196*

Selected Bibliography   *217*

Index   *227*

LIST OF ILLUSTRATIONS

"Shall the Negro Rule!" flyer, *La Follette's Magazine,* August 1913   *42*

Protest petition as it appeared in the *Boston Guardian*   *106*

Political cartoon of Trotter meetings with President Wilson,
Boston Guardian   *188*

Plates following page 116

JIM CROW PROPONENTS

Rare picture of Woodrow Wilson, previously unpublished

Ellen Axson Wilson

Albert Burleson

John Skelton Williams, *left,* and William Gibbs McAdoo, *right,* previously
unpublished

JIM CROW PROTESTORS

Rare picture of William Monroe Trotter

Rare picture of W.E.B. DuBois, Harvard entrance photograph

Senator Edwin Moses Clapp. Photo by Charles Zimmerman

Booker T. Washington

Oswald Garrison Villard

Ida Wells-Barnett

Archibald Grimke

IN 1992 I ATTENDED ONE OF THE ANNUAL FORUMS on Woodrow Wilson and his times at Mary Baldwin College in Staunton, Virginia. One of the main speakers that year was the late Dr. Arthur Link. I was honored to have had the opportunity to hear in person this prolific Wilson historian who, in addition to having written a mountain of articles and books on the twenty-eighth president, had edited the enormous sixty-six-volume *Papers of Woodrow Wilson*. After the speakers had finished their addresses, audience members were given the opportunity to participate in a question-and-answer session.

Although numerous questions were asked that day, most of which I have long since forgotten, one in particular, and the vague answer that followed, would stick in my mind for many years. In fact, the unsatisfactory answer to this question from the Wilson scholars eventually inspired me to write my graduate school thesis and this subsequent book on the subject brought up that day. It went something like this: "Could any of the speakers talk about Wilson's racial attitude toward blacks, particularly the enforced segregation of black federal employees during his administration?" This audience member also referred to the inconsistency between Wilson's ardent defense of individual freedom and equality at home and abroad and the poor treatment of blacks in America, especially their declining status in the federal government during his administration.

I did not hear a good explanation that day. Although Dr. Link admitted that this racial attitude was "a blemish on the Wilson administration," it seemed the speakers in general tiptoed around the topic, and the consensus was, in so many words, "Why focus on this negative aspect of the Wilson years when he accomplished so many positive things?"

Almost seven years later, when I finally began to look into federal racial segregation during the Wilson administration, I was astounded by the findings. Not only were African Americans segregated en masse in federal departments during the Wilson years, but in many cases they were harassed, downgraded, and terminated as well. Yet the most amazing thing I found was that African Americans refused to accept the Jim Crow arrangement being forced on them in federal departments without a tenacious fight. African Americans and white sympathizers launched a collective protest, which at its height included tens of thousands of people and strategically challenged the spread of federal discrimination. For a moment in history, moreover, the protestors shook the edifice of American Jim Crow, and they made the world listen. This book will attempt to tell that story.

ACKNOWLEDGMENTS

I AM ENORMOUSLY GRATEFUL for all of the assistance and inspiration I received during this project. My first debt is to the participants in the Wilson protest, not only the leaders but also those who in the course of everyday life lent their voices and energies to protest federal racial segregation by conducting a rally, signing a petition, or writing a letter. Their passion and determination for racial justice in an early-twentieth-century America dominated by powerful racism are inspiring to say the least. These, along with their predecessors, were the prophets of freedom foretelling the end of racial oppression in their land.

I cannot express enough appreciation for my academic advisers when this book was in its earliest stages as a graduate thesis. Historian Donald Ostrowski, research adviser in social sciences at Harvard Extension School, and Stephan Thernstrom, distinguished Winthrop Professor of History at Harvard College, were very supportive and made their wisdom available at every step of the research process. I am humbled to have had men of their caliber as mentors.

Throughout this project, Sandy Crooms at the University Press of Colorado (UPC) and Kerry Callahan, formerly of UPC and now with the University of Illinois Press, were very enthusiastic and offered much encouragement. I owe them and the entire staff of UPC a dept of gratitude for their patience with my never-ending requests for extensions and for guiding the intensive review process.

I am thankful to the following for their assistance in finding materials, answering questions and requests by postal mail and e-mail, and opening their facilities to me during this project: the staff in the Manuscript Division at the Library of Congress, Leida Torres and the staff at the Moorland-Spingarn Research Center at Howard University, Cathy Lynn Mundale of the Robert W. Woodruff Library at Atlanta University, John C. Johnson of Mugar Memorial Library at Boston University, Robert Chapel of the University of Illinois at Urbana-Champaign, Al Thibeault and John Cronin at the Boston Herald Traveler Library, the staff at Houghton Library of Harvard University, and Lucinda Eddy and the staff at the Woodrow Wilson Birthplace Museum in Staunton, Virginia, for giving me access to their sixty-six-volume *Papers of Woodrow Wilson*. I also thank the staff at the Main Reading Room of the Library of Congress for their assistance; the staff at Widener Library of Harvard University, especially one enthusiastic librarian who eagerly helped me find some elusive material and whose name I do not know; Walter Hill at the Civil Service Commission; John K. VanDereedt and Wayne DeCesar at the National Archives; and the William Monroe Trotter Institute in Boston, Massachusetts.

Enough cannot be said about the wonderful personal support and assistance I received during this project. First and foremost, I express my sincere gratitude to my dear friend Hilary Fuksa of Wichita, Kansas, who cheerfully gave invaluable assistance by meticulously reviewing this book for structure and format. Her stimulating comments led me to view some aspects of my research from a different perspective. Thomas Burress of Staunton, Virginia, a black historian and intellectual who participated in the modern civil rights movement, read drafts of this book and provided encouragement in my research. Burress, in my opinion, is one of the great thinkers on issues that affect his race, and it is a travesty that he lives in relative obscurity. I feel honored to know him. I warmly thank my aunt, Dr. Laten Bechtel of Staunton, Virginia, for reading drafts of this book and providing invaluable insight. She and my uncle, Charles Bechtel, made it possible for me to finish this book as well as my graduate studies after a long illness. I am forever grateful. My mother, Alice Patler, was a source of inspiration during my graduate academic career and was a sounding board while I was writing the thesis and this book. I cannot find words to express my deep appreciation for her support. And my friend, the Rev. Ted Koehl, formerly of Fishersville, Virginia, gave much support—technical and moral—during the earliest stages of this project. His pastoral gifts have since taken him to upper Michigan.

I do not want to leave out my two good friends, Yvonne Mussington, whose unique life experiences as an African American woman stretch from the streets of Harlem to the rural landscapes of the Deep South where she adamantly refused to go to the back of a bus during the days of segregation in Tuscaloosa, Alabama, and Kim Craig, a single mother who struggles to make it from day to day. They both listened intently as I often rambled on about discoveries in my research, and they provided stimulating exchanges. I would also like to mention two courageous African American women. The first, Rita Wilson, is from my hometown, Staunton, Virginia—the same small town, incidentally, where Woodrow Wilson was born a few years before the Civil War. One day in 1965, years before becoming the first female African American to serve on the city council, Mrs. Wilson took her two daughters to an all-white school and managed to enroll them as students, thus helping to bring about integration in the Staunton Public Schools. Her quiet yet powerful presence and determination have always been an inspiration to me. And I wish to honor my friend Margaret (Peggy) Trotter Dammond Preacely of San Pedro, California, grandniece of the most courageous fighter for black equality of the early twentieth century—and perhaps the most courageous ever—William Monroe Trotter. Mrs. Preacely boldly carried her great-uncle's passion into the modern civil rights movement as an active member of the Student Nonviolent Coordinating Committee and a dedicated Freedom Rider, and, like her great-uncle, she was jailed while trying to bring freedom to her people. She continues to be a civil rights, freedom, and peace activist to this day.

Last but not least, I thank my God who lifted me out of an abyss to inspire me throughout this project and beyond.

A Note on Usage

THE READER SHOULD BE AWARE of the way in which several terms are used in this book. First, *federal Jim Crow*, a term used over and over in this book, refers to the segregation, downgrading, harassment, and dismissal/termination of African Americans with civil service status because of their race. Also, I often refer to the protest of federal Jim Crow as the *Wilson protest*. This does not imply that Woodrow Wilson was entirely responsible for federal Jim Crow. Taking his involvement for granted, it simply denotes the fact that the protest was directed at his administration.

I have chosen to use the terms *African American, black,* and *black American* interchangeably in this book. My desire was to utilize the most appropriate term that seemed best suited for the word/sentence structure and the context of the topic in which the term is used. Also, since the Wilson protest occurred so long ago, quotations and remarks from that time period will reflect the language of the day. Some of these are *colored, Negro* or *negro,* and *Afro-American,* as well as a few racist expletives mostly from southern newspapers. And although I use the term *race* in this book, I am at pains to do so.

Race seems mostly a negative concept that has no basis in reality other than as a historical phenomenon. That is because the term has been misused historically and even today to designate a fixed biological meaning or physical fact, and it has created division after division among humanity in designating and often demonizing the other.

In this book the term *liberal whites* refers to those whites who supported and advocated equal rights for African Americans during the Progressive Era. I also use this term interchangeably with *white sympathizers* when referring to these white protestors.

Although the term *liberal* has sometimes been applied historically to the leaders who advocated, supported, and implemented the system of Jim Crow during the Progressive Era, most historicism has referred to white racial reformers as *liberal whites*. I have chosen as well to use the same reference within the context of this book.

Finally, the protestors in this book are often referred to as *radicals*. It seems odd at first that such a term should designate those who advocated democratic rights for African Americans—normative rights all Americans cherished. That seems hardly a radical notion. But the fact that 90 percent of African Americans were driven by force to relinquish these rights and to challenge and resist such injustice, which had been accepted by much of the white majority, was nothing short of radical. Moreover, protestors such as William Monroe Trotter and W.E.B. DuBois even called themselves *radicals* to revive the spirit of the old abolitionist days in the new movement demanding black equal rights and an end to racial injustice.

JIM CROW AND THE WILSON ADMINISTRATION

INTRODUCTION: "SET APART AS LEPERS"

FEDERAL JIM CROW WAS THE CULMINATION OF A SOUTHERN TREND and in many respects a national trend as well. In 1896 the judicial branch of the federal government, in the notorious decision *Plessy v. Ferguson* (163 U.S. 537), had given its blessing to the customary segregation practices states and localities had been engaging in for years. And interestingly, in a court dominated by men from the North and the West, the lone dissent in this decision came from one of only two southerners sitting on the highest bench in the land—a former slaveholder who blamed his colleagues and southern states for stamping African Americans with "a badge of servitude." By 1910, black disfranchisement had almost completely swept the South under the silent and sometimes not too silent approval of the North—including the U.S. Supreme Court, which turned the other way as African Americans suffered political repression in a region that held their rights as citizens, if not their humanity, in utter disdain. And although the federal legislative branch had not passed any discriminatory legislation before the Wilson years, various members of Congress—including some from the

North—frequently sponsored Jim Crow bills. About a month before Woodrow Wilson's inauguration, the House of Representatives, controlled by the Democrats, passed a bill making it a felony for whites and blacks to marry in the District of Columbia. Although the bill failed to pass in the Senate, one racial reformer called it "the most extreme piece of legislation along the color line acted upon favorably by either branch of Congress since slavery was abolished."[1]

Yet during this time, the executive branch of the federal government, perceived by many African Americans as a "court of last resort where equal and even-handed justice would be given," had to some degree transcended racial prejudice by opening the gates of federal employment to all races. Moreover, there seemed to be much less discrimination against African Americans here than in the private sector.[2] During the 1880s and 1890s, as states and localities in the South began the codification process of segregating and disfranchising African Americans and sought to remove the black officeholders of Reconstruction, the federal government—or more specifically the executive branch—moved in the opposite direction by appointing African Americans to federal and diplomatic offices and employing increasing numbers in the executive departments. What is more, African Americans were sometimes the direct target of federal recruitment campaigns, and legal and policy changes that occurred in federal job sectors—particularly in the late nineteenth century—along with the efforts of friendly politicians who lobbied on their behalf for federal employment (often at the insistence of black constituents), gave African Americans access to thousands of jobs previously off limits.

The chief executive's role in regard to Jim Crow is a little more ambiguous. He at times openly challenged the racist norms of the day, at others pandered to white supremacists, and sometimes simply remained aloof. But it appears that no president going back to at least the Chester Arthur administration had officially sanctioned a Jim Crow policy. This would change once Woodrow Wilson entered office. The early Wilson years saw for the first time leaders in the executive branch of the federal government, including the president, openly support and directly implement a Jim Crow course of action in federal departments.

Before the Wilson years, the civil service examination had created if not an even playing field for blacks and whites in federal job competition, at least the best means of economic advancement for African Americans where the two races interacted competitively in any significant number. This process of competition and subsequent advancement was severely curtailed for African Americans almost everywhere else. In their groundbreaking 1931 study, *The Black Worker,* Sterling Spero and Abram Harris found that the "most distinctive characteristic of the Negro's position in the world of labor is his relegation to occupations in which he does not compete with white workers."[3] In contrast, the practice of using merit testing in filling federal job vacancies and needs had largely erased the color line. Although there was certainly racial discrimination in federal employment practices prior to Woodrow Wilson's presidency, as would remain long after, the exam had made it much more difficult for Jim Crow to become the norm. In open and fair competition, thousands of African Americans had demonstrated that they were not only as good as their white counterparts but in many cases even better by outscoring whites on civil service exams.

In the opinion of A. L. Glenn, a historian and one of the founders of the first black federal labor organization, the National Alliance of Postal Employees, the exam had "given the Negro a splendid opportunity to compare his mental and physical capabilities with the Anglo-Saxon."[4] Blacks regularly scored as well as whites on civil service examinations and in some cases made the highest scores in the country. The civil service exam was the one unbiased test, when administered fairly and impartially to both blacks and whites, that in retrospect reversed the findings of the many popular racist scientific studies of the day that claimed over and over that African Americans had low IQs. As a result, by 1912 the federal government was the largest single employer of African Americans in the country, and they occupied numerous positions in almost every area of the government—a striking refutation of the then all-encompassing myth of black inferiority.

With Wilson's victory in 1912, the South was swept into power for the first time in fifty years, and Jim Crow became more widespread than ever before in the federal government. There appears to have been a real movement in Washington and federal departments throughout the South to segregate African Americans regardless of their meritorious achievements and in some cases to downgrade or eliminate them altogether. "Here for the first time since slavery days," wrote Morton Sosna, "the Negro's traditional and only source of hope in a hostile white society—the federal government—had turned against him."[5] This was made even more painful by the fact that for the first time in U.S. history, the largest segment of the eligible voting black population—an estimated 20 to 30 percent—had defected from the party of Abraham Lincoln and instead supported the Democrat Wilson for president.[6] Once proud of their small role in Wilson's victory and looking forward to a New Freedom—Wilson's ubiquitous campaign slogan—the African American leadership now felt embarrassed and betrayed. Not only was Jim Crow mustering its way into the executive branch, but their active support of Wilson during the election had contributed inadvertently to their demise in federal departments.

This time, however, Jim Crow would face its greatest challenge to date. African Americans and liberal whites launched a collective protest—on a scale not seen since the abolition movement—that strategically challenged federal Jim Crow by means of petitions, pamphlets, appeals in the press, publicity campaigns, mass meetings, letters, lobbying, and direct confrontation and by galvanizing communities. In one case, protestors marched through Boston to express their opposition. Remarkably, the numbers of those attending mass protest meetings in the Wilson years were sometimes commensurate with those in the modern civil rights era.

Of course, by this time aggressive protest had historical precedents in black history, some in the not too distant past. In addition to the active black opposition to colonization schemes in the early 1800s and militant black protest and leadership in the abolition movement—both using the methods and tactics listed in the previous paragraph—not to mention the slave insurrections and escapes, African Americans in the late nineteenth and early twentieth centuries openly protested against racial injustice, sometimes sporadically and sometimes collectively, through careful planning. Interestingly, some of these protests used sit-ins and boycotts to challenge Jim Crow rules, statutes, and laws. Beginning in the 1870s, African Americans made deliberate attempts to sit in the white sections of trains, streetcars, restaurants, and theaters or refused altogether—individually and collectively—to patronize discriminatory white businesses. These protestors included the tenacious black equal rights leader Ida Wells-Barnett, who famously refused to give up her seat to a white man on a Tennessee train in 1884, and many lesser-known everyday rebels such as the burly Laura Smith, weary from the daily grind and blistering heat one summer day in 1904, who snapped, "I ain't gwine to do it" when instructed to go to the back of a streetcar in Richmond, Virginia. And incredibly, between 1900 and 1906, fifty years before the modern civil rights movement, African Americans strategically boycotted Jim Crow streetcars and trolleys in more than twenty-five southern cities—including Montgomery, Alabama, where in 1902 the local streetcar company was "so hard hit that it temporarily suspended enforcement" of the Jim Crow ordinance.

Most of these boycotts were organized around packed mass meetings held in churches, given publicity by the black and sometimes white press; some even attracted national attention and support. The white Richmond *News Leader,* keeping an eye on the boycott in the former Confederate capital in 1904, expressed amazement at the dogged determination of its African

American citizens—"young and old, little and big"—who daily "marched" with their feet in protest of Jim Crow "street-car rules."[7]

During the entire history of black protest in America—whether moderate or aggressive and regardless of the methods and tactics used, and even when more accommodating attitudes or positions were adopted toward racial exclusion—African Americans always felt racial injustice was "humiliating" because it presumed they were inherently "inferior." This was expressed over and over in the historical literature, perhaps nowhere with such passion and consistency as in the protest of federal Jim Crow in the Wilson administration. With this in mind, the title of the Introduction to this book, "Set Apart as Lepers," was an often-used idiom with which African Americans described their humiliating treatment by Jim Crow in the federal government. For African Americans, steeped in the language and imagery of the Holy Bible, the term *leper* had a powerful symbolic and negative connotation. In the pages of the Old and New Testaments, those with leprosy were forced to live in virtual isolation—set apart from their family, friends, and community, indeed forbidden any human contact at all. To depict their mistreatment by the government with such a dreadful comparison meant African Americans took that mistreatment very personally.

This book will focus on the protest of federal Jim Crow during the early Wilson years, 1913–1914. It will primarily deal with the two national organizations, fairly new on the scene but ready to fight, that led the protest campaign during those years: the National Association for the Advancement of Colored People (NAACP) and William Monroe Trotter's National Independent Political League (NIPL). Both the NAACP and the NIPL served as umbrella organizations as well as the engines in this protest movement and included thousands of individuals and a multitude of black, white, and interracial groups, societies, leagues, churches, and organizations—many of whose members, brought together to voice their opposition to federal Jim Crow, belonged to one or both of the organizations.

Although this book is primarily concerned with the strategy and methods used in the Wilson protest, one cannot write about this movement without taking into account the backgrounds and personalities of the protest leaders. Like the race leaders in the modern civil rights movement and perhaps even more so, the passions and egos of those earlier leaders are inextricably linked to the protest itself and in some cases were wholly responsible for affecting certain stages of the protest. For example, in his second meeting with President Wilson at the White House, on November 12, 1914, the outspoken and impassioned black leader William Monroe Trotter stimulated national controversy by arguing toe-to-toe with the president over the rampant spread of Jim Crow in federal departments. He boldly declared that African Americans were protesting segregation not in the "attitude of dependent wards of the nation, but as full-fledged American citizens, absolutely equal with all others."[8] Not only had Trotter expressed the defiantly independent spirit arising among the newer generation of discontented black Americans, but he also managed to put Wilson on record as unquestionably favoring federal segregation, and almost every newspaper in the country noted his shocking behavior.

This book also considers the times in which the protest occurred, including the rise of protest and racial uplift organizations and the environment of intense racism that plagued African Americans in the Progressive Era.

Social historians, for the most part, have overlooked the protest of federal Jim Crow during the early Wilson years. Much of the scholarship that has touched upon the subject is superficial and, in the absence of serious research, contains errors in its analysis and conclusions. Many historians have restricted the focus of their analysis to Wilson and the Democratic Congress while ignoring or minimizing the role protestors had in challenging federal Jim Crow. Worse still, any mention of the protest and participants has been generally negative.[9]

Historian Kathleen Wolgemuth, writing over forty years ago, is an exception, and I am very grateful for her early research on the subject. In an article appearing in the *Journal of Negro History* in April 1959, "Woodrow Wilson and Federal Segregation," Wolgemuth wrote a brief yet incredibly accurate account of federal Jim Crow during the early Wilson years and of the protest that followed. "That the protest was a large one was clear," she wrote. "Moreover its weapons were sharp. Its arguments were serious, thoughtful analyses of the present and potential threat federal segregation presented."[10] In many ways Wolgemuth's work served as a model for this book, and although our conclusions differ, it is my ambition to expound on her research and provide an in-depth analysis of the Wilson protest.

The Wilson protest has also suffered from historical obscurity, unable to find a place among latter movements for political and social change, particularly in the postmodern civil rights era. Ira De A. Reid, writing at the dawn of the modern civil rights movement, offers one explanation as to why the first half of the twentieth century posed a problem for his contemporaries, and perhaps for black history in general, in viewing early collective efforts for political and social change: "The patent fact seems that racial leadership has been identified with individual achievement . . . rather than with group activity directed toward group goals."[11] More detrimental in my opinion, however, is the fact that historicism has habitually castigated early-twentieth-century African Americans for their inability to work collectively. They have been too often portrayed as undermining their own group progress by petty squabbles, selfish personal and class ambitions, bitter opposition over racial uplift philosophies, or just plain apathy. Yet the collective movement that protested federal Jim Crow during the early Wilson years, and the networking that occurred among protest and racial uplift organizations during this period, strongly challenge this view.

Preceding the modern civil rights movement by almost fifty years, the Wilson protest brought together tens of thousands of men and women who demonstrated an amazingly uniform approach and shared sense of purpose in protesting against Jim Crow in federal departments. The protest campaign also brought together into a coordinated movement for the first time leaders who had previously disagreed on methods for advancing the rights and upward mobility of African Americans. With most of their race deprived of its rights at the state and local levels, African Americans, along with liberal whites, passionately fought against the spread of racial injustice in the federal government. Moreover, many viewed their efforts as fighting for the freedom of an entire race and were unwavering in their belief that the force and spirit of democracy as manifested in the U.S. Constitution and the Declaration of Independence, as well as the will of God, were on their side.

Although fifty years had passed since the Civil War, in 1913–1914 the first emancipation remained fresh in the hearts of these men and women who still enthusiastically celebrated the birthdays of the liberators—William Lloyd Garrison, Wendell Phillips, Frederick Douglass, and Abraham Lincoln, among others. Clubs, associations, and organizations were named after these heroes of freedom and served to keep alive the sacrifices they had made to abolish slavery. In one case, the Boston School Committee requested that "on Nov. 29, 1913, the anniversary of the birth of Wendell Phillips, teachers in all the schools should speak for fifteen minutes on the life of Phillips and some of the lessons derived from it."[12]

The protestors, moreover, took seriously the principles established by their founding fathers—particularly the American creed that all men were created equal—in a way most whites did not. As DuBois reminded his contemporaries during the Progressive Era, "There are today no truer exponents of the pure human spirit of the Declaration of Independence than the American Negroes."[13] The torch of freedom had been passed to African Americans and white sympathizers because most of the white majority had miserably failed to work out a universal application of democratic equality. The protestors during the early Wilson years were American patriots to say the least and regarded themselves as such. This is their story.

NOTES

1. August Meier, *Negro Thought in America, 1880–1915: Racial Ideologies in the Age of Booker T. Washington* (Ann Arbor: University of Michigan Press, 1963), 162. Justice John Marshall Harlan of Kentucky strongly dissents in *Plessy.* See Jerome R. Corsi and Matthew Ross Lippman, *Constitutional Law: A Political Science Textbook* (Englewood Cliffs, NJ: Prentice-Hall, 1985), 439–441. Incidentally, all three Westerners on the U.S. Supreme Court who ruled in favor of segregation on public transportation in the Plessy case were born and/or raised and educated in the North. For a biographical summary of each justice, see *Congressional Quarterly's Guide to the U.S. Supreme Court* (Washington, DC: Congressional Quarterly, Inc., 1979), 821–822, 825–826, 829–833. William Monroe Trotter to President-elect Wilson, February 12, 1913, Trotter Correspondence, Woodrow Wilson Papers, Seeley G. Mudd Library, Princeton University, Princeton, NJ.

2. National Independent Political League to President Wilson, September 22, 1913, Trotter Correspondence, Woodrow Wilson Papers, Seeley G. Mudd Library, Princeton University, Princeton, NJ.

3. Sterling Spero and Abram Harris, *The Black Worker* (New York: Columbia University Press, 1931), 180.

4. A. L. Glenn, *History of the National Alliance of Postal Employees, 1913–1955* (Cleveland: NAPE, 1956), 26.

5. Morton Sosna, "The South in the Saddle: Racial Politics During the Wilson Years," *Wisconsin Magazine of History* 54 (Autumn 1970): 35.

6. Although precise statistics are unavailable, several historians speculate that Wilson received a higher share of the black vote than previous Democratic candidates had. This is dealt with in Chapter 1, notes 23 and 24.

7. Benjamin Quarles, *Black Abolitionists* (New York: Da Capo Press, 1991), 4, 6, 10–13, 18; Linda O. McMurray, *To Keep the Waters Troubled: The Life of Ida B. Wells* (New York: Oxford University Press, 1998), 22–31; August Meier and Elliott Rudwick, "The Boycott Movement Against Jim Crow Streetcars in the South, 1900–1906," *Journal of American History* 55 (March 1969): 756–775; Richmond *News Leader* quoted in James H. Brewer, "The War Against Jim Crow in the Land of Goshen," *Negro History Bulletin* 24 (December 1960): 53–57.

8. *Crisis,* January 1915, 120.

9. Two of these are Kendrick Clemants, *Woodrow Wilson: World Statesman* (Boston: Twayne, 1987), 99; Sosna, 37–39.

10. Kathleen Wolgemuth, "Woodrow Wilson and Federal Segregation," *Journal of Negro History* 44 (April 1959): 168.

11. Ira De A. Reid, "Negro Movements and Messiahs, 1900–1949," *Phylon: The Atlanta University Review* 10 (1949): 363.

12. *The Guardian,* November 22, 1913, in Box 6, Moorfield Storey Papers, Manuscript Division, Library of Congress, Washington, DC.

13. W.E.B. DuBois, *The Souls of Black Folk* (Grand Rapids: Candace, 1996), 13.

THE RETURN OF THE SOUTH

> [T]he flavor and the color of things in Washington are Southern . . . you feel it in the air, you note it in the changed and changing ways of business.
> —JUDSON C. WELLIVER, SHORTLY AFTER WILSON'S INAUGURATION

"THE GRANDEST DEMOCRATIC VICTORY SINCE THE WAR," declared the Richmond (Virginia) *Times-Dispatch* in rapturous delight the morning after Woodrow Wilson was "swept into office on [the] crest of a great popular wave."[1] That Wednesday morning, November 6, 1912, was undoubtedly unlike any other America had seen for over half a century. The nation awoke that day to find that the first southerner since Abraham Lincoln and the first Democrat since Grover Cleveland had been elected president of the United States. This time, however, there was a feeling of jubilant victory all over the South instead of the dread and whispers of war that had followed Lincoln's election in 1860; and a southern Democrat was about to enter the White House rather than a northern Democrat, as Cleveland was in 1885 and 1893.

But white southerners were not the only ones hailing the new chief. Many African Americans, particularly those groups and individuals from the North who vociferously advocated black equality, celebrated Wilson's victory as the dawn of a new era of race relations in America. The National Independent

9

Political League (NIPL), whose "mission" was the "political emancipation of the colored man of America" and which had enthusiastically campaigned on his behalf, sent the new president-elect a congratulatory telegram on his triumphant election.[2] Seldom if ever had a presidential candidate attracted the patronage of such divergent groups—in this case white southerners and northern black radicals—with utterly conflicting belief systems and so diametrically opposed to each other down to their core that to satisfy either group politically as far as the race issue was concerned would mean deeply offending the convictions of one or crushing the aspirations of the other.

The spoils, however, along with most everything else, would go to the white South. Woodrow Wilson, a native-born Virginian who had spent his formative years in Georgia and South Carolina, won the election with just a little more than 42 percent of the popular vote yet with an overwhelming 435 electoral votes. With most of the eastern states going to Wilson, including Massachusetts and New York, it was the former Confederacy that united the most strongly behind its native son. Democrats carried the "solid South" as every state below the Mason-Dixon line threw its support to Wilson, and to say that he received clear majorities in these states would be an understatement. Incredibly, the number of votes cast for Wilson in every southern state surpassed the combined totals in each of those states for the Bull Moose Teddy Roosevelt and the Republican William Howard Taft.[3]

The 1912 election gave the Democrats control not only of the presidency but of Congress as well. They now had a crushing majority of 164 in the House of Representatives and a majority of 7 in the Senate, with southern Democrats accounting for two-fifths of the members in the former and more than half in the latter. Furthermore, twelve of the fourteen Senate committees would soon be chaired by southerners, as would eleven of thirteen in the House. The counsel from these southern leaders in Congress, not to mention the influence of a strongly southern cabinet, would guide the president for the most part. "Southern influence had been decisive in nominating Wilson and directing his campaign," explained Arthur Link in noting the changing of the guard, "and southerners would soon be given the same share in formulating national policies that their grandfathers once enjoyed." A major shift in geographic control of the federal government had taken place.[4]

BLACKS AND THE CIVIL SERVICE IN THE PROGRESSIVE ERA

Almost three decades earlier, on January 16, 1883, President Chester Arthur had signed the Civil Service Act, thereby creating the Civil Service Commission. This act set in motion the gradual process by which most nonappointive federal positions would require competitive examinations designed to take into account only test performance in determining eligibility for filling federal job vacancies.[5]

The Civil Service Act opened the doors of advancement to many African Americans who were held back elsewhere because of their color. Although it would take several decades for the thousands of federal jobs to be phased into the Civil Service, the benefits of the act for African Americans were almost immediate. During the first six years after the act was signed, the number of black federal government workers increased from 620 to 2,393.[6] The *Eighth Report of the Civil Service Commission* declared, "It is impossible to overestimate the boon to these colored men and women of being given the chance to enter the Government service on their own merits in fair competition with white and colored alike."[7] Around the same time, one newspaper claimed that "seventy-five per cent more Afro-Americans have been given clerkships in the Departments in Washington and in the civil service generally through the operation of the Civil Service Law than were ever given to that class before."[8] By 1912, excluding the 8,000 black military personnel, roughly 12,000 African Americans were employed by the federal government with civil service status, and they were receiving more than $8.2 million annually in salaries.[9] Although the number of black federal appointments to such positions in the diplomatic and consular services, for example, had already been in a steady decline, the relatively color-blind civil service examination still provided the greatest opportunity for black advancement in a Jim Crow world.

Shortly after Wilson was inaugurated as president, the *Washington Post*, after printing the names of the hordes of federal office seekers, raised this question: "How is the Negro citizenship going to fare under the Democratic Administration?"[10] The new administration soon answered that question in regard to its black federal employees as Jim Crow was introduced or increased in federal departments in Washington and throughout the South. The largest amount of Jim Crow was concentrated in the Treasury and Post Office departments where by far the largest numbers of African Americans worked. Here they were grouped together on jobs by race, partitioned off from whites in rooms where the two races had previously worked together, assigned the least desirable jobs, and forced to use separate toilets and lunch tables, inferior work spaces, and unsanitary makeshift dining rooms. In some cases African Americans were downgraded or dismissed/terminated from their positions.

Federal Jim Crow had appeared as early as Theodore Roosevelt's second term but lacked the intensity and tacit approval of leaders in the executive departments—including the chief executive—along with the organized white support that marked the Wilson years.[11] Thus, although federal employment practices had never been entirely free of racial discrimination, Jim Crow in the federal departments was greatly expanded with more consistency during the Wilson administration and now seemed like an official policy backed by the federal government. Prior to this, with the exception of sporadic attempts to segregate black and white workers, the civil service had been relatively free of the overt and systematic racial discrimination so prevalent almost everywhere else. Black federal government employees themselves believed the "merit system transcended race prejudice," and with good reason. It was here that they had the best opportunities, hardly imaginable before the Civil Service Act, for equal access to economic advancement and professional development. Yet the color line, so ubiquitous in political and social life, was now threatening to halt the progress made by men and women irrespective of color within the federal government. Moreover, such a policy ironically contrasted starkly with the Progressive belief in unrestricted freedom to prove one's merit (although, as we shall see, most southern leaders considered Jim Crow not only a progressive policy but by far the most important reform cause of the day).[12]

The Wilson administration also bode ill for the future of federal employment practices in regard to African Americans. By 1914, the civil service required all applicants to submit photographs with their applications for federal jobs. With southern sentiment now prevailing in federal departments, many feared this policy was instituted as an easy way to identify and purge black applicants regardless of their test scores.

Although black federal appointments had been steadily declining for over a decade, Wilson, caring little about rewarding black Democrats for their patronage during the election, removed the majority of black officeholders from positions they had traditionally held—such as minister to Haiti and register of the Treasury—and replaced them with whites. Of the thirty-one highest appointments held by African Americans when Wilson was elected president in 1912, four years later only one black Democrat and one black Republican had been appointed by his administration and confirmed by the Senate, and eight black Republicans had been held over from the Taft administration in offices that, with one exception, were basically obscure consulates. Even these latter positions had all but disappeared by the end of Wilson's second administration, as only three black appointees could be counted among the hundreds of Americans in the U.S. consular service.[13]

The consensus among most southern Democrats had long been that African Americans should be segregated from whites and denied access to the ballot. Although John Cell and others offer half-convincing arguments that disfranchisement was directed just as much, if not more, toward poor whites as at blacks in the South,[14] proportionally African Americans overwhelmingly bore the brunt of the systematic efforts to restrict suffrage beginning in the late nineteenth century. Here there can be no comparison, as the real and potential black vote in the South was all but wiped out. "The purpose of the Mississippi Constitutional Convention," reminded James Vardaman regarding the efforts of the first southern state to restrict suffrage, "was to eliminate the nigger—not the ignorant but the nigger."[15] Other leading southern politicians of the day also openly touted their desire—and worked diligently—to implement various schemes, mostly illegal and unethical, for totally excluding African Americans "without disfranchising a single white man." Moreover, no overt de facto or de jure segregation, not to mention violence, was aimed at poor whites as there was at African Americans.

As is well-known, there had been a growing movement in the South since the end of Reconstruction—swelling to a massive tide of legal proscriptions during the first decade of the twentieth century—to impose severe restrictions on African Americans in regard to the ballot, education, transportation, public places, residential areas, and employment. These restrictions were often reinforced by the threat of violent penalties in what amounted to physical and psychological terrorism for those who dared cross the line. "The extremes to which caste penalties and separation were carried out in parts of the South," said C. Vann Woodward, the often-quoted sage of American de jure racial segregation, "could hardly find a counterpart short of the latitudes of India and South Africa."[16]

Southern members of Congress such as Pitchfork Ben Tillman of South Carolina, Hoke Smith of Georgia, James Vardaman of Mississippi, and a host of others had made the utter subjugation of blacks—and not poor whites—the cornerstone of their political platforms, overtly exploiting racial tensions in their appeals for votes and political power. As one racial reformer succinctly put it, they were "[p]olitical demagogues risen to eminence on the backs of the negro."[17] The severity with which blacks were regularly vilified and dehumanized not only from the political pulpit but in the southern white press as well cannot be emphasized enough. During the 1912 campaign Josephus Daniels—in charge of the publicity bureau of the presidential campaign and Wilson's secretary of the navy—represented this mind-set, albeit mildly, when he wrote in his North Carolina newspaper that "the subjection of the negro, politically, and the separation of the negro, socially, are paramount to all other considerations in the South short of the preservation of the Republic itself."[18] With Wilson's victory around the corner, such views

13

would soon find a new and tangible outlet within federal departments at Washington and throughout the South.

BLACK CIVIL SERVICE EMPLOYEES BEFORE 1915

Black civil service employees considered themselves the same as any other civil service employee, whatever the race, and deserving of equal treatment and consideration. A majority had high school diplomas, and several were graduates not only of black colleges but also of top northern white universities and law schools. It was not uncommon for African Americans in the civil service to have impressive personal and professional credentials, and some had the highest scores on civil service examinations in the country.

Although no official average of scores based on race exists for this period, in part because the exam was conducted at least theoretically on a basis of racial anonymity, a few indicators and citations give an idea as to African Americans' progress in the civil service. On the eve of Woodrow Wilson's election, as mentioned, the total number of African Americans in the federal civil service was 12,000, an enormous increase from the 620 working there when President Arthur signed the Civil Service Act just under thirty years earlier. African Americans were working in practically all departments of the government, including in supervisory and managerial positions. These jobs ranged from skilled laborers and clerks to auditors and the assistant attorney general.[19] Robert R. Jackson, a black assistant superintendent with the Postal Department from 1888 to 1902, for example, had nearly perfect scores on a series of promotional exams, with averages of 99.40, 98.12, and 98.32, respectively.[20] And Louis Harper, an employee in the Railway Mail Service (RMS) and one of the founders of the National Alliance of Postal Employees—an organization founded in 1913 to represent black postal employees—had an average score of 99.90 on his exams. W.E.B. DuBois conducted a case study in 1914 of African Americans recently hired in the Railway Mail Service in St. Louis and concluded that of the "fifty-two colored clerks" training in that city,

> [O]nly one has less than a high school education; fourteen have college degrees; twenty-one own or are buying real estate, and the average assessed value of these holdings is $2,700; thirty-two have families; all belong to civic organizations; one, Mr. William Humphries, has the best examination record in the United States, having to his credit twenty-one examinations of 100 percent each.[21]

This case is not exceptional. It appears that black federal employees were, in general, either middle-class or potentially middle-class. The merit-based federal service, not to mention appointive offices, attracted the most educated African Americans as compared to whites, since opportunities for employment commensurate with blacks' educational attainment were severely limited in the segregated white private sector and the poverty-stricken black community. Within their communities black federal employees were often associated with the professional class and were involved in civic and church affairs. The steady income from federal employment enabled them to buy homes, educate their children, and make investments. And because of the perceived stability of federal employment, they could get easy credit and substantial loans. Also, many photographs of black federal employees taken in the early twentieth century, including the ones in DuBois's St. Louis study, show distinguished men and women fashionably dressed in middle-class attire.

I do not intend to overstate the success of African Americans in the civil service prior to the Wilson years or to paint a utopian picture. As a *Washington Post* article pointed out just before Wilson's inauguration, many blacks occupied the lowest positions there and were not promoted or given salary increases because of their color.[22] Instances of discrimination had always existed—whether by sporadic attempts to segregate blacks in a department here and there, as Elliott Rudwick and August Meier have shown in their article "The Rise of Segregation in the Federal Bureaucracy, 1900–1930,"[23] or in the form of personal insults such as racial slurs, sneers, petty annoyances, and being rebuffed. Even in some cases where merit actually triumphed over severe racial prejudice in the Deep South—such as in Yazoo, Mississippi, where African Americans who scored higher on an examination were appointed as postal deliverers over whites with failing scores on the exam—angry local whites promised violent resistance if any blacks dared show up for work.[24]

Yet in 1912 more African Americans worked in the federal government than in any other sector, having obtained their positions either by outperforming the competition on civil service exams or by being appointed based on political contacts and qualifications. Most important, the liberal civil service had given African Americans an opportunity to develop and use their skills side by side with white employees as equals. These work environments were unique because they were relatively integrated even in most Railway Mail Service runs in the South, and both races worked together at many post offices in large southern cities, including Montgomery, Mobile, Houston, and Jacksonville. Even in Atlanta, which had become notorious before the Wilson years for its racial tension and violence, it appears that black and white postal workers performed their duties together in the city's main post office.[25]

15

In most cases, blacks and whites did share the same work spaces in federal departments at Washington and performed their job functions as an integrated team. Henry Lincoln Johnson, an influential black Republican leader in Georgia politics during the late nineteenth century and the recorder of deeds in Washington, D.C., during the Taft administration, expressed that before the Wilson years the African American had "worked in friendship and with efficiency alongside of his white brother in the various government departments."[26] The outgoing black auditor for the Navy Department, Ralph Tyler, whose white replacement swiftly initiated Jim Crow in his department, called President Wilson's attention to the fact that the systematic segregation of black federal employees was an abrupt change from the many years the two races had worked together.[27] In challenging the segregation of black employees before a House hearing, Martin Madden of Illinois, representing the "Black Belt" district of Chicago and responsible for helping blacks get over 500 jobs in the city's post office, also stated that black and white workers had "worked side by side" in federal departments for years.[28]

Although it appears that there were only a few black supervisors and appointees in federal departments, those who were there generally managed a department and a workforce that was both black and white and sometimes included women of both races. Once the workday was over, however, the professional contact between races on the job was replaced with the stringent social separation that permeated the capital city (and the nation) outside federal buildings. Blacks and whites went their own ways, locked into their distinctly segregated worlds, until the next morning. Yet the Jim Crow that existed almost universally outside Uncle Sam's doors, and its contrast with the semiequalitarian environment in federal employment, served better than anything else to underscore the fact that, relatively speaking, the federal government had transcended the racist norms of its times.

There were also more opportunities in the federal civil service for economic advancement compared to the color-conscious and often lily-white private sector, and this held true even as conditions drastically worsened for the black federal worker in the Wilson years. "There is little question," stressed Sterling Spero and Abram Harris, "that Negroes in government enterprises like the postal service or in other branches of the public services, despite all sorts of discrimination and inequality in assignments and promotions, are better off than in competitive industry."[29]

Besides the obvious success for a few in being appointed to "high places" by the president, the types of jobs and positions blacks held within the civil service before 1913 were diverse and in some cases impressive. With no available statistics or listings of job promotions based on race, the different types of jobs in which African Americans worked on the eve of Wilson's election, listed by Laurence Hayes, give some hint as to black workers' mobility within the federal civil service.[30] For example, it is a given that black "chiefs of divisions" and "heads of departments" had been promoted. Promotions in regard to the much larger numbers of regular black employees with civil service status are harder to determine. For instance, mail carriers generally remained mail carriers, since it was a static position with almost no opportunity for advancement. For postal clerks, however, ranging from manual laborers to highly trained mail distributors and specialists of various kinds and where the second-largest number of African Americans with civil service status fell, one could potentially qualify for many higher positions.[31]

Based on the common method of using civil service promotional examinations in most cases to secure qualified applicants from clerks to the highest grades of technical, professional, scientific, and executive positions, and in light of the diverse number of jobs held by African Americans in every department of the federal government, many African Americans with competitive scores and good work records likely did in fact make it into higher-skilled and sometimes better-paying positions.[32] It is probably safe to surmise that on the eve of Woodrow Wilson's election, black federal government employees had formed at least a quasi-class structure, most likely a substantial quasi-middle class, within a racially integrated economic framework and thus were less prone to tolerate overt discrimination and better suited than African Americans elsewhere to acquire the resources and sympathy necessary for serious protest in the early twentieth century.

BLACK CIVIL SERVICE EMPLOYEES AFTER 1915

During Woodrow Wilson's presidency, a period tagged the "critical years" for black federal workers, a marked quantitative and qualitative change occurred in the status of black employees and appointees, establishing a negative precedent that would continue largely uninterrupted until the later New Deal years. This change manifested and impacted African Americans in at least three ways: through segregation, reclassification (which usually meant downgrading an employee to a lower pay scale and often a less skilled job with limited opportunities for advancement), and dismissal/termination.

Much of the departmental Jim Crow during Wilson's first two years in office occurred in the Treasury and Post Office departments, which together employed well over 5,000 black workers—far exceeding the number employed by any other federal department. But there were also overt efforts or

17

threats to discriminate against African Americans in the Commerce Department, the Interior Department, the Marine Hospital service building, the Navy Department, and the Government Printing Office.

The Treasury Department, under the direction of the southern-born William Gibbs McAdoo, the son-in-law of Woodrow Wilson, implemented Jim Crow not only in its main building—which included the Bureau of Engraving and Printing, the Registry Division, the Miscellaneous and Examining Division, the Auditors Division, and the Internal Revenue Service—but also in each of its adjunct auditors' offices located in practically every division of every federal department in the city. This wide reach enabled Jim Crow to spread throughout many federal departments during the early Wilson years. Thus, in addition to Treasury's main building, efforts were undertaken to segregate, reclassify, downgrade, and terminate black employees in the adjunct offices located in the Post Office Building and the Interior, Navy, War, Agriculture, Commerce and Labor, and State departments. Although it appears that most of these separate departments did not overtly imitate Treasury's policy—except for the Post Office Department—none, with the exception of black federal employees (covertly) and one assistant secretary of the treasury, resisted the spread of Jim Crow in its buildings and offices.

Likewise, the Post Office Department enforced Jim Crow in its main building and throughout its branch offices in the city, including the City Post Office Annex. This policy also affected black civil servants throughout the South who were employed in the post offices and the Railway Mail Service. In the latter, where an acrimonious battle to reform dangerous and unsanitary conditions in the mail boxcars had reached its climax, some southern whites—taking advantage of the momentum and given impetus by the advent of a southern administration—combined or linked their reform campaign with rigorous efforts to segregate African Americans in work and restroom facilities, to push for a lower pay scale for black employees, or to rid mail runs of their presence altogether. In addition, African Americans were harassed on outrageously trumped-up charges and endured repeated racial slurs and daily humiliations.[33]

With about ten times as many black postal workers employed outside Washington, D.C., as there were within the city, black postal clerks, mail route deliverers, and those employed by the Railway Mail Service in the South were by far the most vulnerable to Jim Crow—particularly in a region that had fully embraced de jure segregation. Moreover, representing this region was Wilson's postmaster general appointee Albert Burleson, a Texas politician who had graduated first in his law school class and who had a history of Negro bashing back home in the Lone Star state; Burleson now enforced or approved discriminatory efforts aimed at African Americans throughout his department in Washington. It appears that Burleson used his influence with the president to fill three of four assistant postmaster general offices with southern men, eventually including one from his home state. Thus, the department employing the largest number of African Americans in the federal civil service was for the first time in history almost completely under the control of white men from the South.[34]

FEDERAL JIM CROW: AN OVERVIEW

Since most of the Jim Crow in the civil service after 1913 appears chronologically throughout this book, it may be helpful to the reader to have at least a summary before going further. Jim Crow was manifested in several ways throughout the federal government, some of which were touched upon earlier. Signs designating separate "colored" and "white" restrooms were put up in the main building and divisions of the Treasury Department and in most of its adjunct offices in federal departments throughout Washington. Where official signs were not displayed or were taken down as a result of protest, black employees were given verbal orders to use separate restrooms, backed by a threat of dismissal if they should disobey. Segregated restrooms were also enforced in the Government Printing Office, the Marine Hospital Service building, the Navy Department, and the Railway Mail Service in the South. The Architects Office of the Treasury Department received instructions to provide separate restrooms in all federal treasury buildings below the Mason-Dixon line. In a few cases, these newly segregated black restrooms were unisex facilities—that is, black males and females shared the same restroom—an unheard-of arrangement for the times and one whites would be aghast to consider for themselves. And in other cases, African Americans were forced out of the main employee dining areas and were required to use their washrooms and restrooms as makeshift lunchrooms. For self-respecting African Americans who had acquired their positions by merit, daily "toilet segregation" was humiliating, degrading, and an offense to their dignity because—they rightly believed—it implied that they were "unclean" and labeled them as "inferior."

Segregation in workplaces spread through the federal departments like wildfire after Wilson's election. Most of this was carried out on a large scale in the Treasury Department and its adjunct divisions; in the Post Office Department, including the Railway Mail Service in the South; and in the Government Printing Office. Black and white federal employees—who had

19

worked together for years at the same machines, desks, and tables—were rearranged to have only segregated white and black workstations and in most cases completely segregated rooms and offices. Although the rationale was sometimes given that the purpose of this restructuring was to reduce friction between the races, African Americans well understood that it was a racist policy directed at them solely because of the color of their skin.

Plans were under way as well, initiated by McAdoo and approved by Wilson, to crystallize the separate but equal doctrine in the executive branch by shifting all black employees of the Treasury Department into one "distinctively colored division." In several cases humiliating partitions, some crude and makeshift and others carefully designed, were put up to keep black workers out of view in offices and departments. To make matters worse, white supervisors in many of these federal departments made no effort to ensure that the separate "black" areas were adequately maintained and safe. They were often dirty, with poor lighting and ventilation, and they were the hottest spaces in the summer and the coldest in the winter. In addition, segregated window service, clearly designated "Colored" and "White," was enforced in all city post offices in Washington. And in at least one case, all black workers in a division of the Post Office Department were intentionally transferred to a city post office that was to be abolished, eventually leaving these workers without jobs.

With their forced segregation into unsanitary lunchrooms and restrooms and into obscure and sometimes dangerous work spaces, besides the humiliation of being "set apart as lepers," black federal employees feared there would be limited opportunity for promotion or advancement. Moreover, if African Americans in any way openly challenged or questioned Jim Crow in their departments, they were threatened with demotion or dismissal and were usually terminated from their positions.

BLACK VOTERS IN THE 1912 CAMPAIGN: BREAKING AWAY FROM A SHORT PAST

During the 1912 campaign, many hopeful African Americans, with no way of foreseeing the dismal events that would rapidly follow, found Wilson an appealing alternative to Roosevelt and Taft. Although the exact percentage of black votes in that election is unknown, it is estimated that between 20 and 30 percent abandoned the party of Lincoln in favor of the progressive Democrat.[35] Whatever the percentage, historians speculate that Wilson received the largest number of black votes garnered by a Democratic presidential candidate to that time.[36] With southern blacks effectively disfranchised, support for Wilson came mostly from northern blacks, many of whom were the most ardent supporters of equal rights for their race. With this in mind, what persuaded so many African American voters, reputed as rubber-stamp supporters of the Republican Party, to switch their allegiance in support of a Virginia-born Democrat at a time when Jim Crow was at its zenith?

Several factors account for this shift. A few days after the election, *La Follette's Weekly Magazine*—imbibing the humanitarian impulse for reform and uplift that was popular among socially conscious progressives and was particularly attractive to African Americans—put the new president-elect's victory in perspective, shedding light on why blacks may have voted for a Democrat: "Oppressed and heartsick, a nation of ninety million people demanding plain, simple justice, striving for educational, political and industrial democracy, turned to Woodrow Wilson as the only present hope."[37] The Wilson campaign's public commitment to raise political contributions solely from the masses, shunning powerful corporations and special interests, had inspired many Democratic newspaper headlines across the country to dub its strategy the "Poor Men's Money for Wilson Fight." This was an eye-catcher for African Americans who were predominantly some of the poorest of the poor because of the crushing effects of systematic racism and who had been all but abandoned by their former friend, the Republican Party. And making the transition to the national level a little easier was the fact that the Democratic political machines in northern cities, such as the infamous Tammany Hall in New York, were no strangers to African Americans and for years had been successfully courting and rewarding black votes (and white immigrants) with patronage and much-needed social services and relief.[38]

Yet the attitudes of some African Americans had long been cooling toward the Republican Party on the national and state levels as they watched the party of freedom, the symbol of their hopes and dreams, move from supporting and protecting their rights to accepting a system of race relations that ardently sought to deny those rights. Beginning as early as the late 1870s, some black leaders, organizations, and newspapers—feeling vulnerable and crushed after the withdrawal of federal troops and the restoration of states' rights and white supremacy in the South during the Republican presidency of Rutherford B. Hayes—advocated a divorce from the party of Lincoln and urged African Americans to support the party that best served their interests, even if it meant a trial run with the moderate but slavery-tainted Democrats in the North. Over the next several decades the Democrats of the war-torn South began to revive, and they beat loudly on the doors of congressional power. This prompted northern Republican leaders—including the once outspoken critic of black disfranchisement and lynching, President

Theodore Roosevelt, along with his handpicked successor, William Howard Taft—in an attempt to avert their party's ouster from power, to woo racist sentiment in the South, often advocating Jim Crow while urging African Americans to stay out of politics, relinquish the vote, and submit to an all-white authority.[39]

Astonishingly, a politician from a political party still associated with slavery in the minds of most African Americans would prove to be liberal regarding his policy toward them in the civil service, despite some black southerners' initial fears that his election would mean a return to slavery or a form of quasi-slavery. In 1885 and 1893, Democrat Grover Cleveland, in an attempt to court disaffected black Republicans, appointed African Americans to federal offices and diplomatic posts. These were token positions to be sure, but nevertheless this surprising move from a Democrat essentially gave Democrat-phobic African Americans confidence that perhaps the once taboo party was beginning to change.[40]

African American leaders were also delighted that President Cleveland seemed to resist the growing tide of Jim Crow. He appointed African Americans to federal offices while ignoring demands from Thomas Hendricks, vice president during his first administration, to eliminate blacks from the civil service and despite the sentiments "of many high in governmental circles"—including the Alabama native Hilary A. Herbert, secretary of the navy during Cleveland's last administration—that "universal suffrage of the Negro was the mistake of the nineteenth century." And at the end of his first administration, President Cleveland issued an executive order placing the Railway Mail Service under civil service regulations, thus opening the door of hope and opportunity to African Americans in what was regarded as one of the fastest-growing job markets in the federal sector.[41]

During the Wilson protest years, Cleveland's name was often invoked, and his reputation perhaps exaggerated, as the shining example of a Democrat who in word and action had helped advance the interests of African Americans.[42] He had become a potent symbol during the Wilson election for blacks who were fed up with the racial politicking Republicans. And it wasn't only racial reformers who brought up Cleveland's liberal race policy. In opposing the appointment of a black lawyer, A. E. Patterson, as register of the treasury, popular racist author and orator Thomas Dixon admonished Wilson in a letter for considering appointing a "Negro to boss white girls." "We have traveled many leagues," wrote Dixon, "from the Negro equality ideas in vogue when Cleveland, a Democratic President, did this thing."[43]

Another thing that pushed some African Americans further into the Democratic camp and was presented as evidence of why blacks should support the Democrat Wilson in 1912 was what would be considered a treacherous act on the part of Republican leadership—whipping into a fury black radicals and conservatives as well as liberal whites, including Senators Joseph Benson Foraker of Ohio and John Spooner of Wisconsin, and even provoking criticism from Booker T. Washington. A few days before the 1906 congressional elections, President Roosevelt ordered that three companies of decorated troops from the all-black Twenty-fifth Infantry Regiment be dishonorably discharged for their alleged involvement in a riot at Brownsville, Texas, although they unwaveringly maintained their innocence and despite the fact that there was no proof they had instigated a riot. An independent investigation turned up evidence that proved none of the discharged soldiers had been involved. African Americans were incensed and outraged by what they labeled a "cruel" act. These soldiers had previously achieved a level of recognition for their performance in battle rarely accorded to African Americans. The Twenty-fifth Infantry had become a shining symbol of black achievement in a Jim Crow world, and now that was taken away because of their color. All efforts to exonerate the soldiers were of little avail. Almost exactly one year after the alleged Brownsville riot, only 14 of the 167 soldiers discharged were declared eligible for reinstatement.[44]

The important symbolic significance of the Twenty-fifth Infantry for most African Americans during this time cannot be underestimated. In a white world where spoils and recognition for African Americans were incredibly rare, the high-profile success of an individual or a group was an achievement shared by most of the race. Likewise, the unjust invalidation of such achievers, as seen by the discharge of the black regiment, was a severe blow to all African Americans.

When Robert Terrell, a black appointee, for example, was finally renominated and confirmed municipal judge of the District of Columbia in April 1914, despite heated opposition led by Senator James Vardaman, African Americans nationwide celebrated the victory. One black editor ecstatically wrote Terrell, describing the judge's triumph with a comparison to a larger-than-life hero: "Boy, you are a record-breaker, an epoch maker, the Ty Cobb of black politics. You handle the white folks like a Napoleon." The judge's nomination, declared another editor, had "become of national importance," and he added, "I think all colored people will breathe easier from now on." E. F. Durant wrote Terrell that his victory should be "heralded from pole to pole," while another informed the judge that the entire race "feels a sense of justifiable pride."[45] Thus, it is easy to understand why some African Americans turned away from the Republicans and toward the Democrats after Roosevelt's handling of Brownsville.

Although the Republican Party still gave lip service favoring black equality in its platforms during election time and hammered away at Democrats for restricting political and civil rights,[46] African Americans, with a keen sense of political reality, understood that words and actions were two different things. There was no escaping the fact that during the fourteen-year period from 1896 to 1910, in which Republicans controlled all branches of the federal government, the social condition and political rights of African Americans drastically worsened. With both Roosevelt and Taft having turned their attention to the amalgamation of their party with southern white supremacy and with the Republican Party's active commitment to black political and civil rights now a thing of the past, more and more African Americans began to reevaluate their commitment to the party that had once been synonymous with freedom.

The philosophy of accommodation to white political control stressed by the most prominent black leader in America, Booker T. Washington, reinforced not only the mushroom growth of Jim Crow legislation in states and localities at the turn of the twentieth century but also the "whites only" Progressive movement that was becoming popular in both parties. With resistance to Jim Crow effectively diminished among former white allies in the South, and in the face of abandonment by an apathetic and increasingly Jim Crow North, Washington, wrote C. Vann Woodward, seemed "unwittingly to have smoothed the path to proscription."[47]

RISING FROM THE ASHES: THE GROWTH OF BLACK PROTEST AND UPLIFT ORGANIZATIONS IN THE PROGRESSIVE ERA

Yet ideology and politicking were not enough to enforce Jim Crow. Some whites would resort to physical and psychological terrorism against African Americans and their communities in an effort to maintain white supremacy. In addition to the large number of black hangings around the turn of the twentieth century, increasing atrocities of mutilation, burning, and beating to death of black men suspected (or used as an excuse) of raping white women seemed to verify for many African Americans that they were becoming increasingly vulnerable in the South and parts of the West without political and civil rights. In 1899, for example, a black man named Sam Hose, an alleged rapist and murderer, was in a horrific and shocking act burned alive in Palmetto, Georgia, as 2,000 white men, women, and children let out "wild shouts of joy." Before the body was even cool, a mob rushed in and began to cut pieces of burned flesh—including his liver and heart—and broke off brittle bones for souvenirs. In many cases white mob rule intentionally attempted (and admitted) both the local slaughter of its native black population through systematic terror and murder and the targeted destruction of black communities in towns and cities. African Americans not only lacked political rights in the South and, in cases such as the one described earlier, had no constitutional right to trial by jury, but their right to life and community could be in jeopardy at the hands of white mobs.[48]

But African Americans would not take their mistreatment sitting down. As Jim Crow rushed forward to dominate American life and devour its darker citizens, blacks collectively, along with white sympathizers, boldly rose to challenge its legitimacy, fight for their rights, and advance the race by any method that seemed viable. Organizations for black equality began appearing with vigor and sought to combat Jim Crow while offering an alternative to Washington.

The usually moderate Afro-American Council (AAC), founded in 1898 by Washington ally T. Thomas Fortune, took a more militant posture in 1899 as it publicly denounced the Sam Hose burning, a horrific event that triggered mass protest meetings in the North. The AAC issued an appeal to southern leaders through such lily-white newspapers as the Montgomery (Alabama) *Advertiser*, asking them to take a stand against wanton acts of violence. The AAC—much like its predecessor, the Afro-American League—was formed to fight for equal accommodations and voting rights and against peonage and lynching. Although the militant feminist Ida Wells-Barnett was secretary of the AAC, the only woman elected to an office, the influence if not direct control by Washington seems to have held its more militant minority in check; and as a result the council adopted a more conservative approach that did very little toward advocating black political and civil rights.[49]

In 1891 the former carpetbagger and one of the most outspoken white advocates for black equality in the late nineteenth century, Albion W. Tourgee, founded the interracial National Citizens' Rights Association. The organization, launched with much support and high ambitions, only managed to initiate the legal action in *Plessy v. Ferguson* during its short three-year existence before finally crumbling under Tourgee's heavy-handed and controlling style of leadership.[50]

Shortly after forming the Boston Suffrage League in 1904, the black equal rights leader William Monroe Trotter attended a meeting of black activists from New England to form the New England Suffrage League (NESL) and was elected its first president. Despite its regional name, the ambitious group hoped "to lay the wrongs and the claims of the race before the American people" and endorsed resolutions asking for federal antilynching legislation, federal compensatory aid to southern schools, the outlawing of Jim

Crow on public carriers, and enforcement of the Fifteenth Amendment.[51] Although the NESL was one of the earliest organizations to have a clear platform demanding social and political change and it held several dramatic mass meetings, the group never had a significant membership beyond a handful of black activists in the New England area.

The culmination of a growing black assertiveness for equal rights into one organization was finally realized in 1905 with the founding of the Niagara Movement. This organization brought together a loosely knit collection of black men "from every region of the country except the Far West." Dubbed "radicals," they sought nothing less than equality for their race and together shared, said David Levering Lewis, "the exhilarating conviction that they were making racial history"—a blossoming feeling among the growing number of aggressive equal rights activists during the first decade of the twentieth century. In the Niagara "Declaration of Principles," DuBois and Trotter boldly declared a sentiment that would echo throughout the twentieth century: "We refuse to allow the impression to remain that the Negro American assents to inferiority. . . . [T]he voice of ten million Americans must never cease to assail the ears of their fellows, so long as America is unjust."[52]

Shortly after the incorporation of the Niagara Movement in January 1906, several members participated in a meeting of the first annual Georgia Equal Rights Convention, held in the Deep South. In front of an audience of 200 black delegates from Georgia's eleven congressional districts and in a state that was moving rapidly toward the most violent racial unrest in its history, the infamous 1906 Atlanta Riot—an event that would thrust its white leaders into a hysterical and bloodthirsty campaign to crush and subjugate black Georgians—the ebony DuBois stood tall and was enthusiastically applauded when he declared that the convention would insist on nothing less than full political and civil rights for African Americans.[53] By 1910 the Niagara Movement had been absorbed into the new organization for racial justice, the National Association for the Advancement of Colored People (NAACP). Meanwhile, Trotter broke off and formed his own organization, the National Independent Political League (NIPL). Although the NAACP proved to be the stronger and more enduring of the two, both organizations answered the call for racial justice by means of strategic and aggressive protest, and they began to challenge Booker T. Washington as the new representatives of African Americans.[54]

Even though leadership in these equal rights organizations was either dominated or led by males, with the exception of most notably the NAACP, black women were involved in their own organizations and activities. Here they worked not only for the social uplift of their gender and "a defense of black womanhood" against scurrilous attacks on their morality but also for equal rights for all African Americans. These women had been struggling since the early 1880s to gain an independent voice and active roles within their churches, and, once achieved, they used that experience and knowledge to spread out and form their own secular organizations—still closely aligned or interlinked with the church but with a broader program of social activism for community uplift and of advocating black political and civil rights. Yet long before this time, black women had been creating voluntary organizations to "charitably watch over each other," and it appears they were the first to establish female antislavery societies. Most striking is the fact that in many "autonomous" and "resilient" black organizations made up of both black men and women after the Civil War, women were the leaders.[55]

Black women in the late nineteenth and early twentieth centuries helped lay the foundation for the social and political activism in regard to black equality, carried out by male and female, white and black, that gained popularity in the first few decades of the twentieth century in such organizations as the NAACP. Beginning from a position that challenged gender subordination within the church, black women gained the confidence and skills and collective strength that enabled them to establish their own religious and secular organizations. For example, in 1896 the National Association of Colored Women (NACW) was launched, bringing together thousands of black women and local clubs from all over the nation—including shared membership and collaborative efforts with its religious counterparts—to work for the elevation of the black family by providing services such as education, child care, charity, and job training. The NACW also used its networks and organizational power to protest racial injustice and demand black equality.[56]

Black women played a crucial and often overlooked role in the formation and development of the NAACP. Many of these black women, such as Nanny Burroughs, Mary Wilson, and for a time Ida Wells-Barnett, maintained their membership and offices in both secular and religious organizations and joined, supported, and worked closely with the NAACP in aggressively protesting lynching and federal Jim Crow in the Wilson government—often overlapping and combining the organizations in the struggles. Dorothy Salem explained that only one year after the equal rights organization began in 1909, "black female leadership was evident in both the Executive Committee and the General Committee of the NAACP." On the national level, by 1914 twenty-nine women were represented as officers, board directors, or committee members. In the NAACP branch offices throughout the country, eighty-two women served as local leaders in such positions as secretary, treasurer, and vice president, as well as on executive committees. One black female, Mrs. Letitia A. Graves, even served as president of the Seattle, Washington, branch. Although a handful of prominent and committed white women served in these positions, black women made up a majority of the female leaders described in this section.[57]

Yet this impressive array of black female leadership overshadowed the much larger number of women who worked mostly at the grassroots level. Black women tapped into the massive religious and secular black women's networks and participated as NAACP branch or affiliate organizers, administrators, writers, fundraisers, investigators, recruiters, field organizers, speakers, conference participants, and lobbyists. Utilizing skills and experience acquired from years of voluntary, club, and religious group activities, they swelled the ranks of the new organization and laid the groundwork responsible for building it into the most viable protest organization working for black equal rights and fighting racial injustice in the twentieth century.[58]

As the social mores of the passing Victorian Era that had sustained female repression lingered in a world that had become viciously intolerant of black equality, black women found themselves in a unique position in which they had two major disadvantages: they were both black and female. In a political sense, they were doubly disempowered. And if the beginning of the twentieth century could be considered one of the worst periods in history for free blacks in America, as historian Rayford Logan maintains, it was perhaps bleakest in a political and social sense for black women. "Once black men were denied the suffrage," said Evelyn Higginbotham, "black women became even more powerless and vulnerable to southern racial hostility." Yet from such a limited sphere of action, not beholden to the world of politics and forced to the margins of American life, black women paradoxically had incredible mobility to work consistently and broadly for changes in American society without trying to balance their convictions with what they could obtain from the white power structure. They did not, said Grace Elizabeth Hale, have to "choose between the fetters" of race and gender oppression like many of their white female and black male counterparts. Moreover, some black female leaders such as Nanny Burroughs believed that since black women were the most "aggressive, progressive, and dependable," black women would be the saviors of their race.[59]

As a result, black women spiritedly influenced social and political activism in the early twentieth century more than they are generally credited with having done. For example, at the NACW national convention in 1914, Ida Wells-Barnett spoke jubilantly about the organization's success in defeating the passage of a Jim Crow bill, and the members attending strongly resolved to advocate the use of boycotts to battle discrimination. With these considerations, along with the need for future research on the impact of black women's organizations in protest activism as well as community uplift during the Progressive Era, what may emerge, if not already apparent in form, is that black women's organizations far excelled over white women's reform groups in dogged activism, and they set the tone and groundwork for African American protest in the twentieth century.[60]

A final point touches on the fusion of class and protest among black leaders during this period. Black leaders during the Progressive Era have been chided for imposing their middle-class values on lower-class blacks. This has sometimes been negatively interpreted as a narrowly conformist and patronizing strategy to black uplift, one that replicated the dominant white cultural norms of gender, racial, and class bias.[61] Yet when some within the black middle class (and potentially middle class) and the much smaller upper class who held many of the same dominant values as their white counterparts were personally confronted with explicit and often hostile disregard for those values by whites, many were motivated to action. Black participation and leadership in protest and uplift organizations such as the Niagara Movement, the NACW, the NAACP, and the NIPL were instigated largely from a clash between black middle-class expectations and racial injustice.

The Wilson protest is perhaps one of the best examples of this conflict in action. Those within the growing black middle-class elite had acquired education and a certain amount of economic security; and they had developed confidence, self-respect, and a strong desire for individual self-determination. With the obvious conflict between a Jim Crow system that sought to crush and retard black growth and aspirations and a middle-class status that by definition should have meant unrestricted growth and development for its members based solely on merit, offended middle-class African Americans rose in protest. Often they were motivated by a personal and embarrassing episode involving their mistreatment at the hands of Jim Crow. Ida Wells-Barnett, William Monroe Trotter, and Mary Church Terrell are examples of black leaders who recounted a pivotal event or events—singed into their consciences—in which they were treated like dirt by prejudiced whites, in disregard of their obvious middle-class status. Moreover, in contrast to E. Franklin Frazier's apathetic black bourgeoisie of the 1940s, many middle-class African Americans during the Progressive Era were acutely sensitive to the cross their race had to bear, and racial injustice fueled their desire to challenge that threat not only to their personal status but to the development and progress of lower-class African Americans as well. They clearly believed their fate was inextricably interwoven with the fate of all their black brothers and sisters, regardless of class.

"NOW MR. BLACK VOTER, WHAT ARE YOU GOING TO DO ABOUT IT?"

With the 1912 campaign approaching, a significant segment of the northern black leadership began to take a closer look at the relatively unknown newcomer on the political scene, Woodrow Wilson. Disenchanted with the stepped-up racial pandering of the Republican Taft and the third-party third-term candidate, Theodore Roosevelt, Wilson seemed an attractive alternative. The Democrat had catapulted onto the national political scene in just two short years and came armed with a progressive doctrine called *The New Freedom*. In it Wilson declared that America should be a land lifting "to the admiration of the world its ideas of absolute free opportunity, where no man is supposed to be under any limitation except the limitations of his character and of his mind; where there is supposed to be no distinction of class, no distinction of blood, no distinction of social status but where men win or lose on their merits."[62]

Governor Wilson's words, described by Oswald Villard as "beautiful and worthy sentiments," gave many African Americans hope that he might be another Abraham Lincoln and help break loose the shackles of their second enslavement, this time to Jim Crow.[63] With Wilson apparently free of the racial political baggage that weighed so heavily upon Taft and Roosevelt, African American support for the progressive Democrat blossomed. African Americans around the country began to organize on behalf of Wilson. "I am very anxious to take the stump in your interest," wrote an enthusiastic organizer of the "Negro Democratic Governor Woodrow Wilson for President Club."[64] Another promised organized support for the Democrat if he would assure "the Negro that you and your party will be our friends."[65] Giles B. Jackson, a former Republican and prominent Richmond, Virginia, attorney, broke ranks with his party and formed the National Negro Wilson League because he believed a Wilson presidency "would result in the greatest possible good" for colored people.[66] Democratic Party approval was, in fact, given to the league to provide black spokesmen for the Democratic National Committee in the North.[67] And for more of a personal than a political motivation, a former slave named John Patillo, who claimed to have been Wilson's childhood playmate back in Augusta, Georgia, just after the Civil War, switched parties and voted the national Democratic ticket in 1912.[68]

Incredibly, some of the most prominent black Republican appointees, who owed their positions to the party in power and some of whom had served for three or more decades, boldly switched allegiance and supported the Democrat Wilson for president. They were dismayed, like many African

Americans, by the disfranchisement of their race in the South under Republican power, the decline of black federal appointments, and the wooing of the racist southern white vote. But uniquely, they felt their roles in the diplomatic and consular service, often in some of the remotest parts of the world, afforded them little opportunity to work for the betterment of their race at home. Moreover, African Americans in the consular service had come to believe there was a fixed and permanent ceiling in regard to their employment and that the federal government had no intention of promoting them into higher positions with more influence.[69]

Yet it was the more aggressive independent leadership for black political and civil rights that reached out to Wilson the most. Early in 1912 Alexander Walters, a prominent bishop in the African Zion Church and a board member of the NAACP, became president of the National Colored Democratic League (NCDL). Once Wilson had entered the Democratic pre-convention campaign and following his nomination, Walters and the NCDL eagerly campaigned on his behalf. On July 17, 1912, a delegation of black men representing the National Independent Political League and endorsed by the NCDL—including two of the leading advocates for black equality, William Monroe Trotter and J. Milton Waldron, the latter also president of the Washington NAACP branch—met with candidate Wilson at his home in Sea Girt, New Jersey. Two years earlier Trotter and the NIPL had endorsed the college president in his bid for New Jersey governor because of his "declaration" to "treat all citizens alike." Now the men prodded the Democratic Party's presidential nominee for his views on issues such as disfranchisement, lynching, and racial discrimination. He told them he was "not in sympathy with race and color prejudice" and promised "even handed justice and equal rights to all regardless of race, color, or nationality."[70]

The next day Trotter followed up with a letter to Wilson, along with a written endorsement from Governor Eugene Foss of Massachusetts, recapping their discussion at Sea Girt and forcefully stressing his "sincerity in trying to do away with color prejudice and its horrible effects in color segregation, disfranchisement and lynching." Trotter meant business, and if Wilson wanted the support of African Americans in a three-way election that could boil down to a small margin of votes for the victor, he had to publicly assure African Americans that they "would not be voting for a President who would disregard" their political rights.[71] Supposedly, a second pre-election meeting occurred at the office of Trotter's *Guardian* newspaper on Cornhill in Boston at which Wilson expressed his intention of helping African Americans.[72]

Trotter eventually felt Wilson could be counted on after the candidate expressed to Alexander Walters in a written pledge that colored people "may count upon me for absolute fair dealing and for everything by which I could assist in advancing the interests of their race in the United States." It was Wilson's "earnest wish to see justice done in every matter, and not mere grudging justice, but justice executed with liberality and cordial good feeling." Taking his assurances one step further and assuaging African American anxiety even more, the candidate boldly stated that the law and the U.S. Constitution guaranteed that justice for "my colored fellow-citizens" would be carried out.[73] Thus encouraged, the NIPL campaigned on behalf of Wilson, supported him in the pages of the *Guardian,* and was recognized by the Democratic National Committee as one of its spokesmen. Even the NIPL's stationery was modified during the campaign to read "Repulse Taft and Roosevelt by Voting for Wilson."[74]

On July 31, 1912, a delegation from the United Negro Democracy of New Jersey, in a meeting with the governor at Trenton, was given assurances by Wilson of his "entire comprehension of the ambitions of the Negro race" and his "willingness and desire to deal with the race fairly and justly."[75] Shortly thereafter, Oswald Garrison Villard, the most vocal white advocate for black political and civil rights, serving as chairman of the NAACP and editor of the liberal *New York Evening Post,* met with Wilson at Trenton. Wilson and Villard had been friends for years, and Villard seemed almost willing to settle for any glimmer of hope that the candidate was concerned about the dilemmas facing African Americans. He desperately wanted to support his friend in good conscience, and the race issue was an important one. Villard came away from the meeting delighted. Wilson had told the editor that he intended to be "President of all the people" and that he would make appointments solely on the basis of merit. Although Wilson claimed that as president he would have no power to stop the lynching of African Americans, he would publicly speak out against it. These were vague promises to be sure, but they were enough for the eager Villard—desperate to force Wilson into the mold of a social progressive—to commit his full-fledged support.[76]

Like Trotter, Villard wrote to Wilson the next day, strongly urging him to make a public announcement to assure African Americans that they would have equal treatment before the law and that he would not discriminate against them.[77] Villard never received an answer. The campaign was consuming the presidential contender's time and energy, Villard reassured himself, and he decided not to read anything into Wilson's silence. Thus, the editor relied for the most part—like Trotter—on the assurances given in the Walters letter, along with the vague promises during his personal meeting with the candidate, as the basis of his support.

W.E.B. DuBois had made his militant mark in black America about a decade earlier with the publication of *The Souls of Black Folk.* One of the most vocal advocates for black equality, DuBois had been moving away from the Republican Party since 1908 when he, Alexander Walters, J. Max Barber, and others supported the election of the Democrat William Jennings Bryan. Actually, DuBois had been flirting off and on, but mostly on, with the Democratic Party since his college days at Fisk. And although he would have preferred the Socialist candidate, Eugene Debs, in 1908, he felt it would be a vote thrown away and committed himself instead—after initial hesitation—to wooing the black vote for the Democrats. The Republican Party, he believed, had long acquiesced in the loss of black political and civil rights, thereby forfeiting its claim to the black vote. Besides, DuBois, like many African Americans, had singed in his memory the Republican Roosevelt's injustice to the black Twenty-fifth Infantry Regiment six years earlier. "If between the two parties who stand on identically the same platform you can prefer the party that perpetuated Brownsville," trumpeted DuBois in Trotter's *Guardian,* "well and good! But I shall vote for Bryan."[78]

By 1912 Taft and Roosevelt's racial pandering had shattered any hopes for black political equality. The last straw for DuBois occurred when Roosevelt's Bull Moose Party refused to seat a delegation of southern blacks at the convention in Chicago. DuBois turned to the Democratic Party once again and was "willing to risk a trial" and support Wilson. He went as far as to resign his membership in the Socialist Party to officially work on the campaign. In *Crisis,* the mouthpiece of the NAACP, DuBois told readers that although Wilson did not "admire Negroes," he would not degrade them with "further means of Jim Crow insult." He believed Wilson, a man he knew by reputation as a fellow scholar and intellectual (DuBois had used Wilson's book, *The State,* in his classes as a teacher), would rise above petty racial prejudices and perhaps give African Americans the equal treatment they deserved as American citizens. DuBois made several campaign speeches and wrote a series of leaflets that were widely distributed among black voters in the North by Tammany Hall. Beginning in September 1912, *Crisis* publicly supported Wilson for president and set about proselytizing black voters in hopes of swaying the electoral vote in some northern states to favor the progressive Democrat. Within the pages of *Crisis,* an enthusiastic DuBois seemed to imply that African Americans had an opportunity to take destiny into their own hands in the 1912 campaign. "Now Mr. Black Voter," the editor expectantly asked his readers, "what are you going to do about it?"[79]

BE CAREFUL WHAT YOU VOTE FOR: WILSON WARNING SIGNS

With serious efforts by blacks and liberal whites to support Wilson for president under way, ominous dark clouds hung over the horizon warning of worse things to come from a Democrat with strong southern roots. Although the most aggressive leaders for black equality were trying to get any positive response from Wilson, the candidate, except for a few vague promises, conspicuously avoided making any direct public statements to African Americans. In addition, he declined all invitations during the campaign to address black groups at conventions and rallies. Even Wilson's letter to Alexander Walters promising justice, the basis of much black support, was written mainly to explain why he could not address an upcoming black conference to which he was invited.

Earlier that summer, one of the most influential black journalists in the country, Fred R. Moore, editor of *New York Age,* had fired off warning shots about Wilson in a scathing article: "The *New York Age* does not see how it will be possible for a single self-respecting Negro in the United States to vote for Woodrow Wilson. . . . Both by inheritance and absorption he has most of the prejudices of the narrowest type of Southern white people against the Negro." Moore also informed readers that although Wilson was president of Princeton University, it was the "one large institution in a Northern state" that did not admit Negroes. As governor, continued the editor, "Mr. Wilson . . . has not by a turn of the finger recognized a single Negro in New Jersey." And to top it off, Moore reminded readers that the Democratic convention in Baltimore "absolutely refused to recognize" African Americans' attempts to get "a line or two in their platform regarding the rights of the Negro."[80]

In his bid for the Democratic presidential nomination, Wilson had "appealed especially to the progressive Democrats in the South for support," a faction that had made black disfranchisement and segregation its great reform causes. Regardless of his intentions as president, many blacks feared the presence of a southerner in the White House would give impetus to Jim Crow, and they felt uneasy about southern white men such as William McCombs and William McAdoo running his campaign. And notwithstanding Villard's enthusiasm for the New Jersey governor, his uncle, Francis Jackson Garrison, wrote his nephew that blacks would be Jim Crowed by Wilson and his "Georgian wife."[81]

Perhaps the most disturbing thing about Wilson for his cautious supporters was what the candidate did in fact say, or rather deny, during the campaign. After Trotter and Waldron had met with Wilson on July 16, 1912, Waldron wrote up an account of the meeting in a memorandum for Oswald Villard. Waldron wrote that Wilson had told him he needed African Americans' support and that he would veto any legislation that was hostile to their interests. In addition, wrote Waldron, Wilson would not exclude African Americans from office on the basis of color. On August 14, Villard forwarded the memorandum to Wilson, asking him to make a public statement similar to the one made to Waldron. Wilson responded on August 23, expressing amazement at Waldron's statements. He, of course, would be president of all the people, and African Americans had nothing to fear from a Democratic Congress. Wilson stressed, however, that he had not promised to veto legislation hostile to black interests; he denied saying that he needed black support, and he made no promises or appeals for black patronage. Villard and DuBois, greatly disturbed by Wilson's letter, drafted a statement forcefully emphasizing that African Americans needed some sort of public assurance from him. They suggested that he say "I shall be, if elected, President of the whole nation and treat every citizen according to the spirit of our institutions" and affirm that he would not be "hostile to the colored people." This was a moderate statement to be sure, but it still went much further than Wilson was willing to go. Needless to say, he never issued any public statement other than the one given to Alexander Walters.[82]

Most of the aggressive black leaders and liberal whites still supported Wilson, however, and felt somewhat reassured by the Democratic National Committee's sympathetic public appeal to African Americans entitled "Quo Vadis," which was published in *Crisis* on the eve of the election. In addition, the Democratic Party recognized black organizations working on behalf of Wilson in Massachusetts, New Jersey, New York, Virginia, and Washington, D.C. In New York, in what appears to have been an unprecedented Democratic campaign maneuver, at least on the national level, the campaign headquarters allocated $52,255.95 for the purpose of obtaining black votes—a substantial sum in those days for a historically detested group, particularly when total Democratic campaign contributions that year only amounted to something over $1 million.[83]

EMERGENCE OF THE DEMOCRATIC FAIR PLAY ASSOCIATION

Sometime between Wilson's election and his inauguration, a clandestine organization calling itself the Democratic Fair Play Association (DFPA) appeared in Washington. Although little is known about its membership or its origins, the association's main objective was unquestionably to promote, through outside agitation, the segregation and removal of black federal employees and to prevent their future entrance into the civil service. The DFPA was, in the words of one writer, "a white supremacist counterpart of the

NAACP."[84] On its professional stationery, directly above a list of twelve obscure vice presidents, was printed its goal in capital letters: "RACE SEGREGATION IN GOVERNMENT SERVICE." In one letter that appears to have been written to First Lady Ellen Wilson pleading for her help in separating "deserving white girls" from "ill-smelling negro[es]" in federal departments, the DFPA ended by proclaiming as its goal "the segregation of the races" and "the complete supremacy of the white race."[85]

The DFPA launched its campaign under the guise of civil service reform with its president, Ernest D. Martin, and secretary, Roy M. Harrop, leading the way. Although little is known about Martin or Harrop, they appear to have been, at most, former state politicians with little clout in the Democratic Party they claimed to legitimately represent. The DFPA had no affiliation with the National Civil Service Reform League (NCSRL) either. That league, made up of liberal reformers such as NAACP president Moorfield Storey, sought "responsible" changes in the civil service and an end to "corrupt" practices in government employment. Unlike the DFPA, which never had a membership worth mentioning, the NCSRL boasted a "prominent" and "widely diversified" list of notables in its organization, including Theodore Roosevelt, William Howard Taft, and Woodrow Wilson.[86]

Most newspapers leery of the DFPA believed the association's real hidden agenda was to obtain federal jobs in Washington at the expense of black employees in the civil service. The DFPA members are "political spoilsmen" disguising themselves as a legitimate organization to end "fraud in the civil service," declared one newspaper. Another newspaper headline read, "Fair Play Association Officers Are Desirous of Connecting With Jobs." In a letter desperately pleading for assistance from the well-connected Washington socialite and activist Charlotte Hopkins, the DFPA admitted that the "complete remedy" was to "purify the institutions of our country," which meant ridding federal departments of African Americans altogether. In affidavits filed by two white female federal employees—obviously instigated by the DFPA, as the witnesses printed on both are Ernest D. Martin and Roy M. Harrop—the women protested against working with "abusive," "diseased," and "overbearing negro men and negro women" and asked for an immediate "remedy," as too many "negros" were employed in their offices. With the Democrats winning control of both the executive and legislative branches for the first time in over fifty years, ambitions for federal patronage were unleashed by those who had spent years on the sidelines and felt deserving of some reward for their loyalty to a party that had been out of power for so long. This was the golden opportunity for a Democrat, and the DFPA was determined not to blow it.[87]

The DFPA claimed to have numerous members and "between thirty-five and forty state organizers at work."[88] In a circular, described by one liberal newspaper editor as "a proclamation of hate," the association announced that it stood for "segregation of the races in government employment, and reorganization of the civil service."[89] The DFPA members effectively used literature, mass meetings, letters, lobbying, and affidavits to acquire support for their cause. Although it appears that the DFPA never enjoyed widespread support, its racist tactics through persistent efforts tapped into white nativist fears and the paranoia of African Americans in Washington. Interestingly, the old raison d'être of innate black inferiority did not carry the same weight in the federal departments at Washington as it had in the South. The presence there of African Americans meant in most cases that they had outperformed whites on civil service exams to get their jobs. This fact strongly challenged, indeed threatened, the white man's sense of comfort in regard to his age-old belief in his racial superiority. Thus, the main focus had to shift to a more defensible argument—the close proximity of white females and black males in the work environment. This was perhaps the most important theme in southern society closely linked with black inferiority.

The main scare tactic the DFPA exploited was the image of white women working either side by side with, or under the domination of, black male supervisors. The supervisors were depicted as lurking sexual predators, desiring either in thought or in action to contaminate the racial purity of helpless white women. At a publicized DFPA meeting, for example, Secretary Harrop explained that during visits to federal departments made by "him and his committee," he was amazed to see "a negro employee leaning over the desk of a white woman, evidently giving her instructions relative to her work." "I could never see my mother or sister subjected to what the women in the government offices are forced to submit to," he declared.[90] If a targeted department or service employed only white and black males, the DFPA described the terrible conditions for whites forced to share the same "washrooms" and work spaces with such "objectionable people."[91]

But perhaps one of the most shocking examples the DFPA used to gain support was a letter reportedly written by a white woman working in the Interior Department. It was read in at least one mass meeting, published in the *New York Times,* and circulated within Washington. The alleged writer found it unbearable that she had to work for a "dark-skinned, wooly-headed Negro." Furthermore, the letter stressed the terrible conditions under which a white woman was subordinated to the authority of a black male and implicitly attempted to instill shame and humiliation in the conscience of the white male in hopes of forcing him to act: "I then felt if a human would ever be justified in ever ending his existence I would then, for I was a Southern woman, my father a distinguished officer during the Civil War."[92]

DFPA officers regularly appealed to white women and groups to, "in their more potent way, arouse the manhood of this country," and the group consistently exploited the "evil" image of offensive black males and "subservient" white females in the federal offices. Through public speeches and meetings; in letters, literature, and flyers; and in lobbying efforts aimed at potentially sympathetic audiences and southern members of Congress, the Cabinet, and the president, the DFPA vigorously strove to enlist support to deliver "these oppressed females" from such a disgraceful condition.[93]

This shocking expression of black phobia in regard to physical or sexual relations between black males and white females, sometimes bordering on hysteria—as demonstrated, for example, by the brutal lynchings and burnings of alleged black rapists of white women—was all too common in southern society. In fact, it appears to have been one of the major driving forces behind segregation, disfranchisement, and lynching after the 1880s. The older fear during slavery times that blacks "would rise massively and kill whites, or do them bodily injury," particularly in the post–Nat Turner era, was replaced around the late 1880s with the fear that blacks would "rise individually and sporadically and rape white women," said Joel Williamson. This became the fundamental fact, and often obsession, of antiblack thought. Inextricably linked to this fear was a belief in the popular "retrogressionist" ideology that maintained that the black race, in the absence of the bonds and structure provided by slavery, is an inferior race that is regressing morally and socially. Thus, the powerful image in the minds of many southern whites was that of the black savage or criminal returning to his normal native condition. To avoid being pulled down in his inevitable demise, so the logic went, whites must stick together and eliminate the black from political life and keep him at a distance by enforcing his segregation from the dominant white culture.[94]

By the time Wilson entered office, southern politicians had years of experience playing the race card by regularly conjuring up fears among their constituents about black fiends who did nothing but roam the rural South lusting after white women. These politicians subsequently portrayed themselves as knights in shining armor who would protect the noble white civilization via white female racial purity against such threats. Some of the major southern figures who exploited and sensationalized such fears over and over in public speeches and in the pages of newspapers were James K. Vardaman, Ben Tillman, Tom Watson, Hoke Smith, and a host of lesser-known politicians. Rebecca Felton of Georgia, who became the first female U.S. senator in 1922, added a feminine voice to the bloodthirsty cries of political demagogues by advocating black lynching to "protect women's dearest possession."[95]

Whether purveyors of this tactic seriously believed their own rhetoric or used it only to obtain power or both is unclear. Racial phobia was, and would be well into the second half of the twentieth century, a powerful tactic in the Deep South for obtaining power. An impressive body of evidence from politicians, scientists, historians, and others around the turn of the twentieth century reinforces the view that many—particularly the elite of southern society and many northerners as well—truly believed the black male was regressing into, at worst, a savagely sexual beast (the retrogressionist ideology will be dealt with more fully in Chapter 3).[96]

The extremely popular and perhaps the most penetrating racist author and orator of the era, and one of the foremost preachers of his day, Thomas Dixon Jr., had exploited this fear around the turn of the century in his famous pseudonovels, *The Leopard's Spots* and *The Clansman.* In these and all of Dixon's other writings, African Americans were depicted over and over as sexual predators, morally and physically repugnant, forever inferior, and a mortal threat to a noble white civilization. He mourned for an imaginary idealistic past, those beautiful days of racial amity on the plantation, and he held beastlike blacks responsible for the destruction of this racial paradise.

Most significant, Dixon's extreme sense of Anglo superiority was shared in one form or another by many elite white Americans, including Wilson. Moreover, he added fuel to the prejudices of his contemporaries during the Progressive Era by skillfully manipulating his audiences and readers in much the same way—through imagery and language—Hitler would do with the German people decades later. He presented an iconic Anglo-Saxon, the great leader of civilization, besieged by an inferior black race that threatened white dominance. The right to rule and the path to greatness were the destiny—indeed, the responsibility—of the superior Aryan race, believed Dixon, and blacks must be subjugated and dominated or their sinister influences would contaminate and ruin civilization, much like Hitler's Jewish "vermin."

In 1915 Dixon's romantic view of the white South as portrayed in *The Clansman,* with its candid defamation of black humanity, became the basis for the controversial and enormously successful screenplay *Birth of a Nation.* It is estimated that over 3 million people saw the film during its first eleven months in New York City alone. The film is dazzling and innovative and uses state-of-the-art cinematography, and millions were mesmerized by this early high-tech marvel. The film even inspired a popular resurgence of the real-life Ku Klux Klan. President Wilson, after a private viewing in the East

Room at the White House, allegedly called the film "history with lightening" and remarked that "it is all so terribly true."[97]

One of the main characters from *The Clansman*, depicted in *Birth of a Nation*, is a southern belle who represents the pinnacle of southern white racial purity and is brutally raped by "four black brutes." Although the film version breaks away before the rape scene, Dixon describes the scene vividly in *The Clansman* as a wild, horrific beast devouring its prey, thus completing the black male's dehumanization and reinforcing his beastly image in the white mind:

> Gus stepped closer, with an ugly leer, his flat nose dilated, his sinister bead-eyes wide apart gleaming ape-like, as he laughed. . . .
>
> The girl uttered a cry, long, tremulous, heart-rending, piteous.
>
> A single tiger-spring, and the black claws of the beast sank into the soft white throat and she was still.

In a chilling and almost divinely destined manner, the heroine bravely decides to end her existence rather than live with the shame of being contaminated, and she, along with her mother, steps off the cliff at "Lover's Leap" and commits suicide. Like the letter cited earlier, alleged to have been written by a white woman in the Interior Department, and like racist diatribes in general, Dixon's purpose was clearly to exploit racial tensions and stimulate white male outrage against any notion of black social and political equality by presenting such as an unnatural and unholy configuration of sex, power, and race.[98]

The importance of depicting African Americans in a fearful and undesirable light, particularly in sexual imagery, cannot be emphasized enough. Here was a tremendously effective tactic for influencing some high-ranking members of the government to take action or, at the least, to justify discriminatory measures taken by their subordinates. The tactic had been used for years in an attempt to maintain white solidarity in southern state and local politics. Now it was arousing white paranoia in Washington. In spring of 1913, Representative J. B. Aswell of Louisiana introduced a bill into Congress that called for the segregation of white and black employees in all government departments. In an interview with a newspaper reporter regarding his bill, Aswell explained that a motivating factor for such legislation was that white women were compelled to work at desks adjoining those of black men. In addition, the congressman stressed his desire to "preserve the integrity and the supremacy of the white race."[99] Treasury Secretary William McAdoo later admitted to Oswald Villard that his motivation for segregation was to rid his department of the "unwelcome juxtaposition" of "white women [and] colored men."[100] The DFPA was right in line with some of the racial demagogues in Congress as well, although it is not clear whether they were members of the association. Whatever the case, the DFPA certainly lent credence to the racist views these men had been espousing for years and gave impetus to the flood of Jim Crow legislation they either proposed or supported following Wilson's election.

The DFPA did reach out to the racial demagogues in Washington. In one mass meeting, Representative Emmet Wilson of Florida delivered an address on "race segregation and reform in the civil service."[101] And the DFPA attracted perhaps one of the most rabid racists ever to serve in Congress, Senator James K. Vardaman of Mississippi, to speak at a much-publicized meeting held on the night of August 6, 1913, entitled Shall the Negro Rule.[102]

The newly elected Vardaman had become one of the leading forces for white supremacy the moment he arrived in Washington—a continuation of his intense racial politicking back home in rural Mississippi. He publicly vowed to oppose the confirmation of every African American for federal office with the exception of minister to Liberia. "More than any other man," explained Vardaman biographer William F. Holmes in describing the Mississippian's legacy to the future of race relations in his state, "he instilled a blatant brand of racism into Mississippi politics that plagued the state into the late twentieth century." Now he was going to attempt to do so in Washington. Vardaman was an impressive-looking figure, standing six feet tall with broad shoulders and long, flowing black hair, and he was always well groomed and impeccably dressed. Nicknamed "The White Chief" by those sympathetic to his racial views, not to mention the fact that he dressed in white suits, Vardaman worked diligently for the segregation of African Americans in all federal offices and their removal and exclusion from any federal or diplomatic appointment.[103]

Interestingly, the Mississippian was an enlightened progressive reformer on most issues, including being an outspoken critic of anti-Semitism, an advocate of women's suffrage, and later a vociferous opponent of America's entry into World War I. Far from being an ignorant "redneck," he fit John Cell's description as one of the progressive and "well-educated" men who were the true architects, as opposed to the illiterate southern masses, of the "flexible and sophisticated" Jim Crow system in the South—although he often played the role of redneck or extremist for his constituents. As a young editor of the Greenwood (Mississippi) *Commonwealth* in the late 1890s, far in advance of most national opinion of his time, Vardaman attributed crime to "countless causes . . . over which they [men] have no control," especially mental illness and environment.[104]

SHALL THE NEGRO RULE!

ALL OTHER QUESTIONS ARE MINIMIZED UNDER THE SHADOW OF

SOCIAL EQUALITY AND PREFERENCE FOR NE- GROES

IN THE EMPLOY OF THE GOVERNMENT OF THE UNITED STATES

SENATOR JAMES K. VARDAMAN

AND OTHER PROMINENT SPEAKERS WILL ADDRESS THE PEOPLE AT A PUBLIC MEETING TO BE HELD UNDER THE AUSPICES OF THE NATIONAL DEMOCRATIC FAIR PLAY ASSOCIATION WHICH STANDS FOR SEGREGATION OF THE RACES IN GOVERNMENT EMPLOYMENT, AND "REORGANIZA- TION OF THE CIVIL SERVICE" AS DECLARED FOR IN THE NATIONAL DEMOCRATIC PLATFORM OF 1912. AT THIS MEETING THE POLICY OF APPOINTING NEGROES TO GOVERN- MENT POSITIONS WILL BE FULLY AND FREELY DISCUSSED

AT OLD MASONIC TEMPLE, COR. 9TH AND F STS. N. W.

WASHINGTON, D. C.

WEDNESDAY NIGHT, AUGUST 6, 1913.

ADMIT BEARER   AT 8 O'CLOCK

"Shall the Negro Rule!" flyer. La Follette's Magazine, *August 1913.*

Yet he went to the other extreme when it came to African Americans, who he adamantly believed were an inferior race. Like most of the racist speeches he routinely barked at crowds in Mississippi, the senator gave a "blistering" antiblack speech to the DFPA that night in August. He manipulated the emotions of his audience by first describing fond memories of the "old colored mammy" who raised him as a child, and in the next breath

he aroused his audience into a fury by depicting black males as sexual predators, roaming free in search of white female victims. They must be controlled
and white dominance maintained at any cost, he counseled. This meant,
urged the senator, the disfranchisement of every black in the country, the
abolition of all black education, and the implementation of quick justice in
the form of lynching for black rapists.[105]

But it wasn't just the Vardamans who thought it was a good idea to Jim
Crow African Americans in federal departments. National Civil Service Reform League president Charles Eliot, when approached by Oswald Villard
for assistance in dealing with federal Jim Crow, responded that he agreed
with the efforts to segregate black and white employees in Washington. Incredibly, Eliot, besides heading a liberal reform organization that ironically
advocated a more unadulterated and nondiscriminatory system of merit for
selecting government employees, had been the groundbreaking president of
Harvard for over forty years. During his remarkable tenure there, he had
transformed a provincial college made up of Anglo-Saxon elites from New
England's upper social class to one that admitted students from other ethnic
and socioeconomic backgrounds—including African Americans such as
DuBois and Trotter.[106] The path of segregation seems to have been smoothed
in this case by the acquiescence of a reformer who would have been expected
to protest such actions.

In addition, the U.S. Civil Service Commission, responsible for the administration of civil service laws and regulations but often criticized by
reformers for closely guarding what many considered to be suspicious activities,
maintained that it had no authority to act in regard to "racial" discrimination in federal departments since civil service law gave it only explicit
authority to investigate political and religious discrimination.[107] And in
1913–1914 black federal workers had no viable federal labor unions to turn
to. Most unions, whether in the public or private sector, either explicitly
denied African Americans membership or allowed them to form their own
Jim Crow affiliate, which was usually ignored. For example, the Railway
Mail Association clearly spelled out who was eligible for membership: "Any
regular male employee . . . who is of the Caucasian race."[108] To make matters
worse, vociferous segregation opponent and NAACP member John P. Gavit
observed that "Southerners in Congress have the tacit support of a large
proportion of men from the North and West."[109] With such a prevailing
atmosphere in Washington and the nation at large, it would take little prod-
ding to convince men who were already bent, and in fact had built political
careers, on eliminating them from political and social life, to take action in
regard to segregating or expunging African Americans from the civil service.

THE WILSON CABINET AND THE DFPA

Navy Secretary Josephus Daniels recorded in his diary the details of a cabinet meeting held on April 11, 1913, soon after Wilson's inauguration. At the meeting Postmaster General Albert Burleson brought up the topic of segregating black and white employees in the Railway Mail Service. He claimed it was "very unpleasant" for whites to have to use the same "drinking vessels," "towels," and "places to wash" as "negro employees" and eagerly expressed his desire to segregate the employees not only in his department but in all departments of the government. Treasury Secretary McAdoo was obviously toying with the idea of segregating black and white employees in his department as well. Despite his expressed apprehension that it may not work in Treasury because it might not be practicable, segregation was shortly instituted throughout his department. When the matter of black appointments came up, President Wilson emphasized that he had made no promises to African Americans, and although he did not wish to see them with fewer positions than they currently had, he wanted the matter "adjusted in a way to make the least friction." Burleson made it clear that he believed "it was wrong to have white clerks, men or women," under a black supervisor. If there was any opposition to Jim Crow, it was not voiced at this meeting.[110]

It appears that Burleson's attention was perhaps drawn to the conditions in the Railway Mail Service by the Democratic Fair Play Association. Four days before the cabinet meeting, the DFPA had circulated a form letter condemning the "low and criminal elements" employed in the Railway Mail Service, and a personal copy was sent to Burleson at the Post Office Department. The letter also called for the segregation and dismissal of black employees because they were driving away all worthy whites.[111] With an arduous campaign for the segregation and removal of African Americans in all government offices under way, the letter and many like it were sent to most southern Cabinet members as well as President Wilson, describing the "UnDemocratic, UnAmerican, and UnChristian" conditions that existed as white men and women were forced to work alongside some "greasy, ill-smelling Negro man or woman."[112]

The election of Woodrow Wilson ushered into Washington unabashed white prejudice against blacks that, until then, had been kept tenuously in check by a gradually deteriorating Republican order. The last vestige of protection for African Americans in the federal government against the effects of rampant Jim Crow elsewhere was gone. "There has been a change in government," declared Wilson in his inaugural address.[113] The South had returned to power.

NOTES

1. Richmond *Times-Dispatch,* November 6, 1912.

2. William Monroe Trotter to Hon. Woodrow Wilson, February 12, 1913, Trotter Correspondence, Woodrow Wilson Papers, Seeley G. Mudd Library, Princeton University, Princeton, NJ.

3. Paul D. Casdorph, *Republicans, Negroes, and Progressives in the South, 1912–1916* (University: University of Alabama Press, 1981), 209; *Historical Statistics of the United States: Colonial Times to 1957* (Washington, DC: U.S. Bureau of the Census, 1960), 687.

4. Arthur Link, *Woodrow Wilson and the Progressive Era, 1910–1917* (New York: Harper and Row, 1954), 22, 24; Morton Sosna, "The South in the Saddle: Racial Politics During the Wilson Years," *Wisconsin Magazine of History* 54 (Autumn 1970): 31, 35; *Historical Statistics,* 691; Thomas A. Bailey, *Woodrow Wilson and the Great Betrayal* (Chicago: Quadrangle Books, 1963), 39.

5. Laurence J.W. Hayes, "The Negro Federal Government Worker, 1883–1938" (M.A. thesis, Howard University Graduate School, 1941), 19. Despite its generalities, this is probably the most thorough source that deals with African Americans employed by the federal government during the first half of the twentieth century.

6. 52nd Congress, House of Representatives, Executive Document, No. 1, Part 8, quoted in ibid., 22.

7. Quoted in ibid., 24.

8. *Ohio Standard,* March 15, 1891, quoted in ibid., 25.

9. Hayes, 34; *Republican Campaign Textbook, 1912* (Washington, DC: Republican National Committee, 1912), 238.

10. *Washington Post,* March 24, 1913.

11. August Meier and Elliott Rudwick, "The Rise of Segregation in the Federal Bureaucracy, 1900–1930," *Phylon: The Atlanta University Review* 28 (1967): 178–184. The writers maintain that federal racial segregation was nothing new by the Wilson years and that "this was a Republican as well as a Democratic policy." They are primarily concerned with challenging the historical claim that federal segregation began under Wilson. Yet in doing so they treat federal segregation efforts, from Roosevelt to Coolidge, as if there was no significant difference during these years. Many sources compiled for this book—including correspondences, newspaper accounts, and President Wilson's own remarks—seem to demonstrate that federal Jim Crow during the early Wilson administration was unique in its expansion, intensity, support, and opposition. Uniquely, Jim Crow during this period went much further than just the segregation of black federal employees, as many were harassed, downgraded, and terminated. In addition, discriminating bills appeared with "greater frequency" during Wilson's first year in office, including for the first time in history bills that sought to segregate "clerks and employees of the white race from those of African descent." H.R. 13772, 63rd Congress, Second Session, February 23, 1914, and H.R. 20329, 63rd Congress, Third Session, December 23, 1914, in Box 39-25, Archibald Grimke Papers, Moorland-Spingarn Research Center, Howard University, Washington, DC.

12. Constance McLaughlin Green, *Washington: Capital City, 1879–1950* (Princeton: Princeton University Press, 1963), 217, 223–225; Sosna, 31; Dewey W. Grantham Jr.,

"The Progressive Movement and the Negro," *South Atlantic Quarterly* 54 (October 1955): 476; Hayes, 33, 57.

13. Sosna, 34; Kathleen L. Wolgemuth, "Woodrow Wilson's Appointment Policy and the Negro," *Journal of Southern History* 24 (November 1958): 467; Allison Blakely, "Black U.S. Consuls and Diplomats and Black Leadership, 1880–1920," *UMOJA: A Scholarly Journal of Black Studies* 1 (November 1977): 11–12.

14. John W. Cell, *The Highest Stage of White Supremacy: The Origins of Segregation in South Africa and the American South* (New York: Cambridge University Press, 1982), 120–122. Also, J. Morgan Kousser believes that the objective of disenfranchisement was to eliminate "potential opposition voters," black or white, *The Shaping of Southern Politics: Suffrage Restriction and the Establishment of the One-Party South, 1890–1910* (New Haven: Yale University Press, 1974), 259.

15. William F. Holmes, *The White Chief: James Kimble Vardaman* (Baton Rouge: Louisiana State University Press, 1970), 186. Also, the more moderate Sen. Carter Glass of Virginia openly stated that the delegation to Virginia's Constitutional Convention had a responsibility "to discrimate to the very extremity of permissable action under the limitations of the Federal Constitution, with a view to the elimination of every Negro voter who can be gotten rid of, legally, without impairing the numerical strength of the white electorate." See John Hope Franklin, *From Slavery to Freedom: A History of Negro Americans* (New York: Alfred A. Knopf, 1967), 341.

16. August Meier, *Negro Thought in America, 1880–1915: Racial Ideologies in the Age of Booker T. Washington* (Ann Arbor: University of Michigan Press, 1963), 39–41; Charles Crowe, "Racial Violence and Social Reform—Origins of the Atlanta Riot of 1906," *Journal of Negro History* 53 (July 1968): 234–256; quotation in C. Vann Woodward, *The Strange Career of Jim Crow* (New York: Oxford University Press, 1974), 101.

17. In address by Oswald Villard Garrison at Baltimore protest rally, printed in the *New York Times,* May 6, 1914, quoted in Charles Flint Kellogg, *NAACP: A History of the National Association for the Advancement of Colored People,* vol. 1, *1909–1920* (Baltimore: Johns Hopkins University Press, 1967), 163.

18. *Raleigh News and Observer,* October 1, 1912, quoted in Sosna, 31; Arthur S. Link, *Wilson: The Road to the White House* (Princeton: Princeton University Press, 1947), 501.

19. Hayes, 19, 31–32, 34.

20. Ibid., 23.

21. A. L. Glenn, *History of the National Alliance of Postal Employees, 1913–1956* (Cleveland: NAPE, 1956), 15, 23–25, 27; DuBois's St. Louis case study in *Crisis,* April 1914, 276. A future leader and secretary of the NAACP, Walter White, was the son of a letter carrier in Atlanta who "gave two sons and five daughters college education[s]"; William C. Bradbury Jr., "Racial Discrimination in the Federal Service: A Study in the Sociology of Administration" (Ph.D. dissertation, Columbia University, 1952), 59; correspondence from Son of a Negro Clerk, "Mr. Burleson and the Negro," *New Republic* 19 (May 31, 1919): 150.

22. "Finds Race Prejudice: Clerkships Hard to Obtain," *Washington Post,* March 9, 1913.

23. Elliott Rudwick and August Meier, "The Rise of Segregation in the Federal Bureaucracy, 1900–1930," *Phylon: The Atlanta University Review* 28 (1967): 178–184.

24. Lorenzo J. Greene and Carter G. Woodson, *The Negro Wage Earner* (Washington, DC: Association for the Study of Negro Life and History, 1931), 121. This study provides a good early account of the overt discrimination faced by blacks in the private sector and, to a lesser degree, in federal and state employment. Also Son of a Negro Clerk, *New Republic,* 150.

25. Glenn, 15; *Republican Textbook for the Congressional Campaign, 1910,* 260. Although this source is as biased as can be expected since its purpose is to promote the Republican Party during election time, much of the information and statistics presented, when cross-checked with other sources such as the *Historical Statistics of the United States,* is surprisingly accurate.

26. Casdorph, 46–47; Johnson cited in *Republican Campaign Textbook, 1916,* 376.

27. Ralph Tyler to Hon. Woodrow Wilson, May 12, 1913, Series 4, 152A, Woodrow Wilson Papers, Manuscript Division, Library of Congress, Washington, DC.

28. House of Representatives transcript entitled "Segregation of Clerks and Employees in Civil Service," undated, Series 4, 152A, Woodrow Wilson Papers, Manuscript Division, Library of Congress, Washington, DC; Green, 223.

29. Greene and Woodson, 116–117, 121, 194; Sterling Spero and Abram Harris, *The Black Worker: The Negro and the Labor Movement* (New York: Columbia University Press, 1931), 468.

30. The positions held by African Americans in the federal government prior to the Wilson years, based on a partisan study by Cyrus Adams in 1912 and substantiated in an "independent investigation" by Laurence Hayes in 1941, are: "Auditor of the Navy, assistant district attorneys, assistant librarians, architects, assistant postmasters, assistant weighers, attorneys, bookbinders, boatmen, collectors of customs, collectors of internal revenues, consuls, chiefs of divisions, compositors, chaplains, custodians, cleaners, caster-helpers, clerks, counters, charwomen, carriage drivers, deputy collectors of custom, deputy collectors of internal revenue, deputy U.S. Marshals, domestics and waiters, draughtsmen, envoy extraordinary and minister plenipotentiary, examiners of merchandise, engineers, elevator conductors, folders, farmers, firemen, floor hands, gaugers, guards, heads of departments, helpers, inspectors of customs, immigrant inspectors, imposers, janitors, letter carriers, laboratory assistant, laborers, minister resident and consul general, musicians, messengers, messenger boys, machine operators, monotype, mimeograph operators, openers and packers, postmasters, keyboard operators, patent examiners, pressmen, press feeders, pay clerks, private secretaries, receivers of public moneys, Register of the Treasury, rural delivery carriers, surveyor-general, superintendents of construction, samplers, shippers, stenographers and typists, storekeepers, skilled laborers, sewers, stablemen, teachers, translators, timekeepers, wagon messengers, watchmen, wrappers, and wagon drivers." Adams, *The Republican Party and the Afro-American: A Book of Facts and Figures* (Washington, DC: Republican National Committee, 1912), 17; Hayes, 31–32.

31. Sterling Spero, *Labor Movement in a Government Industry: A Study of Employee Organization in the Postal Service* (New York: George H. Doran, 1924), 79–80.

32. Darrell Hevenor Smith, *The United States Civil Service Commission: Its History, Activities, and Organization,* Service Monographs of the United States Government, No. 49 (Baltimore: Johns Hopkins University Press, 1928), 56, 68.

33. Spero, *Labor Movement in a Government Industry,* 127–137; Glenn, 17, 56–57.

34. Daniel C. Roper, *The United States Post Office* (New York: Funk and Wagnalls, 1917), 360–361.

35. Leslie S. Fishel Jr. and Benjamin Quarles believe the "election of Wilson was marked by a higher percentage of Negro support, up to 20 per cent of the Negro vote"; in *The Negro American: A Documentary History* (Glenview, IL: Scott, Foresman, 1967), 362; August Meier writes that "though the majority voted for Roosevelt, Negro Democrats claimed thirty percent of the Negro vote"; in "The Negro and the Democratic Party, 1875–1915," *Phylon: The Atlanta University Review* 17 (1963): 190.

36. August Heckscher writes, "[H]e received a larger share of their [African Americans'] vote than any previous Democratic candidate"; in *Woodrow Wilson: A Biography* (New York: Collier Books, Macmillian, 1991), 290. Several sources from 1912, including the *Washington Bee, Richmond Planet,* Kelly Miller's *Monographic Magazine,* and various correspondences and secondary sources, have "convinced" Kathleen Wolgemuth that the "shift in votes was indeed large," as an "unprecedented number of Negroes had cast their vote for Wilson"; in "Woodrow Wilson and Federal Segregation," *Journal of Negro History* 44 (April 1959): 158 and note. "We may be confident that Wilson did receive many Negro votes, more, probably, than any other Democratic candidate had ever received"; in Arthur Link, "The Negro as a Factor in the Campaign of 1912," *Journal of Negro History* 32 (January 1947): 98; Stephen Fox says "the actual voting produced the first considerable black defection from the GOP"; in *The Guardian of Boston: William Monroe Trotter* (New York: Atheneum, 1970), 168.

37. *La Follette's Weekly Magazine* (November 12, 1912): 5.

38. Meier, "The Negro and the Democratic Party," 175–180; John J. Broesamle, *William Gibbs McAdoo: A Passion for Change, 1863–1917* (New York: Kennikat, 1973), 69; *Bath County* (VA) *Enterprise News and Herald,* September 20, 1912.

39. Meier, "The Negro and the Democratic Party," 175–180; Vincent P. Desantis, "The Republican Party and the Southern Negro, 1877–1897," *Journal of Negro History* 45 (April 1960): 71–87; Henry Lee Moon, *Balance of Power: The Negro Vote* (New York: Doubleday, 1948), 76; *Guardian,* November 15, 1913, extract in Box 9, Moorfield Storey Papers, Manuscript Division, Library of Congress, Washington, DC. For President Theodore Roosevelt's controversial role in regard to Jim Crow, see opposition to in C. Vann Woodward, *The Origins of the New South, 1877–1913* (Baton Rouge: Louisiana State University Press, 1971), 463–464; Grantham, 467; David L. Lewis, *W.E.B. DuBois: Biography of a Race, 1868–1919* (New York: Henry Holt, 1993), 324, 330; Hayes, 31; and support of in Seth M. Scheiner, "President Roosevelt and the Negro, 1901–1908," *Journal of Negro History* 47 (July 1962): 169–182; Charles W. Calhoun, "James G. Blaine and the Republican Party Vision," in Ballard C. Campbell, ed., *The Human Tradition in the Gilded Age and the Progressive Era* (Wilmington, DE: Scholarly Resources, 2000), 24, 28; Woodward, *Origins of the New South,* 466; Lewis, 324, 331; Kelly Miller, *Race Adjustment: Essays on the Negro in America* (New York: Arno, 1968), 291–292.

40. Francis L. Broderick, "DuBois and the Democratic Party, 1908–1916," *Negro History Bulletin* 21 (November 1957): 41; Oswald Garrison Villard to Francis Garrison, October 10, 1913, Oswald Villard Papers, Houghton Library, Harvard University, Cambridge, MA.

41. Hilary Herbert quoted in Broderick, 41; Glenn, 18. Although Cleveland's first administration reached out to blacks in terms of federal jobs, it appears that by his second

administration he was more cautious in regard to blacks in high-level civil service positions, particularly when they had charge over white women; see Hayes, 27–30.

42. Green, 223; Joel Williamson, *A Rage for Order: Black-White Relations in the American South Since Emancipation* (Oxford: Oxford University Press, 1976), 80. The *Guardian* later exclaimed, "How different is the second Democratic President in 30 years! The colored man is wishing for one minute of Grover Cleveland in the White House." October 24, 1913.

43. Thomas Dixon to Wilson, June 27, 1913, quoted in Wolgemuth, "Woodrow Wilson's Appointment Policy," 463.

44. Fox, 150–154; Woodward, *Origins of the New South,* 467; Scheiner, 181–182; Lewis, 331.

45. George C. Osborn, "Woodrow Wilson Appoints a Negro Judge," *Journal of Southern History* 24 (November 1958): 485–487.

46. *Republican Campaign Textbooks,* 1910, 1912, 1916.

47. Woodward, *The Strange Career of Jim Crow,* 82. Also, in regard to the northern attitude toward Jim Crow, one observer of the American scene during the early Wilson years remarked that the government's segregation of black clerks would have caused a tornado of protest thirty years earlier. "Now it passes almost unnoticed." Kellogg, 177.

48. Louis R. Harlan, *Booker T. Washington: The Making of a Black Leader, 1856–1901* (Oxford: Oxford University Press, 1972), 262–263.

49. Ibid., 193, 262–266; James M. McPherson, *The Abolitionist Legacy: From Reconstruction to the NAACP* (Princeton: Princeton University Press, 1975), 305; Linda O. McMurray, *To Keep the Waters Troubled: The Life of Ida B. Wells* (New York: Oxford University Press, 1998), 252.

50. McPherson, 317.

51. Fox, 76–77.

52. Lewis, 317, 320–321.

53. Ibid., 322, 326–327; Crowe, 234–256.

54. This does not imply that Washington was not the most influential black leader in America in 1912. I simply point out that the belief in aggressive action for black equality was beginning to dominate the thinking of many blacks and liberal whites, including not only the NAACP and the NIPL but also numerous newspapers and black suffrage and political leagues. Also, Washington did not enjoy the influence with Wilson that he had with previous presidents. In his own words, Washington admitted that he had only been able to "get into a little working touch with President Wilson." Washington to Charles Anderson, April 2, 1914, quoted in Kellogg, 173. Kathleen Wolgemuth says, "Washington . . . had little connection with the Democratic administration, was no longer advisor to the President on matters which affected his race." "Woodrow Wilson and Federal Segregation," 171–172.

55. Gerda Lerner, "Early Community Work of Black Club Women," *Journal of Negro History* 59 (April 1974): 158; Evelyn Brooks Higginbotham, *Righteous Discontent: The Women's Movement in the Black Baptist Church, 1880–1920* (Cambridge: Harvard University Press, 1993), 7–18, 182–183; Anne Firor Scott, "Most Invisible of All: Black Women's Voluntary Associations," *Journal of Southern History* 56 (February 1990): 6–7; Jacqueline Jones, *Labor of Love, Labor of Sorrow: Black Women, Work, and the Family, From Slavery to the Present* (New York: Vintage, 1985), 194.

56. Higginbotham, 1, 8, 12, 221–229, and "Clubwomen and Electoral Politics in the 1920s," in Ann D. Gordon, ed., *African American Women and the Vote, 1837–1965* (Amherst: University of Massachusetts Press, 1997), 135–136, 140–141; Floris Loretta Barnett Cash, "Womanhood and Protest: The Club Movement Among Black Women, 1892–1922" (Ph.D. diss., State University of New York, Stony Brook, 1986), 11–13, 211, 218; Beverly Washington Jones, *Quest for Equality: The Life and Writings of Mary Church Terrell, 1863–1954* (New York: Carlson, 1990), 21, 28–29; McPherson, 318–332; Grace Elizabeth Hale, *Making Whiteness: The Culture of Segregation in the South, 1890–1940* (New York: Pantheon, 1998), 31–35; Kathleen C. Berkeley, "'Colored Ladies Also Contributed': Black Women's Activities From Benevolence to Social Welfare, 1866–1896," in Walter J. Fraser, R. Frank Saunders Jr., and Jon L. Wakelyn, eds., *The Web of Southern Social Relations: Women, Family, and Education* (Athens: University of Georgia Press, 1985), 184–185; Adena C.E. Minot (the Northeastern Federation of Women's Clubs) to Oswald Villard, August 23, 1913, Administrative Files, Box 403, NAACP Papers, Manuscript Division, Library of Congress, Washington, DC.

57. Dorothy Salem, *To Better Our World: Black Women in Organized Reform, 1890–1920* (New York: Carlson, 1990), 145–146, 155–156, 158–159, 164. Salem believes the efforts of black women in the early days of the NAACP determined its "ultimate survival and expansion in black communities," 158; Higginbotham, 4, 143, 150, 158–159, 181–184, 234 note 29, 235 note 33; *NAACP, Fifth Annual Report, 1914,* 3–4, 13–24, Box 9, Moorfield Storey Papers, Manuscript Division, Library of Congress, Washington, DC; *Crisis,* October 1913, 275–277; McMurray, 302–304; *Crisis,* December 1913, 140; Adena C.E. Minot (the Northeastern Federation of Women's Clubs) to Oswald Villard, August 23, 1913, and W.E.B. DuBois to Rolfe Cobleigh, August 28, 1913, Administrative Files, Box 403, NAACP Papers, Manuscript Division, Library of Congress, Washington, DC.

58. Salem, 145–146, 155–156, 158–159.

59. Rayford Logan, *The Negro in American Thought and Life: The Nadir, 1877–1901* (New York: Dial Press, 1954) and *The Negro in the United States* (Princeton, NJ: D. Van Nostrand Company, Inc., 1957), 55; Higginbotham, 4; Hale, 34–35; Nanny Burroughs, "Black Women and Reform," in Herbert Aptheker, ed., *A Documentary History of the Negro People in the United States, 1910–1932,* vol. 2 (Secaucus, NJ: Citadel, 1973), 109.

60. National Convention at Wilberforce, 1914, Reel 1, Records of the NACW, 1895–1992, Manuscript Division, Library of Congress, Washington, DC.

61. Kevin Gaines, *Uplifting the Race: Black Leadership, Politics, and Culture in the Twentieth Century* (Chapel Hill: University of North Carolina Press, 1996), xiv–xv, 12–17.

62. Woodrow Wilson, *The New Freedom: A Call for the Emancipation of the Generous Energies of a People* (New York: Doubleday, Page, & Company, 1913), 14–15.

63. Oswald Garrison Villard, *Fighting Years: Memoirs of a Liberal Editor* (New York: Harcourt, Brace, and Co., 1939), 240.

64. John L.F. Talton to Woodrow Wilson, June 17, 1912, in Arthur Link, ed., *The Papers of Woodrow Wilson,* 63 vols. (Princeton: Princeton University Press, 1966–1977), 24: 484.

65. John H.G. Davis to Woodrow Wilson, July 16, 1912, in Link, *Papers* 24: 553.

66. Giles B. Jackson to Woodrow Wilson, December 12, 1913, in Link, *Papers* 24: 620.

67. Link, "The Negro," 85.

68. W. C. Crews interviewing John Patillo, in "A Tale of Woodrow Wilson and His Negro Playmate," *Virginia WPA Historical Inventory Project,* November 2, 1936.

69. Blakely, "Black U.S. Consuls and Diplomats," 2, 9.

70. William Monroe Trotter to Woodrow Wilson, November 15, 1910, and Trotter to Wilson, July 18, 1912, Woodrow Wilson Papers, Seeley G. Mudd Library, Princeton University, Princeton, NJ; copy of latter also in Link, *Papers* 24: 558–559.

71. Trotter to Wilson, July 18, 1912, and Governor Foss to Wilson, July 15, 1912, Woodrow Wilson Papers, Princeton University, Princeton, NJ; copy of former also in Link, *Papers* 24: 558–559.

72. Charles Puttkammer and Ruth Worthy, "William Monroe Trotter, 1872–1934," *Journal of Negro History* 43 (October 1958): 307. There seems no evidence that the meeting actually occurred, although the source is from an interview with Irma and Arthur Brown who were close to the events swirling in Boston during Wilson's first election. Moreover, considering Wilson's total disinclination to speak before black conferences and clubs during the election, it is unlikely that he would have gone out of his way to stop at the office of an African American newspaper.

73. Wilson to Walters, October 16, 1912, quoted in both Kellogg, 159, and Aptheker, ed., *A Documentary History,* 57–58.

74. NIPL stationery in Guardian of Boston Collection, Department of Special Collections, Mugar Memorial Library, Boston University, Boston, MA.

75. Newspaper extract in Link, *Papers* 24: 574.

76. Villard to Francis Jackson Garrison, August 14, 1912, Folder 1451, Oswald Villard Papers, Houghton Library, Harvard University, Cambridge, MA, partially quoted in Kellogg, 157.

77. Oswald G. Villard to Woodrow Wilson, August 14, 1912, in Link, "The Negro," 89.

78. Broderick, 41–44; *Guardian,* quoted in Lewis, 341.

79. *Crisis,* August 1912, 181; "Now Mr. Black Voter" quote in *Crisis,* September 1912, 236; Kenneth M. Glazier, "W.E.B. DuBois' Impressions of Woodrow Wilson," *Journal of Negro History* 58 (October 1973): 453–455. Also, perhaps a more deeply significant reason African Americans supported Wilson was the candidate's rhetoric, which was often dressed in religious and moral imagery. This probably inspired many African Americans whose roots were deeply embedded in the church. This will be further dealt with in Chapter 4.

80. "Wilson and the Negro," *New York Age,* July 11, 1912, in Trotter Correspondence, Woodrow Wilson Papers, Seeley G. Mudd Library, Princeton University, Princeton, NJ, partially quoted in Link, "The Negro," 87.

81. Link, "The Negro," 82; Francis Jackson Garrison to Villard, July 16, 1912, Folder 1451, Oswald Villard Papers, Harvard University, Cambridge, MA, partially quoted in Kellogg, 157.

82. Villard to Wilson, August 14, 1912, Wilson to Villard, August 23, 1912, and Villard to Wilson, August 28, 1912, all in Oswald Villard Papers, Harvard University, Cambridge, MA, quoted in Kellogg, 157–159. Also Link, "The Negro," 90–91.

83. *Crisis,* November 1912, 44–45; Rolla Wells, *Report of the Treasurer of the Democratic National Committee. Presidential Campaign of 1912* (New York: Democratic National Committee, 1913), 172. Also Link, "The Negro," 85–86, and in Broesamle, 69, 242 note 31.

84. Sosna, 33.

85. The DFPA to "Madam," May 9, 1913, Microfilm, Series 4, Reel 230, Woodrow Wilson Papers, Manuscript Division, Library of Congress, Washington, DC.

86. Correspondence, Box 8, John A. Fairlie Papers, University Archives, University of Illinois at Urbana-Champaign.

87. Undated newspaper clipping entitled "Wearing Mask of Civil Service," and *Washington Herald,* May 15, 1913, untitled newspaper clipping, each in Box 39-38, Archibald Grimke Papers, Moorland-Spingarn Research Center, Howard University, Washington, DC; pamphlet entitled "Segregation of Clerks and Employees in the Civil Service," Microfilm, Series 4, Reel 231, Woodrow Wilson Papers, Manuscript Division, Library of Congress, Washington, DC.

88. Undated newspaper clipping entitled "Gaurdians of Civil Service Want Positions," *Washington Herald,* Box 39-38, Archibald Grimke Papers, Moorland-Spingarn Research Center, Howard University, Washington, DC.

89. Belle Case La Follette, "The Color Line," *La Follette's Weekly Magazine* (August 1913): 6.

90. Undated newspaper clipping entitled "Takes up Race Issue," Box 39-38, Archibald Grimke Papers, Moorland-Spingarn Research Center, Howard University, Washington, DC.

91. Undated newspaper clipping entitled "Keeps Races Apart: Bill by Aswell, of Louisiana, Separates U.S. Employees," Box 39-38, Archibald Grimke Papers, Moorland-Spingarn Research Center, Howard University, Washington, DC.

92. *New York Times,* May 4, 1913, in Wolgemuth, "Woodrow Wilson and Federal Segregation," 159–160.

93. Ernest Martin, DFPA President, to Charlotte Hopkins, May 28, 1913, Box 2, Series 3411, Charlotte Hopkins Papers, Manuscript Division, Library of Congress, Washington, DC.

94. I. A. Newby, *Jim Crow's Defense: Anti-Negro Thought in America, 1900–1930* (Baton Rouge: Louisiana State University Press, 1965), 67, 135–138; Williamson, 94–95.

95. Newby, 67, 135–138.

96. Ibid.

97. Everett Carter, "Cultural History Written With Lightening: The Significance of *The Birth of a Nation,*" *American Quarterly* 12 (Fall 1960): 347–348, 353–357; Maxwell Bloomfield, "*The Leopard's Spots:* A Study in Popular Racism," *American Quarterly* 16 (Fall 1964): 393, 395–400; quotes in Williams, 114–115. There has been much curious debate over whether or not President Wilson referred favorably to *The Birth of a Nation* in his private remarks. While it is true that his alleged remarks were quoted to the press by Dixon and/or Griffith to give the film credibility, it is the opinion of this author that Wilson agreed with much of its historical content, regardless of whether he did or did not use the famous quotes attributed to him. And although Wilson, at the urging of Joseph Tumulty, tried to distance himself from the film after months of intense protest, claiming he was "unaware as to the character of the play before it was presented," this statement appears disingenious. For one thing, as mentioned in the text, *The Birth of a Nation* was based on Dixon's enormously popular book and stage production, *The Clansman.* The author had probably given his friend and classmate from John Hopkins a copy of his best seller when it appeared in 1905 (the success of which helped turn Doubleday & Page into a publishing giant). Even if Wilson had never read the book, he could hardly have missed the storm of public controversy which the stage production had created for almost a decade. And Wilson was sympathetic to the racist portrayal of Reconstruction in the film, which drew on some of his own

views as well as direct quotes from his *History of the American People*. Finally, if Wilson was distressed over the film after the White House viewing on February 18, 1915, he did nothing to interfere with its showing the next night to Washington elite. With all considered, it seems very unlikely that theamactically *The Birth of a Nation* caught Wilson by surprise (although its groundbreaking cinematography certainly did, as it did for most who saw the film), or that he was opposed to the film's portrayal of Reconstruction.

98. Thomas Dixon Jr., *The Clansman: An Historical Romance of the Ku Klux Klan* (New York: Grosset and Dunlap, 1905), 303–308.

99. Undated newspaper clipping entitled "Keeps Races Apart: Bill by Aswell, of Louisiana, Separates U.S. Employees," Box 39-38, Archibald Grimke Papers, Moorland-Spingarn Research Center, Howard University, Washington, DC.

100. McAdoo to Villard, October 27, 1913, Folder 2369, Oswald Villard Papers, Houghton Library, Harvard University, Cambridge, MA.

101. Undated newspaper clipping entitled "Takes up Race Issue," in Box 39-38, Archibald Grimke Papers, Moorland-Spingarn Research Center, Howard University, Washington, DC.

102. La Follette, "The Color Line," 6.

103. Holmes, *The White Chief,* xi, 32, 286–287 (quotation on xi); Cell, 18–19, 120; Osborn, 484.

104. Quoted in Holmes, xi; Cell, 18–19, 120.

105. Holmes, xi, 32, 286–287; Osborn, 484.

106. Villard to Eliot, September 29, 1913, November 10, 1913, Eliot to Villard, November 11, 1913, all in Oswald Villard Papers, Houghton Library, Harvard University, Cambridge, MA, quoted in Kellogg, 172; Miller, 70; Lewis, 81: "The poorest and the richest students are equally welcome here," boasted Eliot (ibid., 84); various correspondences in Box 8, John A. Fairlie Papers, University of Illinois at Urbana-Champaign. The *Chicago Public* declared that "if civil-service reformers shut their eyes to this violation of civil-service reform principles, then they cannot consistently object to a return to the old spoils system," quoted in *Crisis,* November 1913, 332.

107. Smith, 71–73.

108. Samuel E. Warren, "The Development of Negro Labor: An Adventure in Teaching Certain Aspects of American Labor History," *Journal of Negro History* 25 (January 1940): 52–53.

109. John P. Gavit to Oswald Villard, October 1, 1913, Folder 280, Oswald Villard Papers, Houghton Library, Harvard University, Cambridge, MA, quoted in Link, *Papers* 28: 348–350. Overt racial prejudice against blacks was not confined below the Mason-Dixon line during the Progressive Era. When Wilson became president, it was northern legislatures that were flooded with anti-intermarriage and segregated transportation bills. For more on northern attitudes regarding race, see Chapter 5, note 24.

110. E. David Cronon, ed., *The Cabinet Diaries of Josephus Daniels, 1913–1921* (Lincoln: University of Nebraska Press, 1963), 32–33.

111. Wolgemuth, "Woodrow Wilson and Federal Segregation," 159.

112. Democratic Fair Play Association Circular, May 9, 1913, quoted in ibid., 160.

113. Inaugural Address of President Wilson, in Box 39-38, Archibald Grimke Papers, Moorland-Spingarn Research Center, Howard University, Washington, DC.

2

THE COLOR LINE IS DRAWN IN WASHINGTON
The NAACP Prepares for Battle in New York

RUMORS SURROUNDING THE SEGREGATION AND DISMISSAL of black federal employees had been leaking out of Washington for months after Wilson's inauguration. Most of the segregation, however, was being "slowly" introduced and "subtlety" concealed in a low-key approach that made it difficult to attribute it to any specific authority.[1] Nevertheless, the black and liberal white press, along with the African American leadership, began sounding the alarm. Upon learning that the president-elect had appointed southerner Albert Burleson postmaster general in February 1913, William Monroe Trotter, aware of the inherent dangers this appointment presented to black postal employees, expressed his opposition in a letter to Wilson: "I simply ask for such a disposition of your forces that a man from a section of great color prejudice will not have jurisdiction over the largest body of Colored government employees."[2] On May 24, 1913, the Boston *Guardian* printed an article informing readers that "a petition signed by more than 8,000 railway mail clerks," requesting the immediate segregation of African Americans in the Railway Mail Service, was presented to Postmaster General

Burleson.[3] In the June 1913 issue of *Crisis,* readers were warned about the efforts of a "society calling itself the National Democratic Fair Play Association" that sought to use "the Negro as a bait" for promoting federal segregation and getting their jobs within the civil service.[4] And after a black mail clerk in the South wrote a letter to the *New York Globe* explaining how he was marked "incompetent" and recommended for dismissal after he was forty-five minutes late for work one day because of an emergency, the newspaper criticized "a Democratic Administration" that permitted "its subordinates to go on to embarrass and annoy Negro Civil Service Employees who are not wanted in this branch of the service."[5]

Around the same time, an issue concerning black federal patronage provoked comment and protest. Black leaders, some of whom had been lobbying the new president for their share of federal offices, began to grow increasingly impatient as March and April passed without Wilson making any black appointments. Rumors circulated within the black press that the president's failure to appoint African Americans was to be official policy throughout his administration. Calvin Chase of the Washington (D.C.) *Bee* wrote Wilson at the end of March that, based on statements of "those closest to the President," he believed such rumors to be true.[6] By April, letters and editorials criticizing Wilson for making no black appointments began to appear more frequently in white as well as black newspapers such as the *New York Times.*

A new action by the administration soon incensed African Americans even more. To the chagrin of the black press and leaders, the new president began to quietly remove black men from what were considered traditional black posts, replacing them with white men. By September 1913, W.E.B. DuBois was openly protesting the removal of a dozen black officials. These losses included most high-profile black offices such as assistant attorney general, register of the treasury, recorder of the deeds in Washington, and collector of customs in Washington. African Americans were being removed daily from a great number of postmaster positions.[7]

Particularly offensive to African Americans was the appointment of an unqualified southern white man to the traditional black post of minister to Haiti, an all-black nation. Madison R. Smith, a relatively undistinguished one-term congressman from Alabama, replaced Henry W. Furniss who held four university degrees and had been minister to Haiti for almost eight years and who had previously served as consul to Brazil. Although black and liberal white leaders actively worked for the appointment of black Democrats and protested against their exclusion, of the thirty-three highest appointments, only one black Democrat and one black Republican were confirmed during Wilson's first administration—James Curtis as minister to Liberia and Robert Terrell as municipal judge in the District of Columbia, respectively. Seven black Republicans, appointed during the Taft administration, were retained in what amounted to insignificant consulates in little-known parts of the world such as Madagascar and Monrovia. Even black consuls themselves, although sometimes serving in "nice berths," wondered if their service was not just a form of exile or deportation.[8]

With African Americans distressed over the loss of appointments to federal offices and diplomatic posts, particularly considering their symbolic importance, many were becoming increasingly distracted by what appeared to be a Wilson administration policy to segregate black workers in federal bureaus and offices. By early summer, black federal employees were flooding the National Association for the Advancement of Colored People (NAACP) headquarters in New York City with letters, "stirred up over what they considered the hostile attitude of the Administration in regard to colored employees in the government departments."[9]

For the most part, it seemed like provocations to discriminate against African Americans in the federal civil service came solely from white workers or outside influences. Then on July 12, 1913, Assistant Secretary of the Treasury John Skelton Williams sent an official order to his chief clerk and superintendent, James Wilmeth, instructing the arrangement of separate restrooms for "white and colored employees." Almost immediately the order ended up in the hands of racial reformers. Although the NAACP was very careful not to "place the whole segregation issue" on this one written order, it was the first of at least three segregation orders to reach the public and serve as a major impetus for protestors. The other two included one found in September stating that the "notices of July 15" segregating toilets in the Architect's Office of the Treasury Department were "still in force" and an order discovered in October—dated July 16, 1913—segregating toilets in the "Office of the Auditor of the Interior Department," signed by Robert Woolley, chief auditor of the treasury and a close friend and colleague of John Williams. All the other orders to segregate had been oral, or if written orders were given, they were deliberately kept from falling into the wrong hands.[10]

DuBois, frustrated by what seemed an orchestrated plan of secrecy, complained to the editor of the *Congregationalist and Christian World,* Rolfe Colbleigh, that "[t]he actual facts are difficult to get at because there is very little documentary record." This was because "the order has come down from above by telephone and is communicated by word of mouth." Nevertheless, it had been apparent from the increasing number of complaints from black federal employees that segregation was gaining momentum before the first written order was discovered. The Williams order segregating restrooms not only reinforced such complaints but also signaled the advent of what appeared to be an official policy of the new administration. It was now a fact that a highly ranked cabinet official had ordered the color line to be drawn in his department.[11]

Yet the power behind the order issued by Williams, who signed it as acting secretary, carried an almost absolute authority in the Treasury Department that may have even escaped those such as DuBois. Shortly before Wilson's inauguration, the outgoing treasury secretary, Franklin McVeagh, issued an order stating that "[c]irculars promulgating rules and regulations affecting the personnel of the Treasury Department generally" and "circulars establishing departmental policies . . . involving two or more bureaus or divisions . . . will be signed by the Secretary or Acting Secretary."[12] This essentially meant that Williams, in the capacity of acting secretary with the consent of William Gibbs McAdoo (and probably, in some cases, without his consent), could set departmental policy at Treasury—including in all of its adjunct auditors' offices located in almost every federal department. His order to segregate restrooms carried as much authority as if it had come from McAdoo. Thus, even taking the Williams order by itself, Jim Crow restrooms were created at one of the highest levels—indeed, at the cabinet and executive level—of power in the United States.

Like Wilson, Williams was a native-born Virginian. Robert Woolley, his chief auditor at Treasury, although born in Kentucky, had spent most of his life in Virginia. Both men brought to Washington their homegrown racist views in regard to African Americans. They were two of the highest-ranking Treasury appointees. In fact, during the early Wilson years, Williams was second only to McAdoo in power at Treasury. In 1914 he was appointed the comptroller of Treasury, considered the most prestigious position in government finance. A descendant of an old Virginia planter family and an ancestor of Edmund Randolph, secretary of state under George Washington, Williams had attended law school for a few years at the University of Virginia and later became a railroad magnate before losing part of his family fortune in a scuffle over control of his rising empire. His stellar reputation for a consuming love of justice and deep respect for the individual, not unlike other elite southern whites, applied only to whites. Although not as flamboyant as the white-suited James Vardaman, Williams perpetually wore a cutaway coat from a bygone era and walked in a dignified manner, and like the Mississippian, he is described as a self-gratifying, rabid racist. Following his premature death in 1926, one Georgia newspaper romantically eulogized his southern "cavalier spirit," dedicated to helping the South recover from "the horrors of re-construction."[13]

Although Woolley's appointment as chief auditor had less prestige than Williams's, he was a close friend of McAdoo and had worked as an antitrust investigator before serving as publicity agent for Wilson during the presidential campaign. He seems to have been less eye-catching than Williams, but he shared the same racist views.[14]

If Jim Crow in the federal departments had begun to raise its divisive head under Roosevelt and Taft, the recently hastened efforts to segregate black employees took on a new significance, as segregation was being "pushed with greater vigor and rapidity" under an administration dominated by southerners. The Chicago *Defender,* a militant African American newspaper, without any knowledge of the April 11 cabinet meeting in which segregation was proposed, announced to its readers that the segregation order from Williams could not have been put in force without the approval of Treasury Secretary McAdoo. "The fact that McAdoo permits the orders to go into effect is proof," explained the newspaper, "that President Wilson is in favor of them."[15]

Shortly after the Williams segregation order reached the public, a chorus of protest rang out from blacks and liberal whites across the country. The NAACP, organized a little less than three years earlier, was anything but a novice, as it quickly thrust itself into a formidable battle against Jim Crow in the federal departments. It may have seemed like David versus Goliath, and it probably was, but what the new organization lacked in maturity it more than made up for in determination and brilliant leadership. The coterie of impressive and committed NAACP leadership in its early years was made up of what Joel Spingarn dubbed the "new abolitionists"—highly educated professionals and intellectuals who shared the same liberal vision for racial justice and color-blind democracy. These leaders—most of whom, except the women, were listed in *Who's Who in America, 1914–1915*—included Oswald Villard, W.E.B. DuBois, John E. Milholland, Mary Church Terrell, May Childs Nerney, Mary Wilson, Joel Spingarn, Moorfiled Storey, and many, many others.[16]

The NAACP was the outgrowth and coalescence of several organizations—some aggressive and others more moderate—such as the Constitution League, the New England Suffrage League, the National Afro-American Council, and, most notably, the Niagara Movement. Yet others that were not necessarily equal rights organizations—particularly black women's clubs—also contributed to the rise of the NAACP by working for self-improvement in black communities through, among other things, education, thereby building confident black men and women who would be responsive to a national organization for advancing their rights. These groups included the National

Association of Colored Women, the Women's Baptist Convention, and social settlement houses—all of which furnished an untold number to NAACP membership roles. Many of these members became leaders as well and helped lay the groundwork for what would become the most effective organization fighting for black equality and against racial injustice in the twentieth century.[17]

Although most historians believe the NAACP in its formative years was weak and limited in scope, an opinion expressed by a few contemporaries of that period as well, a closer look reveals a visionary organization ready to battle Jim Crow almost from its inception. As the original conference that formed the NAACP came to a close on July 21, 1909, the thousand or so men and women attending voted for a reprimand of President Taft for reducing the number of black officeholders in the South, demanded strict enforcement of civil rights under the Fourteenth and Fifteenth amendments, appealed for black access to the ballot, and called for equal educational opportunities for all Americans.[18]

By the end of 1913, as the battle against federal Jim Crow was at its zenith, membership and branches had more than doubled from eleven branches and 1,100 members the previous year to over twenty branches and 3,000 members nationwide. "The NAACP," remarked DuBois around this time, "is the new abolition society."[19]

With so much energy poured into the fight against federal Jim Crow, it was amazing what else the organization was able to accomplish during this time. Far from being unproductive in its early years, as has been charged, the NAACP—in both its national and local branches from 1912 through 1914—was active all over the country in challenging the constitutionality of numerous segregation ordinances, laws, and proposals in residential areas, public places, and transportation; fighting racial discrimination in employment, restaurants, and theaters; intervening through legal pressure and outside support for the release from prison of innocent blacks falsely charged; campaigning rigorously to drum up membership and increase the number of branches; and actively opposing the onslaught of racist legislation flooding Congress and state legislatures, including the ubiquitous anti-intermarriage bills.[20]

By the end of Wilson's second term as president, NAACP membership reached over 100,000, thus becoming in an era that had witnessed the growth of large farm and business pressure groups the first significant pressure group working for black political and civil rights. NAACP historian Charles Flint Kellogg believes "the reason for this spectacular rise in membership" was the "sanction and extension of segregation . . . during the Wilson administration," which contributed to the "violence and mistreatment of Negros" during those years. The young equal rights organization, along with numerous sympathizers, was gradually becoming a force that could not be ignored. With influential contacts and friends nationwide, coupled with a growing membership, it was the most likely organization to lead the protest against federal Jim Crow, and it wasted little time launching an investigation into the new matter at hand.[21]

The board chairman of the NAACP and liberal editor of the *New York Evening Post,* Oswald Garrison Villard, had been careful not to publicly blame President Wilson when rumors of federal Jim Crow first began spreading. Despite Villard's recollection years later of his boldness in directly confronting and threatening Wilson over the issue, he "delayed" taking any action that might have "hurt the proposal for a race commission"—which he had presented to the president earlier that spring—to "study the status of the Negro in the life of the nation." Besides, his personal friendship with the president reached back to Wilson's days at Princeton, and Villard had been too staunch a supporter in the 1912 campaign to hastily criticize the friend in whom he had such high hopes.[22] The extent of their friendship can perhaps be surmised in a handwritten note Wilson had sent Villard: "You may be sure that I will never think anything you write—in other than an act of frank friendliness—even when I disagree."[23] Like many people questioning the meaning of federal segregation in its early days under Wilson, Villard was reluctant to believe his friend and author of *The New Freedom* could possibly approve of such a policy.

Behind the scenes, however, Villard began to wonder just how much the new president knew about the Jim Crow taking place in his administration. Did Wilson realize the speed with which these actions were taking place and the dangers they presented to African Americans, indeed, to his own administration? Villard was the grandson of the fiery abolitionist William Lloyd Garrison, a powerful influence in his life. During his battles against racial injustice, Villard thought of himself as a latter-day Garrison. He was part of a family tradition that was determined to free African Americans from the shackles of white prejudice, working toward the day when they could freely participate in political life. With such a high standard to live up to and a burning compassion ingrained in him since his youth, Villard would stay close to his roots, letting the ardent passion of his grandfather light his way. When anti-intermarriage bills began to flood state legislatures shortly after Wilson's election, for example, Villard and the NAACP sent an "earnest" protest to all states considering such legislation, quoting Garrison debunking the rationale behind a similar Massachusetts law in 1843.[24]

Villard's background and training gave him an inspired sense of purpose to see justice done for his oppressed brethren. The resulting messiah complex sometimes made the chairman appear condescending and obstinate when it came to sharing his leadership with other members of the NAACP. "He is used to advising colored men and giving them orders and he simply cannot bring himself to work with one as an equal," DuBois told a close friend. The truth was, however, that the controlling Villard found it difficult to work on an even par with just about everybody—black or white—although as was true with many other white racial reformers, a degree of paternalism could be detected in his dealings with African Americans. "From his grandfather," explained James M. McPherson, "Villard seems to have inherited a prickly ego that made it difficult for him to share authority." In addition, his private life may have influenced his professional attitude. Villard's wife had grown up in the South, and she adamantly refused to entertain black guests in their home. How much this may have affected the liberal Villard in his personal relationships with African Americans is unclear. Nevertheless, the color of his skin, not to mention his stellar reputation as an excellent journalist and editor, made him more acceptable to the white power structure than a black protestor of the same temperament would have been.[25]

As letters of complaint flooded NAACP headquarters on Vesey Street in New York City, Villard made several attempts to contact President Wilson about the issue. On July 21, in a letter to the president, Villard respectfully explained that he was receiving "numerous protests" from people "stirred up over what they consider to be a hostile attitude of the Administration in regards to colored people in the government departments." The response to Villard's letter came just two days later and confirmed that the president approved of a policy of separate but equal in the federal government. "My own feeling is by putting certain bureaus and sections of the service in the charge of Negroes, we are rendering them more safe in their possession of office and less likely to be discriminated against," rationalized Wilson. "It is as far as possible from being a movement against the Negroes. I sincerely believe it to be in their interest."[26]

Villard and the NAACP vehemently disagreed with this logic. They understood all too well that this policy was not being carried out in the interest of African Americans, although the president may have sincerely thought so. Segregation "is the very thing that has caused friction," declared a worker in the Government Printing Office.[27] It was a humiliating policy that forced African Americans into the least desirable conditions and jobs, heightened harassment, and paved the way for their termination from the civil service. "That separation leads to subordination is clear from the case of separate cars, schools, etc.," affirmed the NAACP. Segregation has always meant African Americans would be relegated to an "inferior" position. The NAACP further believed Jim Crow was detrimental to both races, since it increased "the already deep feeling of strangeness between whites and blacks." Finally, the young equal rights organization castigated segregation as "evil," since it forced African Americans down into a "lowly" condition without chance for improvement regardless of "merit."[28]

It was obvious by this time that the color line was being drawn in several departments and bureaus in the nation's capital. During summer 1913, NAACP secretary May Childs Nerney, on investigative assignment, made contact with black federal employees in Washington and others who had firsthand knowledge of federal Jim Crow. Hired a year earlier, she is credited for the burgeoning growth that occurred in black membership and branches of the NAACP during its early years, thereby laying the fundamental ground-work for what would arise as the most powerful organization battling racial injustice.[29]

Nerney is a somewhat mysterious historical figure. A librarian who was plucked out of obscurity, she seems to have burst onto the scene out of nowhere, and a short time later she disappeared into anonymity. During her short tenure as secretary, Nerney brought to the NAACP, according to DuBois, an "excellent spirit and indefatigable energy" and a blind passion to battle "vigorously" against Jim Crow—prerequisites that would serve her well in putting together the pieces of the segregation puzzle in Washington. More-over, her confrontational style exploded the meek and passive librarian ste-reotype. Outspoken and hot-tempered, she would face the Jim Crow giant (and any obstacle, for that matter) with her slingshot and never flinch. The early months of the investigation, during mid- to late summer 1913, would be crucial to building a case against the federal government in Washington, and Nerney—fixated on her goal—would lead the charge.[30]

The NAACP would not go too far out on a limb until it had enough information to verify some details of the departmental segregation. "We must get more publicity and to get it we need fresh and up-to-date data," ex-plained the investigator to a black clerk in the Post Office Department. Nerney and the NAACP understood that to acquire support and keep pressure on the Wilson administration, the organization needed to have its facts right; and the more blatant the injustice, the better. Newspapers sympathetic to the cause were more than willing to voice their opposition to federal Jim Crow. In their editorial pages, reports and letters from people lambasting federal Jim Crow appeared on a daily basis. But if proof was found wanting, the newspapers and their readers would lose interest. It was not a matter of embellishing or exaggerating Jim Crow in Washington; that was never a tactic of the NAACP. But Jim Crow was, in most instances, carried out in such secrecy by its perpetrators that only an incessant effort by Nerney had any chance of uncovering the details. She understood, moreover, that those details must be explicated and publicized as much as possible.[31]

Nerney's persistence paid off. Black federal employees, through letters and third parties—often concealing their identities for fear of reprisal—informed the investigator that Jim Crow was in full force in parts of the Treasury and Post Office departments. Although the signs designating separate restrooms for black and white employees had been taken down in parts of the Treasury Department, the order was still in effect. Shortly after the signs were removed, black employees began to resume using the restrooms closest to their workstations. They were immediately "called up before different officials and warned to continue to use the room which had been 'set apart' for them." In the Post Office Department, a black clerk told Nerney that "the colored clerks have been segregated during working hours . . . placed in a corner of the room and separated from the white employees by a partition" made up of a "row of ten lockers ten feet high." Shortly thereafter, an order was issued transferring sixty clerks out of the Post Office Department to city post offices in Washington. All black clerks performing clerical duties were included in the order. It was feared that this was the beginning of efforts to remove black workers from federal departments.[32]

Another contact informed Nerney that racial segregation was on the increase in the Miscellaneous Division and the Examining Division of the Treasury Department. Black employees, who had worked for years in an integrated environment at the same machines and desks, found themselves segregated from their white counterparts in workspaces and in rooms and offices. In the office of the auditor of the Post Office, a branch of the Treasury Department, black women were segregated in a small room where they were kept out of view of "casual observers to the building." And in at least two rooms of the office there were "nothing but colored men employed on the machines."[33]

True to her unscrupulous investigative style, Nerney used whatever means she had at her disposal to acquire information. In a flattering letter, disguising her intentions by appearing naively curious about the segregation rumors coming out of Washington, Nerney wrote to Charlotte Hopkins for information about the Jim Crow policy. It appears that Hopkins was a popular Washington socialite and activist completely sympathetic to the segregation taking place in the government. In a tone of trust and confidence, Hopkins, with the attitude of a paternalistic do-gooder, responded that she had personally gone to the Bureau of Engraving and Printing—a branch of the Treasury Department that designed, engraved, and printed paper money and stamps—to suggest to the director that he segregate black and white employees before he was ordered to do so. But to Hopkins's pleasant surprise, "Mr. [Joseph] Ralph . . . with about 400 colored people in his 4,200 employees," had already "segregated." Although it is not clear why Nerney believed Hopkins had access to information regarding federal Jim Crow, the information she acquired verified one more instance of racial caste in government departments.[34]

One possible explanation as to why Nerney believed Hopkins had information regarding federal Jim Crow is that Hopkins worked on the Alley Campaign to improve living conditions of the poverty-stricken residents living around the nation's capital. This was significant because First Lady Ellen Wilson led the Alley Campaign. A few newspapers during the time—including the black *New York Age* and the white *Boston Transcript* and *New York Times*—attributed the initiation of federal Jim Crow to Ellen Wilson's displeasure over seeing black and white employees working and eating together during a visit to the federal departments. The observant Nerney was probably aware of these reports, and as a social reformer herself, she was familiar with those who worked on the Alley Campaign such as Hopkins. In addition, before his ouster from the NAACP, J. Milton Waldron had led the Alley Improvement Association in Washington, a black organization that preceded the Alley Campaign and whose overtures to work with Hopkins and Wilson seem predictably to have been rebuffed.[35]

Historians Elliott Rudwick and August Meier seem to discount any influence First Lady Ellen Wilson may have had on federal racial segregation, but a few other sources—in addition to the newspaper reports cited previously—verify her deep sympathy for, if not her direct involvement with, drawing the color line in at least one federal department. In a letter addressed to "Mrs. Woodrow Wilson," begging for her "assistance" in the utter segregation of black and white female employees and essentially asking for the dismissal of black female workers and their replacement by whites in the "new bureau of Engraving and Printing," a white female employee reminds the First Lady of her earlier help in the old building. "We think a great deal of you and the President," stressed the writer, "for you had the negro girls separated from the white when you came through."[36]

The First Lady did, in fact, tour the federal departments sometime in early 1913—spearheading, ironically, one of her pet projects to improve the working conditions and pay for white female government employees in Washington. Although this area was in dire need of reform, since women often faced discrimination in federal employment and—if they were lucky enough to be hired—received lower pay than their male counterparts, Ellen Wilson's efforts to uplift her race and gender probably coincided with her wish to segregate black employees.[37] The National Association of Colored Women (NACW) believed so unremittingly in Mrs. Wilson's guilt in the "wholesale segregation of government employees" that when she died prematurely it refused to send condolences to the President.[38] And in an interview historian Ray Stannard Baker conducted with the middle Wilson daughter, Jessie W. Sayre, in 1925, she described her mother as feeling "more strongly than the President about the color line" and added that Ellen Wilson was "hostile to assumptions of equality." Yet in emphasizing this latter point, Wilson scholar Arthur Link points out that both Wilsons were opposed to social relations between the races.[39]

It also appears that the Bureau of Engraving and Printing, in at least one instance, used Charlotte Hopkins as a buffer between a departmental supervisor trying to enforce segregation and black female federal employees who questioned or resisted those efforts in what may have been one of the earliest sit-ins. The progressive and socially conscious *La Follette's Weekly* investigated the incident after receiving a request from a distraught Nanny Burroughs pleading for help in regard to the racial segregation being enforced in the department, and the results were widely published in black and white liberal newspapers and magazines. Mrs. Bella C. La Follette, the recipient of Burroughs's letter and whose husband was one of the most liberal white racial reformers in the West, wrote Assistant Treasury Secretary John Williams "for the facts" regarding the rumored "order to exclude colored girls from lunchrooms." After assuring Mrs. La Follette that "no such general order has been issued," Williams spilled the beans by saying, "however . . . two of the tables were assigned especially for the use of colored girls" and, in so many words, interjected the separate but equal doctrine. The only objections, Williams continued, came from "three colored girls" who were "given positive directions to use the tables assigned" to them.[40]

Shortly thereafter, Mr. Bella La Follette, the editor, interviewed the three girls to get their side of the story. The girls explained that they had refused to leave a segregated white lunch table shortly after "a change" had been made "in the table arrangements." After being asked by two people to move, one of the girls responded in protest: "So long as the food was paid for [we] should be able to eat in any seat not occupied." They told La Follette that they had received their "appointments under the civil service," like the other employees in their department, and likewise were "accustomed" to sit "at any vacant seat."[41]

Sometime thereafter, according to La Follette's investigation, two of the girls were called into the supervisor's office where Charlotte Hopkins met them. She politely told the girls it would perhaps be better for them to consider eating either at a separate table or "in their own lunchroom," as this would provide more "harmony" within the work environment. One girl, feeling powerless and dejected, responded that when she saw the "employees being segregated in the workrooms," she figured it was just a matter of time before her department would attempt to do so in the "lunchroom." Despite the advice from Hopkins, another girl, "Miss R. A. Murraye," continued to resist obeying the lunchroom segregation order and was "dismissed from her position" for "insubordination."[42]

As Nerney pressed forward on her fact-finding mission, Villard, DuBois, and NAACP president Moorfield Storey decided they had enough information from complaints, along with the Williams segregation order and Wilson's acquiescence to the Jim Crow policy in the letter to Villard, to send an official letter of protest to President Wilson. In an August 5 meeting of the board of directors at 26 Vesey Street, it was unanimously decided that Villard present to the president a resolution of protest in the name of the NAACP.[43]

Villard made several more attempts to speak with Wilson about the issue, but the president turned a deaf ear to his requests. Then, on August 15, an eloquent and conscientious protest letter was sent to the chief executive entitled "A Letter to President Wilson on Federal Race Discrimination." Copies were also sent to McAdoo, Burleson, Secretary of the Interior Franklin Lane, and Secretary of Commerce William Redfield. Although it avoided listing the specific instances of racial segregation uncovered to that point (the NAACP refrained from going public with this information until after Nerney's visit to the federal departments at the end of September), the NAACP made it poignantly clear that the organization objected to "such a drawing of caste lines in the Federal Government, and how humiliating it is to the men thus stigmatized." The nation's capital, since after the Civil War, had been a symbol of refuge for a people persecuted "elsewhere because of their dark skins." The NAACP explained that the federal government had entered the arena of racial discrimination, which had been the domain of states and localities. African Americans had made some of their greatest strides in the federal government, and now the future looked bleak. The segregation policy, warned the organization, was the first step toward eliminating them from certain jobs and eventually from the civil service altogether. The most painful thing to deal with, however, was that such a policy implied that African Americans had been "set apart as lepers as if mere contact with them were contamination." With the southern attitude toward African Americans rising in the federal government, the NAACP asked, "How long will it be before the hateful epithets of 'nigger' and 'Jim Crow' are openly applied to these sections?" The black race, the letter continued, "desires a 'New Freedom,' too, Mr. President. Yet they include in that term nothing else than the rights guaranteed them by the Constitution under which they believe they should be protected from persecution based upon a quality with which Divine Providence has endowed them." The NAACP wrapped up the protest in a somber tone and predicted that federal racial segregation would be interpreted as a stamp of approval from the highest office of the land on future acts of discrimination and violence against African Americans through-out the country.[44]

President Wilson, for all intents and purposes, was incidental compared to the targeted audience the NAACP was truly interested in reaching. The letter sent to the president would be futile unless a multitude of voices could be persuaded to join in the protest. The NAACP launched a comprehensive publicity campaign—vigorously driven in no small part by Nerney—to "educate" and motivate organization members, sympathizers, friends, newspapers, members of Congress, and anyone else it could reach who might voice their protest against racial segregation in federal departments. And that was not all. The NAACP clearly understood the far-reaching power of advertising its organization as well as its cause. "All our work might be characterized as publicity work," explained Villard in the Fourth Annual Report. The NAACP was not slow to seize the golden opportunity provided by Wilsonian Jim Crow to "put its program on record" and publicize the young organization "from the Atlantic to the Pacific coast."[45]

NOTES

1. May Childs Nerney to Mr. Henry W. Wilbur, November 20, 1913, Box C-403, NAACP Papers, Manuscript Division, Library of Congress, Washington, DC [hereafter NAACP Papers].

2. Trotter to Gov. Woodrow Wilson, President-elect, February 26, 1913, Trotter Correspondence, Woodrow Wilson Papers, Seeley G. Mudd Library, Princeton University, Princeton, NJ.

3. "Postmaster General Asked to Discriminate for Race," Boston *Guardian,* May 24, 1913, Microfilm, Mugar Memorial Library, Boston University, Boston, MA.

4. *Crisis,* June 1913, 60.

5. *New York Globe,* May 24, 1913.

6. Calvin Chase to Woodrow Wilson, March 29, 1913, Woodrow Wilson Papers, Manuscript Division, Library of Congress, Washington, DC.

7. *Crisis,* September 1913, 233.

8. Kathleen L. Wolgemuth, "Woodrow Wilson's Appointment Policy and the Negro," *Journal of Southern History* 24 (November 1958): 457–471; Morton Sosna, "The South in the Saddle: Racial Politics During the Wilson Years," *Wisconsin Magazine of History* 54 (Autumn 1970): 34; *Crisis,* September 1913, 232–236; Laurence J.W. Hayes, "The Negro Federal Government Worker, 1883–1938" (unpublished master's thesis, Howard University Graduate School, 1941), 45; Allison Blakely, "Black U.S. Consuls and Diplomats and Black Leadership, 1880–1920," *UMOJA: A Scholarly Journal of Black Studies* 1 (November 1977): 2–3, 11, 12, 14 note 3; Thomas G. Patterson, "American Businessmen and Consular Service Reform, 1890s to 1906," *Business History Review* 40 (Spring 1966): 81. Also, the twenty-one highest offices lost by African Americans are as follows: assistant attorney general; register of the treasury; collector of customs in Washington, DC; auditor for the navy; register of the Public Land Office; special agent for the Department of Agriculture; internal revenue collector, Honolulu; recorder of deeds in Washington, DC; receiver of Land Office, Jackson, MS; deputy collector, Los Angeles; inspector at New York; assistant district attorney, Chicago; assistant district attorney, Boston; internal revenue collector, Beaufort, SC; minister to Haiti; internal revenue collector, New York; internal revenue collector, Jacksonville; district attorney, Washington, DC; internal revenue collector, Brunswick, GA; postmistress, Mound Bayou, MS; postmaster, Boley, OK; and numerous other postmaster positions, listed in Wolgemuth, 467, and Hayes, 42.

9. Oswald Villard to His Excellency President Woodrow Wilson, July 21, 1913, Series 4, Reel 230, Woodrow Wilson Papers, Manuscript Division, Library of Congress, Washington, DC.

10. J. S. Williams to James L. Wilmeth, July 12, 1913, and Executive Officer to Superintendents and Chiefs of Divisions, both printed in *New York Evening Post,* September 9, 1913, in Administrative Files, Box C-403, NAACP Papers; R. W. Woolley to the Chiefs of Divisions and other officers of the Office of the Auditor for the Interior Department, July 16, 1913, printed in *Guardian,* November 15, 1913, in Box 6, Moorfield Storey Papers, Manuscript Division, Library of Congress, Washington, DC.

11. W.E.B. DuBois to Rolfe Colbleigh, August 28, 1913, Box C-403, NAACP Papers; May Childs Nerney to Archibald Grimke, undated, Box 39-25, Archibald Grimke Papers, Moorland-Spingarn Research Center, Howard University, Washington, DC.

12. Department Circular no. 9, *Circular Instructions of the Treasury Department, William G. McAdoo* (Washington, DC: Government Printing Office, 1915). This source was obtained from National Archives II, College Park, MD.

13. Two-page Biographical Sketch of John Skelton Williams taken from "Men of Mark in Virginia," Box 39, and *New York Times,* February 1, 1914, Box 87, and In Memoriam, Supplement to November 1926 *Georgia and Florida Railway Bulletin,* and *Outlook,* June 5, 1918, 23, Box 93, MSS 10040, all in John Skelton Williams Papers, Special Collections, University of Virginia Library, Charlottesville, VA; John J. Broesamle, *William Gibbs McAdoo: A Passion for Change, 1863–1917* (New York: Kennikat, 1973), 79–80, 160.

14. Broesamle, 160.

15. Chicago *Defender,* September 27, 1913, untitled clipping in Administrative Files, Box C-432, NAACP Papers.

16. B. Joyce Ross, *J. E. Spingarn and the Rise of the NAACP, 1911–1939* (New York: Atheneum, 1972), 25–26; *Who's Who in America, 1914–15* (Chicago: A. N. Marquis, 1915), 678, 1619, 2205, 2261, 2419. Although *Who's Who* during this time claimed to be "a biographical dictionary of notable living men and women of the United States," it appears few women and no black women are listed in this enormous volume.

17. James McPherson, *The Abolitionist Legacy: From Reconstruction to the NAACP* (Princeton: Princeton University Press, 1975), 153, 368–393; B. Joyce Ross, 26; Mary White Ovington, "How the National Association for the Advancement of Colored People Began," *Crisis,* August 1914, 185–186; Ruth Worthy, "A Negro in Our History: William Monroe Trotter, 1872–1934" (M.A. thesis, Columbia University, 1952), 85, 87, 88, 91; Louis R. Harlan, *Booker T. Washington: The Making of a Black Leader, 1856–1901* (Oxford: Oxford University Press, 1972), 193, 262–267; Floris Loretta Barnett Cash, "Womanhood and Protest: The Club Movement Among Black Women, 1892–1922" (Ph.D. diss., State University of New York at Stony Brook, 1986), 11, 13, 50, 211, 218; Fox, 28, 76–77, 123–124.

18. David L. Lewis, *W.E.B. DuBois: Biography of a Race, 1868–1919* (New York: Henry Holt, 1993), 396.

19. NAACP Fourth Annual Report, 1913 (January 1914), Box 9, Moorfield Storey Papers, Manuscript Division, Library of Congress, Washington, DC.

20. NAACP Third Annual Report, 1912 (January 1913), Fourth Annual Report, and Fifth Annual Report, 1914 (dated 1914), Box 9, Moorfield Storey Papers, Manuscript Division, Library of Congress, Washington, DC.

21. Wolgemuth, "Woodrow Wilson and Federal Segregation," 173; *Crisis,* December 1913, 88; Charles Flint Kellogg, *NAACP: A History of the National Association for the Advancement of Colored People,* vol. 1, *1909–1920* (Baltimore: Johns Hopkins University Press, 1967), 154; Professor Bill Toll, University of Michigan, to Stephen Fox, December 6, 1968, Trotter File, Guardian of Boston Collection, Mugar Memorial Library, Boston University, Boston, MA.

22. For Villard's personal account of his role in challenging federal segregation, see *Fighting Years: Memoirs of a Liberal Editor* (New York: Harcourt, Brace, 1939), 236–242. Also NAACP Fourth Annual Report, 11–12. The *New York Evening Post* also supported Wilson's candidacy for governor of New Jersey in 1910. When Wilson announced his candidacy for president, Villard, along with William F. McCombs and William G. McAdoo, helped plan the campaign strategy.

23. Wilson to Villard, April 2, 1913, Folder 4234, Oswald Villard Papers, Houghton Library, Harvard University, Cambridge, MA.

24. Stephen Thernstrom, "Oswald Garrison Villard and the Politics of Pacifism," *Harvard Library Bulletin* 14 (Winter 1960): 127–128; Wolgemuth, *Woodrow Wilson and Federal Segregation,* 162. William Lloyd Garrison argued that it is absurd for the government to decide who should or should not be united in "wedlock" based on color: "It may as rationally decree that corpulent and lean, tall and short, strong and weak persons shall not be married to each other as that there must be an agreement in the complexion of parties"; quoted in NAACP Fourth Annual Report, 9.

25. DuBois to Ovington, in Herbert Aptheker, ed., *The Correspondence of W.E.B. DuBois,* vol. 1, *Selections, 1877–1934* (Amherst: University of Massachusetts Press, 1973), 189–191,

although DuBois admits "there are not in the organization two persons in closer intellectual agreement on the Negro problem than Mr. Villard and myself"; quoted in James M. McPherson, *The Abolitionist Legacy: From Reconstruction to the NAACP* (Princeton: Princeton University Press, 1975), 389 note 44. McPherson quotes an "unpublished manuscript," published since then, that deals with the paternalism of Villard and other white founders of the NAACP written by Victor M. Glasberg and entitled "Black Liberation and White Liberalism: The Founders of the NAACP and American Racial Attitudes," 389 note 44. Also Stephen R. Fox, *The Guardian of Boston: William Monroe Trotter* (New York: Atheneum, 1970), 142–143.

26. Villard to Wilson, July 21, 1913, and Wilson to Villard, July 23, 1913, Oswald Villard Papers, Houghton Library, Harvard University, Cambridge, MA. In addition, Wilson had earlier assured racist author Thomas Dixon that federal Jim Crow was "a plan of concentration"; Wilson to Dixon, June 29, 1913, in Wolgemuth, "Woodrow Wilson's Appointment Policy and the Negro," 463–464.

27. A. L. Tulghman to Archibald Grimke, June 4, 1914, Box 39-25, Archibald Grimke Papers, Moorland-Spingarn Research Center, Howard University, Washington, DC.

28. Untitled document arguing against racial segregation, Administrative Files, Box C-403, NAACP Papers.

29. August Meier and Elliott Rudwick, "The Rise of the Black Secretariat in the NAACP, 1909–1935," in Meier and Rudwick, eds., *Along the Color Line: Explorations in the Black Experience* (Urbana: University of Illinois Press, 1976), 95–98.

30. Ibid., 95–98; DuBois quoted in Lewis, 472; for Nerney's role in Washington, see her correspondence with Archibald Grimke in Box 39-25, Archibald Grimke Papers, Moorland-Spingarn Research Center, Howard University, Washington, DC.

31. May Childs Nerney to Mr. Oliver Randolph, September 10, 1913, Administrative Files, Box C-403, NAACP Papers; Lewis, 472.

32. Untitled document in Administrative Files, Box C-403, NAACP Papers.

33. Thomas Clarke to May Childs Nerney, September 6, 1913, Clarke to Nerney, September 11, 1913, Stella Arrington to Thomas Clarke, September 19, 1913, all in Administrative Files, Box C-403, NAACP Papers.

34. Charlotte Hopkins to Nerney, undated, Administrative Files, Box C-403, NAACP Papers; Ralph to Hopkins, July 19, 1913, Box 1, Series 3411, Charlotte Hopkins Papers, Manuscript Division, Library of Congress, Washington, DC.

35. Constance McLaughlin Green, *Washington: Capital City, 1879–1950* (Princeton: Princeton University Press, 1963), 223. Also see *New York Age,* September 11, 1913; letter to *New York Times,* May 4, 1913; Kellogg, 162; Sosna, 33; Hopkins to Nerney, undated, NAACP Papers; Waldron to Hopkins, undated, and others, Alley Campaign, Box 1, Series 3411, Charlotte Hopkins Papers, Manuscript Division, Library of Congress, Washington, DC; Boston *Transcript* clipping dated November 14, 1914, entitled "Apportioning Blame," Box 87, MSS 10040, John Skelton Williams Papers, Special Collections, University of Virginia Library, Charlottesville, VA.

36. "A poor widow" to Mrs. Woodrow Wilson, March 20, 1914, Microfilm, Series 4, Reel 231, Manuscript Division, Library of Congress, Washington, DC.

37. The First Lady may have influenced her husband to use his executive authority to

hire and promote women in the federal service. It appears that President Wilson regularly issued executive orders to personally assist women in federal employment in Washington and throughout the nation.

38. Various letters, Box 1, Series 3411, Charlotte Hopkins Papers, Manuscript Division, Library of Congress, Washington, DC; Wilberforce National Convention, 1914, 89, Records of the NACW, 1895–1992, Microfilm, Reel 1, Manuscript Division, Library of Congress, Washington, DC.

39. Memorandum of an interview with Jessie W. Sayre, December 1, 1925, in the Ray Stannard Baker Papers, Manuscript Division, Library of Congress, Washington, DC, quoted in Worthy, "A Negro in Our History," 112 note 45; Arthur Link, "The Negro as a Factor in the Campaign of 1912," *Journal of Negro History* 32 (January 1947): 87.

40. LaFollette and Williams cited in *Crisis,* October 1913, 275–277; Hopkins to Nerney, undated, Box C-403, NAACP Papers.

41. *Crisis,* October 1913, 277.

42. Ibid.

43. Minutes of the Meeting of the Board of Directors, August 5, 1913, NAACP Microfilm, Manuscript Division, Library of Congress, Washington, DC.

44. "A Letter to President Woodrow Wilson on Federal Race Discrimination," August 15, 1913, Administrative Files, Box C-403, NAACP Papers. Carrie Allen McCray quotes her mother, who protested federal segregation during the Wilson era, as saying, "When President Wilson let them segregate those government offices, he gave a green light to segregation all over the country"; *Freedom's Child: The Life of a Confederate General's Black Daughter* (Chapel Hill, NC: Algonquin, 1998), 150.

45. NAACP Fourth Annual Report, 11, 15.

3

JIM CROW IN THE WHITE HOUSE

URING THE EARLY PROTEST IN LATE SUMMER 1913, some letters arriving at Pennsylvania Avenue and a few newspapers held out hopes that President Wilson was either unaware of the extent of Jim Crow taking place in his administration or was somehow duped by prejudiced cabinet members into acquiescing to the color line in federal departments. Even W.E.B. DuBois, in an open letter to the president that appeared in the September issue of *Crisis,* asked rhetorically, "Mr. Wilson, do you know these things? Are you responsible for them? Did you advise them? Do you consent to this, President Wilson? Do you believe in it?"[1]

Following the release of the National Association for the Advancement of Colored People's (NAACP) letter of protest to the public, however, more and more protestors were laying blame for the Jim Crow policy at the president's feet. "He seems to have been led by his own prejudice or that of others, into a serious mistake for which he cannot, however, escape the responsibility," declared the *New Haven Register.*[2] The *Congregationalist and Christian World* warned its readers of more things to come from a chief executive who shared the prejudices of the typical southerner against blacks after Wilson told the paper he did "approve of the segregation that is being attempted in several of the departments." The paper rallied its readers to "protest against the wrong; demand justice; keep on demanding it until we win."[3]

Although Wilson knew at least of the segregation in the Treasury Department, in its bureaus and divisions, and in its various adjunct auditors' offices and essentially sanctioned it, he did not perceive it to be discrimination against African Americans. As his correspondence with Oswald Villard demonstrates, Wilson had given his nod of approval to the policy and vigorously defended it as being in blacks' interest. He could not understand or would not admit that segregation was a discrimination that relegated African Americans to an inferior status, thereby perpetuating a system of intense subordination and oppression and violence. Moreover, the leader, by his own admission, habitually submitted to the majority view; and in this case most people either supported or, at the least, were ambivalent toward racial segregation in any form. Wilson accepted at face value the fact that prejudice existed, and in defending federal Jim Crow, he maintained that the races should be kept separate to reduce friction until time could ameliorate the prejudice whites felt toward African Americans. Thus, because Wilson was unable to understand the dire consequences of such an arrangement, racial segregation was essentially benign in his view.[4]

Like Booker T. Washington, Wilson felt the best way for African Americans to move forward was to "go about the work . . . and see that the race makes good and nobody can say that there is any kind of work that they can't do." In fact, the only black leadership the president recognized was that of the black conservatives who regularly reinforced, in personal letters of sympathy and newspaper clippings, his conviction regarding the slow process of change and his view that protest would be detrimental to African Americans. Wilson eschewed agitation in any form that sought racial justice. "[M]ark these pages," he assured William Monroe Trotter, "it [justice] will come quickest if these questions aren't raised." Yet racial prejudice was deep-seated in the white American psyche, and economic prosperity for African Americans would not only fail to mitigate white racism but intensify it.[5]

Woodrow Wilson came of age in a culture where the dominant and ubiquitous theme of black inferiority, earlier used as a major defense of slavery, would be enshrined through the dissemination of "retrogressionist" ideology. This was made all the more respectable in an empirical sense by the large numbers of prominent scientists, psychologists, historians, academics, businessmen, and religious figures who claimed to have some sort of expertise in their support of the ideology. This belief, as mentioned in Chapter 1, maintained that Negroes were a naturally inferior race and, in the absence of the structure once provided by slavery, were quickly regressing to a state of barbarity and resorting instinctively to sexual predation.

Many of those who promulgated black inferiority within their respective genres and who called for segregation were, like Wilson, from the middle and upper classes—a fact that underscores John Cell's thesis that the system of segregation that developed during the early Progressive Era, far from being driven by the "crude and irrational prejudice" of the lower class, was largely the achievement of a progressive and educated elite.[6] In addition to the U.S. Supreme Court (and lower courts) and the prominent lawyers who defended Jim Crow there, a cursory glance at the authors of the historical and professional literature of the day trumpeting black inferiority reveals names of individuals who were at the forefront of their professions and eager to apply their expertise on the "Negro problem": Nathaniel Shaler of Harvard, John Roach Stratton of Mercer University, historians William Dunning and John Burgess of Columbia, anthropologist Charles Davenport, Edward Drinker Cope of the University of Pennsylvania, steel magnate Andrew Carnegie, psychologist G. O. Ferguson, novelist Thomas Nelson Page, and Episcopal clergyman Joseph Louis Tucker.

The latter, the Rev. Joseph Louis Tucker, an Episcopal clergyman in Jackson, Mississippi, has been too often overlooked in discussions of racism; and although not an intellectual per se, he held a doctorate in divinity, and he seemed to exercise considerable influence not only in the South but in the entire nation. Born in the North, he initially gained prominence within religious circles in 1882, and eventually with whites in the South and North, by arguing that free blacks were "retrograding morally" and that slavery had imposed "outward restraint" upon "absolute barbarians." Making his public debut before a large white audience at the elite Protestant Episcopal Church Congress in Richmond, Virginia, Tucker drove home to his overly sympathetic listeners the belief that African Americans were by nature morally depraved, vulgar, and dishonest and that it was imperative that they be controlled by white southerners without interference from the North. An avalanche of endorsements from white churches all over the South immediately followed what amounted to his call to arms, which was widely distributed as a pamphlet; and although Episcopal African American clergy and others publicly debunked and protested Tucker's diatribes, white "experts" from all over the nation soon jumped on the black retrogression bandwagon.[7]

Tucker was thus one of the first, if not the first, to synthesize the theme of black retrogression that became popular in one form or another in the late nineteenth and early twentieth centuries. The 1884 edition of the *Encyclope-*

dia Britannica gave some idea as to his early influence, not to mention the growing popularity of the retrogressionist ideology, when it cited Tucker as an expert on the fact that "negroes" are "nonmoral" (a year earlier, in the 1883 edition, Francis Galton had coined the term *eugenics* as "the science of the improvement of the human race germ plasm through better breeding"). And Tucker's name became part of the racist vernacular in the South, as more cultured southerners—including Wilson—would refer to the most assertive blacks, ironically, as "Tucker[s]" or "Tucker darkey[s]," thus masking the more traditional racial slur while retaining every bit of its degrading meaning.[8]

As the chorus of professional voices codified the inferiority of blacks in American culture and law, companies were creating or reinforcing powerful black stereotypes in the minds of whites—surpassing even those of racist narrative and minstrel shows—by creating fictitious, distorted, and often grotesque black images and personalities to advertise and sell their products. The technological advances of the expanding industrial order, Grace Elizabeth Hale has emphasized, made the cheap mass production of this visual imagery possible, reaching potential millions through sophisticated marketing that was rapidly becoming more and more innovative. African Americans were portrayed with out-of-proportion heads and features—such as large fire-red lips, enormously disproportionate smiles, and bulging eyes—and were depicted as submissive, docile, laughable, silly, poor, and ugly. "The negative portrayals of blacks," said David Milgrim and Phillip Middleton, "were both reflected in and shaped by everyday material objects: toys, postcards, ashtrays, fishing lures, children's books."[9]

This was the world in which Woodrow Wilson lived. It was one so saturated with racism that black Americans' most ardent and optimistic white defender in the South, George Washington Cable, prophesied in 1885, "We may reach the moon someday, not social equality"— never dreaming that years into the future these two momentous events would happen at almost the exact same time.[10]

Whether Wilson wholeheartedly embraced the black retrogressionist-inferiority dogma is uncertain, but it does appear that he was strongly influenced by it, as evidenced in his writings, correspondences, and recorded statements. In a more optimistic tone, Henry Blumenthal believed Wilson dimly viewed a far-distant day of better race relations in the country, but if that was the case, there is no record as to what "better" meant.[11] It seems likely that better probably meant some form of indefinite black subordination in a white world.

Although one important Progressive Era historian maintains that Wilson had no strong racial views, he did, in fact, express very clear opinions about blacks in the South, an issue to which he admittedly gave a "great deal of thought."[12] In Wilson's political writings dealing with the South, a common theme arises stigmatizing African Americans with such terms as *ignorant and inferior, dark minded, uneducated, menace, dangerous, shiftless, indolent,* and *incompetent.*[13] Wilson's racial sentiments could also be seen in some of his campaign speeches while running for governor of New Jersey, in which he jokingly conjured up images of a comedic or docile "Sambo" or "darky" to drive his point home regarding some current issue. There are several recollections of him imitating a demeaning "darky" dialect in front of friends for laughs; and, to the chagrin of the *New York Age,* he referred to his messenger in the governor's office as a "good darky." When Joseph Tumulty urged Wilson to withdraw his endorsement of *Birth of a Nation,* the president responded that he would do so if he could "do it without seeming to be trying to meet the agitation . . . stirred up by that unspeakable fellow Tucker"—a degrading reference to William Monroe Trotter and a more gentlemanly way of demeaning the black equal rights leader.[14]

In a letter to his second wife, Edith, the president expressed his strong disapproval over her niece's desire to marry a Panamanian man because "there is the presumption that the blood is not unmixed." And like a true southern aristocrat of his time, he believed there were certain jobs that white people should not do. In deflecting a request that white students should wait on tables in the school cafeteria at Princeton, Wilson hastily responded that this type of work was "ordinarily" rendered by "Negroes," and for whites to do such work would mean "an inevitable loss of self-respect" and "social standing."[15]

Although Wilson had at one time proposed aid for southern blacks, the constant theme throughout many of his political writings—sometimes expressed with forceful conviction—was that southern whites should have complete political control over the black minority within their borders. Emphasizing the absolute consensus theme among retrogressionists, he believed this was necessary to manage a weak race that was prone to crime and idleness without the "tutelage" of its former masters. The South had determined by the disfranchisement of blacks "never to suffer themselves to be ruled by another race in every respect unlike themselves; and in that resolve they cannot be, should not be, shaken," wrote a young Wilson. "Any enlightened people," he believed, would not be subjected to an "ignorant and inferior race." Furthermore, southerners "do not object to the votes of negroes because they are negroes, but because their minds are dark, because they are ignorant, uneducated, and incompetent to form an enlightened opinion."[16]

With his publication of the well-received *Division and Reunion* in 1893, the ambitious professor helped usher in an enduring era of racist post-

Reconstruction historiography that promoted the myth of black rule, denounced Reconstruction as an utter failure, and derided black participation in these efforts as a menace to democratic government in the South.[17] Here Wilson acknowledged that slavery was bad in some respects, but overall he was, in the words of one biographer, "curiously indifferent to the moral iniquity of slavery," questioning and even minimizing its hardships on black slaves.[18] Wilson seemed irritated that this trivial issue of slavery, as he saw it, an institution he believed was "protected by every solemn sanction of the Constitution," should disrupt the great experiment in democracy. "This view of slavery," wrote Charles Ballew in pointing out Wilson's lack of human sensitivity, "was completely divorced from any thought of its injustice to the individual."[19]

To the aloof professor, *Uncle Tom's Cabin* (a book that was in his father's library when Wilson was growing up) was more a theoretical treatise than a real-life glimpse into the evils of human bondage. Wilson was more sympathetic, however, to the economic degradation and plight of the poor whites he believed the system of slavery had produced, while at the same time he held slaveholders in high esteem for being "intelligent, alert, and self-conscious."[20] Moreover, the plantation illusion—a romantic love for a fictitious, happy-go-lucky antebellum South—longed for by many of his southern contemporaries, held him in its deceptive grasp as well. There was an order and a sense of family in the special bond between master and slave, Wilson believed, rather than a forced association maintained by violence and fear. Even in his biography of George Washington, the scholar found it more noteworthy to discuss the gallant horses that served Washington than the numerous human beings of African descent who toiled for him in human bondage.[21]

Although Wilson believed southern blacks were not ready to participate in political life, he was unwilling to help prepare them. Princeton remained one of the few colleges in the North that did not admit African Americans to its undergraduate program with Wilson at the helm. "I would say that, while there is nothing in the University to prevent a negro's entering, the whole temper and tradition of the place are such that no negro has ever applied for admission," Wilson wrote in a private letter, "and it seems extremely unlikely that the question will ever assume a practical form."[22] And he made sure it never would. When a black seminary student from Lynchburg, Virginia, later wrote Wilson expressing his interest in attending Princeton, the college president responded that "it is altogether inadvisable for a colored man to enter Princeton," and he recommended that the student try "Harvard, Dartmouth, or Brown."[23]

The Princeton policy of excluding African Americans would continue for several decades, making it, according to a 1942 article in the *Daily*

Princetonian, "the last of the leading institutions outside the deep South which still adheres to this faith in racial superiority." In contrast, many of Wilson's colleagues at other northern universities had been admitting African Americans for years and were quick to criticize the chief executive for allowing federal racial segregation in government departments. He did, however, get support from the Commission of Southern Universities. The commission's 1914 annual report stated that "race segregation in public service departments . . . may be expedient and just in solving the problems by race adjustment."[24]

Woodrow Wilson, the leader, seemed distressingly void of the admirable humanitarian quality historically attributed to him when it came to understanding and dealing with the problems faced by his "fellow-colored citizens." One of Wilson's most comprehensive biographers, August Heckscher, believed the Democrat "had largely transcended his southern upbringing," but *Crisis* was probably more accurate, putting Wilson's political motivations aside when it stated, "the only possible explanation of President Wilson's attitude is that of early environment, and the traditions of his youth . . . race prejudice was inherited by [him], as a boy, to an extent which still tinges his views of men and things."[25] Reluctant to contradict the image of Wilson as a progressive reformer and a man of great idealism, most writers have treated his utter failure in regard to federal Jim Crow as an embarrassing secret, or, when his racial views have been mentioned, they have been quickly dismissed without serious consideration as common prejudices of the times. There seems to have been nothing to salvage or no way to reconcile Wilson's treatment of blacks with his often expressed noble sentiments of justice, liberty, and equality. He not only failed to uplift African Americans, but he enabled forces to crush them even further with his approval of federal Jim Crow—all this as he preached to the world the importance of serving humanity.

The proud Scots-Irishman, suffering from a bad case of Anglophilia, simply could not relate to a demoralized people of African descent. He could not cross over from his white privileged world and put himself in the shoes of others, and he had no desire to do so. His muddled conception of African Americans was that of the typical white stereotypes derived from published cartoons, minstrel shows, "darky" jokes and stories, and demeaning advertisements that used a distorted and ridiculous black caricature to sell a product.

Wilson's strong Anglo-Saxon sentiments thrashed against other ethnic groups as well. During the 1912 campaign, at a time when Indian Hindus—proportionally the least tolerated minority in the United States—were being attacked, beaten, and driven from their communities in the Northwest, the candidate reassured a former mayor of San Francisco by approving a hotly debated and strongly supported policy that sought to prohibit the immigration of Chinese and Japanese peoples to the West Coast. "We cannot make a homogeneous population out of people who do not blend with the Caucasian race," warned Wilson. "[I]t will give us another race problem to solve and surely we have had our lesson."[26] A decade earlier, in *A History of the American People,* the Princeton professor had described the dark-skinned European immigrants arriving at Ellis Island in search of a better home as swarthy and undesirable.[27]

But like most WASPs (White Anglo-Saxon Protestants), Wilson had never personally experienced any of the suffering and oppression, not to mention the daily humiliation, endured by African Americans and other impoverished ethnic groups. Moreover, he was the quintessential reserved southern Presbyterian—a denomination that was the privileged elite of American Protestantism and was criticized by many for failing to "come down" to meet the needs of the "common man."[28] The Presbyterian Church of the South, not unlike other denominations, had earlier split with its northern brethren over slavery; and despite overtures for reconciliation from the latter during the Reconstruction period, the southerners refused because to do so would "involve a practical recognition of the equal manhood of the inferior race."[29] Wilson, coming from a long line of Presbyterian ministers and scholars—including his father, the Rev. Joseph Ruggles Wilson—grew up in a southern parsonage and church that seems to have been more of a haven for the haves than for the have-nots in the war-torn South. And in his sheltered youth and early adult life, rather than sympathize with a people suffering in a land decimated by war, he seemed instead repulsed by the sometimes crude survival habits of his poor southern neighbors and leaders, black and white. DuBois was right on the mark when he indicted Wilson as being "by birth and education unfitted for largeness of view or depth of feeling" on the race issue.[30]

Even though the progress of Western Civilization impressed Wilson, he seemed unable to appreciate the enormous obstacles African Americans had overcome in the half century since he was born.[31] Conversely, Henry L. Morehouse, a white racial reformer during the Progressive Era whose name and efforts would transform the black Atlanta Baptist College into the famous Morehouse College—the black Harvard, as it one day came to be known—echoed the sentiments of several others when he said the progress made by African Americans so soon after slavery was "greater than that of any other people similarly handicapped by unfavorable conditions."[32] Only fifty years after having spent two and a half centuries in physical bondage, African

Americans owned millions of dollars' worth of property and assets; worked in a relatively integrated federal government; had created their own autonomous institutions in education, religion, and social services; and had established community-based businesses along with legal and medical practices. Denied a political voice by Jim Crow, African Americans were sharpening their own impressive democratic mechanisms within the church—"the black communities['] most independent enterprise"—and voicing their opinions and activity through numerous organizations and publications both religious and secular.[33]

Yet Wilson only saw black progress in America through a lens in which white civilization always remained the backdrop. Although he could vaguely appreciate the accomplishments of African Americans, in the larger scheme of things their progress was meager and inconsequential at best. In *Mere Literature and Other Essays,* while discussing the racial composition of late-nineteenth-century America, Wilson neglected to even mention the millions of African Americans who lived there. But why would he discuss them? For him, modern civilization was synonymous with the "stronger and nobler" Aryan race—a view perhaps inherited from his boyhood hero William E. Gladstone, prime minister of Victorian England, whose mystic view of Anglo-Saxon superiority justified the imperial domination of non-Westernized continents such as Africa and Asia. Wilson believed that historically, African Americans had nothing meaningful to contribute; and like the superior Englishmen in Gladstone's scheme, he believed American whites—the rulers and active participants of what he perceived as an advanced social and political order—were obligated to provide "tutelage" for the "less civilized" blacks in their own country.[34]

But this tutelage went much farther than a paternalistic effort to uplift others. In his *History of the American People,* Wilson defended and at times romanticized the oppressive and violent methods, such as the Black Codes and the Ku Klux Klan, used to control the freedmen and restore "civilization" in the South. Although he eschewed the worst aspects of lawlessness—pointing the finger of blame at both the KKK (or some ambiguous aberration of the KKK) and reconstructed southern governments—he felt compelled to justify the actions of the KKK as that of a powerless white majority following its "mere instinct of survival" (there was nothing but condemnation for the reconstructed southern governments and legislatures, however).[35] With Jim Crow and horrific racial violence still rampant at the end of the first decade of the twentieth century, Wilson abandoned African Americans to the utter and often dangerous subjugation by southern whites, saying, "I feel that men resident among the Southern Negroes are the only men" who can determine what is best for them "with any degree of confidence."[36] These words must have tickled the ears of southern leaders such as James K. Vardaman, perhaps the black American's most bitter opponent, who had been preaching for years that "only southerners understood the Negro and could deal with him properly."[37]

Louis Auchincloss, in regard to Wilson's attitude toward African Americans, recently wrote that "[n]ine out of ten men raised as he was would have thought the same [way]."[38] Yet in a sense, Woodrow Wilson was not nine out of ten men. He was a man of high ambition; a fresh newcomer on the political scene, arising from the realm of liberal academia—unheard of in American politics; for many an inspiring man to believe in; and the author and expositor of *The New Freedom.* "I find many Colored men ready to vote for you," wrote Trotter to the New Jersey governor, and "they sincerely desire that you will be the democrat to begin the end of democratic aggression against their political and civil rights."[39] The popular *Harper's Weekly* believed so strongly in Wilson during his Princeton days that, incredibly, in 1906 it began to print "Woodrow Wilson for President" across the top cover of each issue and over the next several years introduced the unknown academic to the public through a series of articles and biographies.[40]

Ironically, Wilson's disloyalty to one group of supporters actually enhanced his reputation as a liberal reformer seeking a change from the old way of doing things. The editor of *Harper's Weekly,* George Harvey, along with political bosses from New Jersey, essentially offered Wilson the Democratic nomination for governor of the Garden State with the belief that they would pull the strings of the inexperienced puppet. But even before his inauguration Wilson turned against the bosses, dealing a blow to their grip on power and thereby making it clear that no political machine would control him.

Once he was in the political arena, many of Wilson's speeches were replete with words filled with hope about making democracy work for the average citizen, politically lost in a morass of powerful special interests, by giving him "justice" in the form of equality and opportunity. "I tell you the men I am interested in," explained the newly elected president in an interview, "are the men who . . . never had their voices heard." Even his first inaugural address must have seemed like a sweet melody of justice to a beleaguered black race when he proclaimed, "Justice, and only justice, shall always be our motto."[41] With the exception of women in a white male–centric society, who could have possibly needed more justice—any justice—than the black man who was often regarded with fear and suspicion?

For the ancestors of slaves, however, justice would not be forthcoming. It quickly became apparent that Wilson had only the white man in mind. The disfranchised southern black man probably never even crossed Wilson's mind when, during a campaign speech in New Jersey, he told an audience, "When the slightest suspicion rests upon any man of tampering with the ballot, then I cease to regard him as worthy from any consideration as an American citizen." (Yet as president he considered two men convicted of ballot tampering "worthy" of clemency.)[42]

Moreover, the term *progressive* in Wilson's mind meant economic reform and not social justice. Thus, it was an unfortunate but expected travesty, given the times, that an enlightened scholar of governments and political institutions should be sucked into the vortex of racial prejudice, unable to see beyond the black stereotype perpetuated by southern society. Even the most eloquent protest of the Wilson years left the provincial southerner in the White House more irritated and offended than anything after a black visitor declared, "We come to you . . . as full fledged American citizens, absolutely equal with all others."[43] The growing protests of African Americans may not have succeeded in breaking down the barriers of racial prejudice in the Wilson years, but neither would the voices for change cease—indeed, they would only grow stronger—in demanding that African Americans be treated as free men, accorded the same rights and privileges as any other citizen with a lighter complexion. The most important lesson of a people determined to be free was not to be found in a textbook. It was staring the new president straight in the face.

Wilson was likely not prepared to act on his personal sentiments in regard to African Americans when he became president, nor was he willing to resist the southern conviction that was swept into Washington with his election. He would have been satisfied to leave the status quo intact, as he strongly desired not to "rock the boat."[44]

And although a major Wilson biographer recently wrote that upon "entering politics he assumed the position of one sympathetic by every instinct of justice and liberality to the betterment of race relations,"[45] there appears to have been very little evidence in Wilson's words or actions that this was the case. The progressive Democrat, in hindsight, offered nothing more than empty platitudes. The promises he had made to African Americans during the campaign were vague, with the Waldron incident a sure sign as to his true lack of intentions to help the race once he became president. The fact that men like DuBois and Villard supported him anyway represented wishful thinking on their part. Wilson did make a few positive remarks privately about African Americans in general, but they were always in the context of an explanation as to why he could not or would not stop segregation in federal departments or approve the NAACP's National Race Commission.

His attitude toward African Americans was at best overwhelmingly paternalistic.[46] Wilson's idea of better race relations was one that strongly supported the most limited interaction possible between whites and blacks.

But aside from his personal views, there were political realities that could not so easily be ignored. When Jim Crow took hold of the federal departments, backed by racial demagogues in a Congress dominated by southerners, Wilson told protestors that any opposition on his part could mean a loss of support for his legislative agenda. Even during the Democratic pre-convention campaign of 1911–1912, some southern political opposition to Wilson's nomination had put the progressive Democrat on the defensive with its public statements that he was "ravenously fond of the Negro," rumors he denied. This rhetoric quickly petered out, as pro-Negro hazing was a common ritual of the times that southern candidates often had to endure—even such fire-breathing racists as James Vardaman, Ben Tillman, Hoke Smith, and Tom Watson. Smith and Watson, in fact, were two of the loudest voices that had charged the Virginia-born Democrat with accusations that had once been levied against them.[47] When Wilson became president, he was keenly aware that he had to work in "cooperation" with the same type of men who "sit in the government" and who represented a majority party dominated ideologically by the southern wing.[48]

Those congressional influences were unquestionably an important factor in Wilson's political mind. The Democrats had a crushing margin in both the House and the Senate, and southerners controlled most key committees. "With the tariff and currency bills then before Congress, and many other reform measures yet to follow," explained Henry Blumenthal, "the President did not want to lose Southern support by starting a bitter controversy."[49]

Yet blacks and liberal whites believed, and correctly so, that Wilson would not be playing the game of racial politics unless he personally felt separation of the races was morally right. Regardless of his personal sentiments, however, protestors clearly understood that the president's approval of the policy gave impetus to federal segregation and, most dishearteningly, contributed to an atmosphere of segregation and violence against African Americans in general.[50] Wilson "has certainly made conditions much worse than they have been for years," a despondent editor told Nerney.[51] Jim Crow was in the White House.

NOTES

1. *Crisis,* September 1913, 233; Constance McLaughlin Green, *Washington: Capital City, 1879–1950* (Princeton: Princeton University Press, 1963), 224.

2. October article quoted in *Crisis,* December 1913, 69.

3. Rolfe Colbleigh, "Turning the Negro Back," *Congregationalist and Christian World* (September 18, 1913): 357, 359.

4. Wilson to Villard, July 23, 1913, and Wilson to Villard, August 29, 1913, in Woodrow Wilson Papers, Manuscript Division, Library of Congress, Washington, DC; Henry Blumenthal, "Woodrow Wilson and the Race Question," *Journal of Negro History* 48 (January 1963): 2; Edith Bolling Wilson, *Selected Literary and Political Papers and Addresses of Woodrow Wilson, Volume 2* (New York: Grosset and Dunlap, 1927), 15.

5. Wilson quoted in Christine Lunardini, "Standing Firm: William Monroe Trotter's Meetings With Woodrow Wilson, 1913–1914," *Journal of Negro History* 64 (Summer 1979): 258; Wilson's recognition of black conservatives in Charles LeBron Ballew, "Woodrow Wilson and the Negro" (M.A. thesis, University of Maryland, 1965), 7.

6. John W. Cell, *The Highest Stage of White Supremacy: The Origins of Segregation in South Africa and the American South* (Cambridge, UK: Cambridge University Press, 1982), 18–19.

7. Alexander Crummell, *A Defence of the Negro Race in America From the Assaults and Charges of Rev. J. L. Tucker, D.D., in His Paper Before the "Church Congress" of 1882, on "The Relations of the Church to the Colored Race"* (Washington, DC: Judd and Dutweiler, 1883), stored on Microfilm no. 18176E, Library of Congress, Washington, DC; Tucker's personal profile and *Encyclopedia Brittanica* cited in Elazar Barkin, "Appendix C: A Brief Note on Late-Nineteenth-Century Racial Ideology, Retrogressionist Beliefs, the Misperception of the Ex-Slave Family, and the Conceptualization of Afro-American History," in *The Retreat of Scientific Racism* (Cambridge, UK.: Cambridge University Press, 1992), 533–534.

8. Crummell; Barkin, 533–534.

9. Grace Elizabeth Hale, *Making Whiteness: The Culture of Segregation in the South, 1890–1940* (New York: Pantheon, 1998), 8, 51, 138, 151–168; David Milgrim and Phillip Middleton, Ferris State University, "Jim Crow Museum of Racist Memorabilia," http://www.ferris.edu/news/jimcrow/caricature (accessed March 23, 2002). Also, it is interesting that in the only motion picture about Woodrow Wilson, an award-winning yet sanitized film made in 1944, there is a scene in which the presidential candidate and his wife are relaxing from the rigors of campaigning in a theater, waiting patiently for the live production to begin. Suddenly, as "Dixie" begins to play, a white performer comes out on stage dressed like Teddy Roosevelt in his safari gear but wearing a painted dark-black shining face with huge white lips and pulling a small dog with a fake lion's mane around its neck. After smiling at the applauding audience for a few seconds, the actor, in a demeaning and imitative black dialect, barely intelligible, squeals, "Weely, weely. I'm delighted." The Wilson actors, along with the rest of the audience, roared with laughter. Darryl F. Zanuck, prod., Henry King, dir., *Wilson* (Hollywood, CA: 20th Century Fox Films, 1944).

10. George Washington Cable, "The Freedman's Case in Equity," *Century Magazine* 29 (January 1885): 417.

11. Blumenthal, 2.

12. Wilson to Louis Edelman, September 20, 1909, in Arthur Link, ed., *The Papers of Woodrow Wilson,* 63 vols. (Princeton: Princeton University Press, 1966–1977), 19: 386. John Milton Cooper, honorary president of the Woodrow Wilson Foundation, maintains that Wilson had no strong racial views in *Pivotal Decades: The United States, 1900–1920*

(New York: Norton, 1990), 184. In addition, a serious critique of Wilson, particularly in regard to his racial views, has been prevented by the disproportionate focus on his achievements in the historical literature. Many Wilson historians have been blinded by his legislative success and vision for world peace and seem to feel, to a lesser or greater extent, like McAdoo when he expressed that there was "no truer, nobler and braver soldier in the cause of humanity . . . since the death of Lincoln." McAdoo to Villard, October 27, 1913, Oswald Villard Papers, quoted in Kathleen L. Wolgemuth, "Woodrow Wilson and Federal Segregation," *Journal of Negro History* 44 (January 1959): 167 and note 23.

13. Unpublished articles/writings, February 22, 1881, in Link, *Papers* 1: 27, 51; Woodrow Wilson, *A History of the American People, Volume 5* (New York: Harper and Brothers, 1902), 18, 20, 46, 49, 58, 60, 194, 195; Ballew, 15.

14. Campaign Speech in Phillipsbury, NJ, October 22, 1910, and Campaign Speech in Salem, NJ, October 25, 1910, both in Link, *Papers* 21: 390, 423; *New York Age,* July 11, 1912, in Trotter Correspondence, Woodrow Wilson Papers, Seeley G. Mudd Library, Princeton University, Princeton, NJ; Alexander L. George and Juliette L. George, *Woodrow Wilson and Colonel House: A Personality Study* (New York: Dover, 1964), 19; Louis Auchincloss, *Woodrow Wilson* (New York: Penguin Putnam, 2000), 6; Stephen R. Fox, *The Guardian of Boston: William Monroe Trotter* (New York: Atheneum, 1970), 189.

15. Ray Stannard Baker, *Woodrow Wilson, Life and Letters: Youth, 1856–1890* (New York: Doubleday, Page, 1927), 150, 231–232; Wilson to Morgan Poitiaux Robinson, October 30, 1905, in Link, *Papers* 15: 32. The latter demonstrates a striking parallel between the racial views of Wilson and Vardaman. The belief that there were certain things whites do not do, particularly ones relegated to blacks, was a common theme in southern society. A case emphasizing this point can be seen in Vardaman's bitter opposition to white Mississippi teachers holding summer school for black teachers: "Now it is an almost unpardonable offense for a white man or woman to teach in the ordinary nigger school . . . to do it means social ostracism"; quoted in William F. Holmes, *The White Chief: James Kimble Vardaman* (Baton Rouge: Louisiana State University Press, 1970), 89.

16. Woodrow Wilson, "The Reconstruction of the Southern States," *Atlantic Monthly* 87 (1901): 6; a young Wilson encourages "liberal and systematic aid" for southern blacks, in "The Politics and Industries of the New South," April 30, 1881, in Link, *Papers* 2: 54; unpublished article/writings, February 22, 1881, in Link, *Papers* 1: 27, 51; Wilson, *History of the American People, Volume 5,* 18–20; Ballew, 15 note 13.

17. Woodrow Wilson, *Division and Reunion, 1829–1889* (Gloucester, MA: Peter Smith, 1974), 109–119, 227. "Beginning with Woodrow Wilson," explains Anthony Lewis in his introduction to DuBois's *Black Reconstruction in America, 1860–1880,* "white historians and political scientists documented, denounced, and derided African-American ignorance, venality, and exploitation under Reconstruction" (New York: Simon and Schuster, 1995), vii. Lewis maintains that by the 1960s the "war against racist Reconstruction historiography had been won" following the "revisionist" histories that disputed the dominant racist interpretations; xvi–xvii. It seems, however, that this war has been won more in the field of academia, and primarily at more liberal institutions, than in the minds of the general white majority. It appears that the general views of racist Reconstruction historiography still persist in large degree even today. Interestingly, the distinguished Harvard historian Albert

Bushnell Hart, under whom men such as DuBois and Villard completed graduate studies, also served as editor for Wilson's *Division and Reunion.* Hart applauded DuBois's reinterpretation of black contributions during Reconstruction in a paper written in the 1890s that later became the basis for *Black Reconstruction,* and he even paid the latter's traveling expenses to have the paper presented at a meeting of the American Historical Association in 1909. Although it seems strange that Hart would devote himself to two radically different interpretations of Reconstruction, he seems not to have been completely comfortable with either interpretation, although he leaned more toward that of DuBois. Later, however, Hart would join the racist school. Lewis, "Introduction," in DuBois, *Black Reconstruction,* viii.

18. August Hecksher, *Woodrow Wilson: A Biography* (New York: Macmillan Publishing Co., 1991), 111.

19. Woodrow Wilson, "The Course of American History," in Wilson, *Mere Literature and Other Essays* (New York: Houghton, Mifflin, 1896), 238; Ballew, 16.

20. Lewis, *W.E.B. DuBois,* 85.

21. Ballew, 13–14; Woodrow Wilson, *George Washington* (New York: Harper and Brothers, 1897), referenced in Ballew, 14 and note 9.

22. Excerpt in Link, *Papers* 15: 262.

23. G. McArthur Sullivan to Wilson, December 3, 1909, and Wilson to Sullivan, December 6, 1909, in Link, *Papers* 19: 550, 557–558; *New York Age,* July 11, 1912, in Trotter Correspondence, Woodrow Wilson Papers, Seeley G. Mudd Library, Princeton University, Princeton, NJ. Just a couple of months after rejecting Sullivan because of his race, Wilson amazingly wrote, "Learning knows no differences of social caste or privilege." Wilson himself did, however; "The Country and the Colleges," in Link, *Papers* 20: 160–161. See also John M. Mulder, "A Gospel of Order: Woodrow Wilson's Religion and Politics," in John Milton Cooper Jr. and Charles E. Neu, eds., *The Wilson Era: Essays in Honor of Arthur S. Link* (Arlington Heights, IL: Harlan Davidson, 1991), 235, 246.

24. "White Supremacy at Princeton," condensed article from the *Daily Princetonian,* in *Negro Digest* (January 1943): 60–61; Commission of Southern University's 1914 annual report quoted in *Washington Herald,* December 16, 1914.

25. Heckscher, 291; *Crisis,* January 1914, 124.

26. Wilson to James Duval Phelan, May 3, 1912, in Link, *Papers* 24: 382–383; Gerald N. Hallberg, "Bellingham, Washington's Anti-Hindu Riot," *Journal of the West* 12 (January 1973): 163–175. Henry W. Bragdon says that "for years he [Wilson] taught his classes that a homogeneous population was a pre-condition of successful constitutional government. . . . But eventually he came to a conclusion that even with a mingling of races, a democratic nation could be formed as long as the other race conforms." *Woodrow Wilson: The Academic Years* (Cambridge: Belknap Press of Harvard University, 1967), 260. Yet as of 1912, in regard to Chinese and Japanese immigrants, this was not the case.

27. Wilson, *History of the American People, Volume 5,* 59–62. The policies and actions of the Wilson administration unleashed negative forces on some of the most vulnerable people and groups in early twentieth century America. The Committee on Public Information (CPI), established by Wilson in 1917 ostensibly to rally American support for WWI, was more or less a propaganda machine that promoted hyper-nationalism. The CPI fueled an intense suspicion of the actions, beliefs, and interests of any person (s), and ethnic, political,

and civic groups that appeared to even superficially challenge this rigid and exclusive definition of patriotism. Congress quickly followed suit by passing the Espionage and Sedition Acts—both of which gave the federal government arbitrary power to subvert civil liberties. These actions, along with Wilson's own publicly harsh remarks questioning the loyalty of immigrants and others, not only attempted to discourage and crush dissent, but resulted in thousands of American immigrants being taken from their homes, and either held as detainees with no rights or deported from the country. In addition, not only were immigrants under intense scrutiny, but many pacifists, socialists, and others were susceptible to and were the victims of discrimination and violence. Frederick Howe, the Commissioner of Immigration at Ellis Island during the Wilson years, was utterly discouraged by an administration that "encouraged these excesses . . . abandoned the liberty . . . and it lent itself to the stamping out of . . . freedom." Author's paper/remarks on the negative treatment received by African Americans, immigrants, and women during Woodrow Wilson's presidency. Princeton University Colloquium on Public and International Affairs, "Woodrow Wilson: In the Nation's Service," April 28–29, 2006, in honor of the 150th anniversary of the birth of President Woodrow Wilson.

28. Ernest Trice Thompson, *The Changing South and the Presbyterian Church* (Richmond, VA: John Knox, 1950), 24–27.

29. Unnamed author, "The Southern Situation," *American Missionary* 43 (January 1889).

30. Baker, 58, 62–63, 70, 84, 231–232; DuBois quoted in "William Monroe Trotter," *Crisis,* January 1915, 82.

31. This is not because of a lack of information on the progress of African Americans at that time. There were several studies, including a 1910 Department of Commerce, Bureau of the Census release, that statistically demonstrated an enormous decrease in the illiteracy rate among the black population in the South. In addition, President Wilson had friends, such as Ray Stannard Baker, who were interested in the progress of blacks. Baker, in fact, wrote in 1908 that many whites in the South felt threatened by the sweeping increase in black education and ownership of property and assets and desired to keep them poor and ignorant; the South wanted "negroes who are really inferior and feel inferior." See *Following the Color Line: American Negro Citizenship in the Progressive Era* (New York: Harper Torchbooks, 1964), 54, 78, 84–85, quote here from 241–242, 282. Although DuBois cited the 1910 Bureau of the Census report when stating that the total value of farm property in the South operated (owned, part ownership, managed, share tenant, or cash tenant) by blacks amounted to $1,116,641,576 that year (*Crisis,* March 1914, 248), it appears that his impressive number falls short of the official Census number given in its release for that year, which was estimated to be $1,144,181,000. "Negroes in the U.S.," Department of Commerce, Bureau of the Census, release no. 8-4499, in Box 74, John Skelton Williams Papers, MSS 10040, Special Collections, University of Virginia Library, Charlottesville, VA.

32. Morehouse quoted in James M. McPherson, *The Abolitionist Legacy: From Reconstruction to the NAACP* (Princeton: Princeton University Press, 1975), 357–358.

33. Virgil A. Wood, "The African American Experience," Introduction, in *Holy Bible: African American Jubilee Edition* (New York: American Bible Society, 1999), 28. For an excellent study on the growth of self-sufficient black enterprises within the church impact-

ing secular life, see Evelyn Brooks Higginbotham, *Righteous Discontent: The Women's Movement in the Black Baptist Church, 1880–1920* (Cambridge: Harvard University Press, 1993).

34. Woodrow Wilson, *The State* (Washington, DC: Heath, 1918), 1–2, and *Mere Literature and Other Essays,* 222; John M. Blum, *Woodrow Wilson and the Politics of Morality* (Boston: Little, Brown, 1956), 10; Ballew, 13–14.

35. Wilson, *History of the American People, Volume 5,* 20, 59–62.

36. Wilson to Louis Edelman, September 20, 1909, in Link, *Papers* 19: 386. Also, a brief summary of the development of Wilson's political thought can be found in Katherine L. Brown, *Woodrow Wilson on the Constitution: Son of the Staunton Manse* (Staunton, VA: Woodrow Wilson Birthplace Foundation, 1988). See also Interview with Wilson by the United Negro Democracy of New Jersey, as reported in the *Trenton Evening Times,* July 31, 1912, also copy in Link, *Papers* 24: 574. Here Wilson is more indirect, but his belief that the South should be left alone to deal with blacks is clear; he stated that the races in the South "understand each other better than elsewhere." And in a speech before the Southern University Commission on Race Problems, Wilson said that "as a Southern man" he knew "how sincerely the heart of the South desires the good of the Negro and the advancement of his race on all sound and sensible lines"; *Crisis,* February 1915, 172, quoted in Charles Flint Kellogg, *NAACP: A History of the National Association for the Advancement of Colored People,* vol. l, *1909–1920* (Baltimore: Johns Hopkins University Press, 1967), 175.

37. Vardaman quoted in Holmes, 90.

38. Auchincloss, 6.

39. Trotter to Wilson, July 18, 1912, Wilson Papers, Seeley G. Mudd Library, Princeton University, Princeton, NJ.

40. Auchincloss, 29. For two examples of *Harper's Weekly* articles on Wilson, see "Qualities of Woodrow Wilson," May 26, 1906, and "Considerations of Woodrow Wilson," April 7, 1907.

41. Edith Bolling Wilson, 6, 22.

42. Campaign Speech in Salem, NJ, October 25, 1910, in Link, *Papers* 21: 433; *Congressional Information Service Index to Presidential Executive Orders and Proclamations, April 30, 1789, to March 4, 1921, George Washington to Woodrow Wilson* (Washington, DC: Congressional Information Service, 1987), 1915-44-175.

43. "Mr. Trotter and Mr. Wilson," *Crisis,* January 1915, 119. This meeting is the theme of Chapter 7.

44. Morton Sosna, "The South in the Saddle: Racial Politics During the Wilson Years," *Wisconsin Magazine of History* 54 (Autumn 1970): 32.

45. Heckscher, 291.

46. Grantham, 470. In perhaps the most favorable consideration of Wilson's racial views, he could be placed in the category described by social reformer Mary White Ovington as one of those "kindly and intelligent people" who in defending segregation "believe that they have the colored man's welfare at heart"; *Crisis,* January 1915, 142.

47. Arthur Link, "The Negro as a Factor in the Campaign of 1912," *Journal of Negro History* 32 (January 1947): 82–84; Charles Crowe, "Racial Violence and Social Reform—Origins of the Atlanta Riot of 1906," *Journal of Negro History* 53 (July 1968): 241–242; William E. Reynolds to Booker T. Washington, May 22, 1912, Booker T. Washington

Papers 11: 541. Yet both Watson and Smith, along with the rest of the South, rallied behind Wilson once he had won his party's nomination.

48. Wilson to Villard, August 29, 1913, quoted in Wolgemuth, "Woodrow Wilson and Federal Segregation," 164.

49. Blumenthal, 6. Also, Wilson may very well have believed southern senators would attempt to obstruct his legislative agenda if he did not abide by their demands for racial exclusiveness when it came to federal appointments. J. Clay Smith Jr. notes that "the drama surrounding Judge Terrell's nomination was so intense that the key senators blocked all other pending nominations until the Terrell matter was favorably resolved." *Emancipation: The Making of a Black Lawyer, 1844–1944* (Philadelphia: University of Pennsylvania Press, 1993), 173 note 108. Morton Sosna believes "Southern votes played a crucial role in the passage of Wilson's legislative program," and possibly "Southerners were the prime movers behind reform legislation under the New Freedom"; Sosna, 35 note 12.

50. Charles Anderson believed the Wilson administration "inspired enemies of the Negro to run amuch at any time without fear of punishment and notified the oppressor that oppression was safe and protected by the highest authorities in the land"; Kellogg, 166–167 and note 45. Also, racism and violence cast its shadow on the Wilson administration from the international level as well. Overlooked by Wilson scholars, the first horrific genocidal campaign of the twentieth century, the official efforts of the Turkish government to "exterminate entirely all the Armenians living in Turkey," which resulted in the murder of seventy percent of the Armenian population, occurred in 1915. Top Turkish officials did not try to conceal their genocidal actions from Henry Morgenthau, Wilson's ambassador to Turkey during this time. In fact, Morgenthau says they talked of the slaughter casually, and he sent their statements, along with numerous other eyewitness accounts describing the carnage, in a stream of reports to the U.S. State Department while trying to persuade an unwilling U.S. government to intervene on behalf of the Armenians. See Morganthau, *Ambassador Morgenthau's Story* (Garden City, New York: Doubleday, Page & Co., 1919), 307, 323–324, 325, 328, 333, 339, 351–352.

51. Rolfe Colbleigh to May Childs Nerney, October 22, 1913, Administrative Files, Box C-403, NAACP Papers, Manuscript Division, Library of Congress, Washington, DC. This chapter does not propose that Wilson's racial sentiments were entirely responsible for federal Jim Crow during his presidency. Rather, they were one of the contributing factors that included the racial views held by some of his cabinet—particularly Burleson, McAdoo, and Daniels; racist senators and House members, motivated by their own racial prejudice and that of their constituents to push Jim Crow policies and legislation; and external pressure from white groups such as the Democratic Fair Play Association and the White Railway Workers Union, among others. The main purpose here was to demonstrate that Wilson's thinking throughout most of his life supported the doctrine of racial separation he later approved of as chief executive.

THE NAACP LAUNCHES ITS CAMPAIGN
AGAINST JIM CROW

The protest to President Woodrow Wilson against the segregation in the Federal offices in Washington . . . is justified by the laws of the land and the dictates of freedom and fairness.

—*TACOMA NEWS*

O N AUGUST 18, 1913, three days after "A Letter to President Wilson on Federal Race Discrimination" was sent to Wilson and members of his Cabinet, the National Association for the Advancement of Colored People (NAACP) sent out a mass form letter to all association members, branch offices, friends, and sympathizers. In it the organization instructed them to "write at once a letter of protest—first, to your representative in Congress, second, to both your state Senators, and third to the President of the United States." The letter went on to ask, "Will you not try to secure at least five of your friends to do the same." Copies of the official protest sent to President Wilson were also included with the letter. The form letter concluded by offering copies of the letter upon request for distribution.[1]

The response was overwhelming. People from all walks of life—laborers and professionals, men and women, blacks and whites—wrote the NAACP asking for more copies of the protest letter to distribute to friends and colleagues at meetings, churches, and clubs; informed the organization of their commitment to individual and mass protest efforts; and often expressed a fiery determination to educate the public and their representatives of the injustice in Washington. In addition, numerous U.S. senators and representatives who had received or read the protest letter wrote the NAACP expressing their personal opposition to federal Jim Crow, and some even offered their assistance in protest efforts.[2]

Although the NAACP was at the forefront in this stage of the protest, it was strategically important that the protest appear to be a grassroots effort, carried out on the initiative of citizens opposed to the Jim Crow policy. The organization was still much too small and embryonic to be taken seriously as a single powerful force. "It is not intended that members should notify the President that a copy of the letter to the President was being sent to each member with the request that protests be made . . . it weakens the force of the protest," explained a concerned Oswald Villard to a protestor who failed to understand the dynamics of the protest. The communication of the masses, and the powerful symbol of protest such united voices of opposition represented, believed Villard, must be tactically directed at President Wilson and officials of the white power structure to convince them that Jim Crow was not a benign and accepted arrangement but a serious injustice to African Americans. Moreover, if the protest appeared to be the work of a small group of troublemakers, the president—already disposed to accept the conservative viewpoint as representative opinion among African Americans—might be led to believe the objections to federal Jim Crow were not widespread and therefore nothing to be concerned about.[3]

The day after the form letter was sent to members and friends, the NAACP sent out mass form letters along with copies of the protest letter to newspapers across the country. According to NAACP files, the protest or parts of the protest letter were widely published and sent to 338 black newspapers, 50 white religious papers, and 16 editors. Seventy-five copies went to William Monroe Trotter's National Equal Rights League, newspaperman Charles Hallinan of the *Chicago Evening Post,* and another editor, John Nail.[4]

The protest, astonishingly, was also printed in numerous black newspapers in every state below the Mason-Dixon line, most of which were humble weeklies consisting of no more than four pages. For example, the Greensboro (North Carolina) *Herald,* an African American weekly, printed the protest letter in its entirety, and the paper's editor jubilantly expressed his desire to participate in the "movement." The most militant black northern newspapers, such as the Indianapolis *Freeman,* and more conservative rags like the *New York Age*—faithful critics of Wilsonian Jim Crow that had printed the protest letter—also found their way south where their articles were regular topics of conversation in African American communities. Although illiteracy was high in many parts of the South, groups would congregate in barber-shops or other meeting places to hear the latest news read aloud, including the calls for protest.[5]

The NAACP used two different mass form letters for its nationwide news-paper campaign. One was directed at small newspapers with limited space and requested that they "print in the most conspicuous place . . . the en-closed protest to President Wilson." The other form letter was sent mostly to large newspapers. It praised the particular paper's "spirit of fair play towards the Negro," hoped that the "enclosed open letter to President Wilson . . . will find a place in your columns," and requested "editorial comment" from the publisher—clearly a potent tactic for influencing public opinion.[6]

Black and religious white newspapers were not the only ones to print the letter. The protest, along with editorial comment, also found its way into the pages of several liberal newspapers, including the widely circulated *New York Times*. In the South the controversial *Lexington* (Kentucky) *Herald* quoted the entire letter and printed a favorable editorial. As a result, it is safe to say that tens of thousands of people probably read the letter, and an untold number of them were persuaded to join the protest, including many illiter-ate black southerners who had their names added to letters and petitions.[7]

THE PROTEST AND BOOKER T. WASHINGTON

Shortly after newspapers received the protest letter, the NAACP sent "an earnest appeal" to sympathetic members of Congress asking for their assis-tance in putting pressure on the Wilson administration. "Will you lift up your voice" in opposition to a policy that withholds "justice and fair play to the Negro," pleaded the organization. What makes this particular letter unique is that the NAACP attempted to use the name of its ideological adversary, Booker T. Washington, to strengthen its arguments and gain support from white politicians. With his glory days passing away, Washington was still considered by and large the most respected black leader in America. Most important, because of his strategically employed rhetoric placating the South, he posed no apparent threat to the white power structure.[8]

Although the NAACP was formed in part to fill the void created by Washington's overt neglect of black political and civil rights, the seemingly irreconcilable philosophies of the Tuskegeen and the NAACP have been much overblown. Putting personal feelings aside, the organization and even the impatient agitator and Washington nemesis William Monroe Trotter were not opposed to vocational training that would enable many poor blacks to become economically self-sufficient. With the demand for black political and civil rights the cornerstone of the NAACP, the activist organization also supported and promoted industrial education—reflecting the often historically overlooked fact that many shared aspects of, and often shifted between, economic improvement, with its emphasis on self-sufficiency, and agitation and protest.[9]

Responding to claims that it was "opposed to industrial education," the NAACP Third Annual Report made it clear that "[n]othing could be farther from the truth." Many of its directors and members, the report emphasized, regularly contributed money and in some cases leadership to the work of industrial schools such as Hampton and Tuskegee. The following year, in its Fourth Annual Report, the organization jubilantly informed members of its support for a new organization "comprising the principals or managers of small schools in the South, doing an industrial work after the fashion of Tuskegee." "The secretaryship," continued the report, "has been taken over by Mr. Leslie Pinckney Hill, a member of the National Association." If this could be interpreted as a power play by the NAACP to chisel away some of Washington's influence in his own backyard, it cannot be overlooked that whatever their motives, the NAACP members clearly understood the benefits derived from an education that trained those for a trade who might otherwise have ended up as impoverished sharecroppers under the domination of a white landlord or overseer.[10]

But most within the NAACP felt industrial training alone would never improve the lot of the African Americans unless they had equal political and civil rights, and they condemned Booker T. Washington for seeing only one side of the coin. The secretary of the Tacoma, Washington, branch, Nettie J. Asbury—one of the coterie of black female leaders in the early years of the NAACP and one who helped pioneer the organization in the West—criticized Washington in a letter for not speaking out against federal Jim Crow: "[W]e are more than mere *money making machines*," stressed Asbury.[11] A few years earlier, DuBois as well had written that "the question as to whether the Negro should have simply an industrial education or . . . the highest training depends entirely upon" whether the "Negro" is being trained "for his own benefit or for the benefit of somebody else."[12] Trotter underscored this point by objecting to what he felt was the conventional moralizing of the times that sought to mold every unsophisticated black child in the image of Tuskegee for "practical" use while balking at higher education.[13] And long-time friend Oswald Villard, in a candid letter, explained to Washington that African Americans had made some progress under his leadership but added that "prejudice and discrimination" had increased even more rapidly, and he laid some of the blame at his friend's feet.[14]

Although competition between Washington and the NAACP had kept them mostly apart (particularly for the Tuskegeen, who was not willing to let loose of the reins of power for even an inch and who had developed a mild obsession with covertly tracking the equal rights organization), the NAACP wisely used him to grab the attention of white leaders. "Dr. Booker T. Washington writes me," Villard informed New York senator Elihu Root, "that never in his experience has he seen the colored people in Washington so depressed and so bitter as at the present, and he finds that they are subject to great humiliation and needless petty vexations." Villard forwarded to Wilson the entire letter from Washington asking for a change from the "hurtful" policy before it went any further. In addition, Washington's letter was published in the *New York Times*. It would be easier for members of the political establishment to respond out of sympathy for Washington than to openly align themselves with more aggressive organizations such as the NAACP and Trotter's National Independent Political League. Most important, if the passive leader were disturbed over federal Jim Crow, perhaps the issue would be perceived as more serious than unsubstantiated news stories.[15]

Washington was not opposed to protest efforts aimed at Jim Crow in government departments. He strongly believed such a policy was "persecuting the colored people" and creating much "harm" for both races. If Washington had at times, as James McPherson pointed out, "used Villard as a proxy spokesman for positions he could not afford to take publicly," his recent protests showed a more aggressive leader who now came out of the shadows and publicly put his name behind his criticisms.[16]

The Tuskegeen expressed his discontent with the Jim Crow policy in the *New York Evening Post*—a well-respected newspaper with a wide circulation that aggressively sought political and civil rights for African Americans. Washington also praised Villard's August 4 article in the *Post,* which lambasted federal Jim Crow, and he called on President Wilson to take action against it through the same newspaper—a move Villard's uncle Francis Garrison called "interesting, in view of his past attitude." In a tone sounding more like one of the "radicals," Washington wrote to a friend that Treasury Secretary McAdoo was guilty of "high crimes and misdemeanors" for allegedly leading segregation efforts in the federal departments. And in response to an inquirer who wanted to carry out a protest against federal Jim Crow, Washington wrote that he felt "reasonably sure that a carefully planned protest" would "prove effective."[17]

Federal Jim Crow caused some in the Tuskegee camp to join the NAACP as well. For example, Roscoe Conkling Bruce, an assistant superintendent of schools in Washington, D.C., who had served as the head of Tuskegee's academic department, became an active member of the city's NAACP branch.

"I am Mr. Washington's friend and admirer," affirmed Bruce, but he added, "I am also a loyal supporter of the principles for which Mr. Villard stands."[18]

Yet if Washington supported protest activities through his own resources during the Wilson years, it was done in secret. Although the National Negro Press Association—reputed as supporting the policies of Washington and representing over 126 publications—protested in a letter to Wilson in a surprisingly militant tone, it appears the only time the Tuskegeen publicly raised his voice against racial caste in the federal bureaucracy was in the *New York Evening Post.* Whereas most of his criticisms of federal Jim Crow and support of the protest remained within the confines of personal correspondences, there is evidence that Washington may have expressed his displeasure directly to McAdoo and Wilson. If nothing else, this verified that blacks and whites with different philosophies regarding black advancement, including many in the Washington camp, were largely in agreement and remarkably united when it came to opposing federal Jim Crow.[19]

In the weeks following the release of the August protest letter, the NAACP recruited a newspaperman from Chicago with "considerable experience in publicity work" to help direct its publicity campaign. His duties were to inform the public about the spread of Jim Crow in federal departments and give credibility to the report in the protest letter. Charles Hallinan of the *Chicago Evening Post* was responsible for finding writers to contribute articles for national magazines. After securing the agreement of magazine editors, Hallinan found writers with knowledge of and experience with federal Jim Crow to write articles for such popular magazines as *Harper's Weekly, Collier's Weekly,* the *Saturday Evening Post,* and *La Follette's Weekly.* In addition, Villard soon wrote an article on the effects of federal Jim Crow for the influential *North American Review.* And Nerney, after approaching Archibald Grimke about writing an article for the *Atlantic Monthly,* asked if he "would mention the NAACP." Publicity for the organization was secondary only to publicity for the injustice in Washington. Publicizing federal Jim Crow in the pages of newspapers and magazines, Nerney believed, ideally went hand in hand with publicizing the young equal rights organization she believed was leading the fight.[20]

From autumn 1913 on, as data on the size and extent of the Jim Crow policy in Washington mounted, black and liberal white opposition was united, hitting hard at what was felt to be the most serious blow to African American rights since the days of slavery.[21] "I fear this land is facing a similar crisis to that of 1860–1863," lamented Cicely Gunner, a black equal rights and women's suffrage advocate and president of the Northeastern Federation of Women's Clubs, in a letter to Villard.[22]

Thousands of people from all walks of life had received the letter of protest and the appeal for participation in the fight against federal Jim Crow. Shortly after the NAACP protest was sent out, editorials condemning the injustice grew sharper in their criticisms, mass meetings in cities increased, and letters of protest flooded the White House and the offices of Jim Crow Cabinet members. Public recognition of the NAACP's leadership in the Jim Crow protest was growing as well. The *Savannah Tribune* was one of many newspapers that praised the NAACP for doing "a great and grand work" in helping the "Negro" to "secure his social and political rights."[23]

NAACP MASS MEETINGS AND PETITIONS OF PROTEST

Throughout 1913 and 1914, numerous mass meetings were held all over the country to protest by petition against federal Jim Crow. Amazingly, some of these meetings compared in numbers to those held in the modern civil rights era. Petitions were signed at mass meetings held in Baltimore, Boston, New Haven, New York, northern California, Portland (Maine), Providence, Tacoma, Topeka, and Washington, D.C. Almost half the signatures on the anti–Jim Crow petitions found in the Woodrow Wilson Papers at the Library of Congress appear to be those of women, and many if not most were signed at mass meetings held in black churches and sanctuary halls.

Dynamic speakers of both races who were either leaders of the community or members of the NAACP at the local or national level often led these "enthusiastic" meetings. In addition, NAACP national officers toured such eastern cities as Boston, New York, and Washington to arouse and inform the public. Even though most meetings were sponsored by or affiliated with the NAACP, people who were not members of the organization packed crowded halls and sanctuaries to hear the latest on Jim Crow in the nation's capital and voice their opposition as well. These protests were generally registered on petitions and sent directly to the president by telegraph.

Mass meetings were more numerous in the Northeast and parts of the central United States, since those regions had far more NAACP branches compared with other areas. In addition, in those areas lived most of the organization's national officers, plus the national headquarters was located in New York City. With such a cluster of leaders in one area, particularly in the Northeast, protest strategy and efforts often emanated from that part of the country. In the Midwest and the western seaboard region, however, branches were popping up all over and were eager to lend their energies to protesting Jim Crow in federal departments. And although the Deep South appears to have had only one active branch in 1913—the "most Southern outpost" in

Talladega, Alabama—southern preachers used their pulpits to rake federal Jim Crow over the coals. This is astounding in light of the fact that most rural black pastors in that period did not usually, in the words of Alabama native Coretta Scott King, "discuss from their pulpits the rights of blacks or the issues of segregation."[24] But it does appear that black southern ministers, who—with the exception of those in the elite denominations in the border and northern states—by and large had been conservative and cautious in speaking out against the more extreme forms of racial injustice (although a decade or so earlier many did, in fact, lead and participate in the boycotts of Jim Crow streetcars that had swept across the South), were by the second decade of the twentieth century becoming increasingly vocal from the pulpit in their opposition to Jim Crow.

Southern newspapers, almost all black, were quick to recognize the NAACP efforts against segregation while voicing their own opposition as well. With this in mind, protesting Jim Crow in Washington provided a relatively safe target for African Americans in the Deep South—who were reluctant to openly criticize the racism in their own backyard for fear of violent reprisal, an almost daily occurrence since the beginning of the century—to vent their pent-up frustrations. Thus, adding their name to a petition or writing a letter that would end up hundreds of miles from home in Washington, or writing an article in a local black newspaper that was ignored by whites, was much safer than condemning the homegrown Jim Crow in a local white southern paper or requesting a reverse in local custom on a petition widely circulated throughout a southern community.[25]

Although it would be a few years until the NAACP printed its official instructions on how to conduct a successful mass meeting, these early efforts, which brought together a collective chime of African American voices in protest—whether in newspapers, in mass meetings, in churches, or on petitions—were marked by an amazingly uniform approach and a shared sense of purpose. Interestingly, in what was perhaps one of the first instances of national networking in African American protest, many NAACP branches corresponded with branches in other cities, often to assist them in arranging their own protest meetings and to stay informed of other protest activities and efforts. Moreover, this successful early networking occurred at a time when technological mass communication was still in its infancy and when African Americans were relatively disconnected (the Great Migration and the rise of the Associated Negro Press were still a few years off) and had not yet discovered their collective potential.

In late August 1913, the president of the Cincinnati NAACP branch and national organizer, Dr. M.C.B. Mason, eagerly sent a telegram to the headquarters on Vesey Street requesting "immediately" more copies of the letter of protest to distribute at an upcoming mass meeting at which a large attendance of blacks and whites was anticipated.[26] Dr. Mason was one of the NAACP's most effective organizers, having arranged mass meetings to protest federal Jim Crow in at least five cities during fall 1913. He was also a featured speaker at some of those meetings. In Portland, Maine, for example, Mason addressed a "large audience" at a meeting he had helped organize, and he spoke at another in Cincinnati, along with former senator Joseph Benson Foraker who had ardently defended the black soldiers discharged at Brownsville. In addition, Mason organized mass protest meetings in Atlantic City, New Jersey; Columbus, Ohio; and New Haven, Connecticut.[27] During a protest meeting in New Haven, the eloquent Rev. George W. Crawford, an NAACP national director and one of the original founders of the Niagara Movement, delivered an "inspiring speech" that brought the audience to its feet.[28]

At the Park Street Church in Boston on October 20, a large audience was stirred by the impassioned speeches of several notable speakers. They included Senator Edwin Moses Clapp of Minnesota, the underdog's most persistent champion in Congress; Albert Pillsbury, a former Massachusetts attorney general who earlier that summer had resigned his membership in the American Bar Association after it had refused to admit black members; and Rolfe Cobleigh, assistant editor of the *Congregationalist and Christian World* and faithful Wilson critic.

With eloquence and foreboding, Senator Clapp, the most vociferous advocate for black equality in the Senate, drew thunderous applause as he warned his audience of the dangers presented to the entire nation by Jim Crow: "When men . . . are struck a blow like this, they are putting back on the black man the bloody shackles which four years of bloody warfare struck from his ankles!" "It is not the question of the Negro," the senator continued, "but that of the progress of our great nation. The moment you have thoroughly forced into the consciousness of the black or white man that there can be no progress, you have laid the foundation for class distinction." Following other impassioned speeches condemning federal Jim Crow, the mass meeting in Boston telegraphed protest resolutions to the president. "Such action by the Government, or by any officer thereof," the protest declared, "is in open violation of the principles of equality upon which the Government stands." Letters were also forwarded to President Wilson from Governor Eugene Foss and Congressman Augustus Peabody Gardner, both of Massachusetts, asking that he "take . . . action" and "bring an end to race discrimination in any department of government."[29]

In early November, NAACP national officer Dr. Joel E. Spingarn—an energetic modern-day Renaissance man who was a poet, essayist, publisher, orator, and leader and was independently wealthy—addressed an "enthusiastic" protest meeting attended by over 600 African Americans at the Beneficent Congregational Church in Providence, Rhode Island. Protest meetings sponsored by the NAACP national headquarters were held at several churches in New York as well, including the Rev. John Haynes Holmes's racially diverse Community Church of New York City and St. Mark's Guild, led by NAACP board director and militant feminist Florence Kelly.[30]

The cradle of American abolitionism, where the antislavery oratory of such giants as Frederick Douglass and Wendell Phillips once echoed across the nation, was the home of another enormously successful mass meeting held December 1. This meeting in particular was unique because it was here that one of the first organized modern protest marches took place. An hour before the scheduled meeting in Boston's historic Faneuil Hall, a large procession—including hundreds of people belonging to the Odd Fellows lodge and led by the Rev. Samuel A. Brown of the Congregational Church—marched from the west end of town. From the south end, the Rev. B. W. Swain of the Zion Church led numerous protestors belonging to different faiths, denominations, and organizations toward the same destination. Braving the biting northeast winds gusting off the Atlantic, the two columns of bundled-up marchers, which included people from different socioeconomic backgrounds, merged halfway and sung spirituals as they slowly made their way to Faneuil Hall.[31]

By three o'clock Faneuil Hall and the adjacent square were packed. The leaders of the black churches of Greater Boston, who were also members of the NAACP, had organized the massive protest meeting. One of the main speakers, the white president of the NAACP, Moorfield Storey, drew a "great burst of applause" when he declared, "Our colored citizens are not inferior, and are progressing so fast that they will soon present themselves as the white man's equal!" "The national government sanctions and approves the race prejudice which is the greatest handicap to Negro progress today," continued Storey. Rabbi Eichler, the next speaker, after telling the audience that blacks and Jews had suffered similar prejudice and assuring them that he was in this "fight" all the way, lambasted federal Jim Crow as "wrong" and "unjust."[32]

Oswald Villard was the last speaker, and it was interestingly reported that many in the audience had heard "his distinguished" grandfather, the great abolitionist William Lloyd Garrison, "in this very hall pleading for justice to the Negro." When Villard stood to speak, the hum of whispering voices swirling around the giant hall was abruptly interrupted by thunderous applause. Many in the audience appreciated the historical significance of the grandson standing where the grandfather had once stood, pleading justice for the same ebony brethren. The modern-day abolitionist told the audience that the "victims of this segregation plan are no corner loafers, they are educated citizens who have passed the same civil service examinations as their white associates." He criticized the hypocrisy of those who trumpet freedom and yet deny it to millions of black citizens. African Americans have made exceptional progress within the federal government, and the forces of race prejudice are seeking to crush them, Villard continued. The proponents of such a "plan" are determined to force "the Colored people out of the public service entirely." Following Villard's speech, a telegram was read from Boston mayor John Fitzgerald (grandfather of future president John F. Kennedy) stating that he had taken up the segregation matter with the authorities in Washington. Resolutions of protest, signed by those attending the meeting, were then sent to President Wilson, Postmaster General Burleson, and Secretary of the Treasury William McAdoo. Later that day the Cambridge Lyceum held another energetic mass meeting for the hundreds of people who had been turned away from the packed Faneuil Hall.[33]

The western part of the country contributed its share in protesting federal Jim Crow as well. In Tacoma, Washington, on the evening of September 26, several speakers took turns electrifying a large audience of blacks and whites at a mass meeting held at the city's First Baptist Church. Speakers included the Rev. J. A. Nelson, president of the Tacoma branch of the NAACP; W. W. Seymor; and the mayors of Seattle and Tacoma. When the last one had finished speaking, over 500 men and women rushed to the front of the room and signed resolutions of protest to be delivered to President Wilson. This "far Western outpost" also "corresponded with Seattle, Spokane, Portland, Denver and Ogden, and succeeded in arranging meetings of protest in both Ogden and Seattle." About a month later, another well-attended mass meeting was held in Tacoma and was coordinated by both the Seattle and Tacoma NAACP branches. Following the meeting, resolutions of protest were forwarded to the Canadian-born Jacob Falconer, now a member of Congress representing his district in Washington state, who personally delivered them to the chief executive.[34]

The newly formed NAACP branch in northern California sponsored several protest meetings. This branch also conducted an energetic grassroots campaign to arouse local opposition and sent a continuous stream of letters and telegrams to officials in Congress.[35] In Topeka, Kansas, a large audience estimated at 400 people attended a protest meeting sponsored in late September 1913 by the city's NAACP branch. Several distinguished speakers, white and black, drew roaring ovations as they raked Wilson, Burleson, and McAdoo over the coals for opening the floodgates of racial discrimination in the federal government. After the meeting ended, the protestors signed resolutions of protest, which were sent to President Wilson.[36]

In January 1914, Joel Spingarn, perhaps the most militant white member of the NAACP, launched what William Monroe Trotter dubbed the "tour against segregation." This was unique in the sense that most organized tours in the past advocating black equality and battling racial injustice—beginning in the abolition movement—were primarily confined to the Northeast, with the exception of a few journeys to Europe. Other groups with their own agendas, such as the National Woman American Suffrage Association, however, had been making nationwide tours for years to acquire members and support. The NAACP appears to have been the first equal rights organization to send a spokesman west on a major scheduled tour. Spingarn visited NAACP branches and potential branches and spoke before numerous audiences in Detroit; Chicago; Quincy, Illinois; Kansas City; Topeka; St. Louis; Indianapolis; and Cleveland. Although one of the purposes of the tour was to acquire new members, Spingarn's most important goal was to motivate audiences to work against Jim Crow at all levels, including in the federal government.[37]

His work paid off. Several of these branches, inspired by Spingarn's fiery appeal, spoke out in protest. Shortly after his visit, the Indianapolis NAACP branch held several meetings protesting federal Jim Crow and sent numerous letters and petitions of protest to Washington. An energetic mass meeting was held in Kansas City during Spingarn's visit, and resolutions of protest were wired overnight to the president. Fired up after his visit, the branch sent over a hundred letters to various members of Congress in hopes of persuading them to join the fight. The smallest NAACP branch, in Quincy, Illinois, motivated by Spingarn's call to arms, held numerous mass meetings. Here New York national director Charles Edward Russell and NAACP publicity coordinator and Chicago newspaperman Charles Hallihan addressed audiences on the Jim Crow issue in Washington. Although it is not clear whether the Detroit NAACP branch held mass meetings in 1913, the branch was reported to have vigorously protested federal Jim Crow by bombarding President Wilson and members of Congress with telegrams, letters, and signed resolutions."[38]

Throughout 1913 and 1914 the articulate Mary Wilson—social reformer and wife of Boston NAACP branch president Butler Wilson—traveled through Ohio, New York, New Jersey, and Pennsylvania delivering speeches for the NAACP at black churches and women's clubs. In addition, she had visited numerous cities to help arrange speaking engagements for Spingarn's tour. Always resourceful and making friends wherever she went, Mary Wilson used her network of black women's secular and religious organizations, along with black churches, to obtain speaking engagements and spread the word regarding the work of the NAACP, including its protest efforts against federal Jim Crow. She was so successful in organizing branches, pledging members, and raising money that Nerney asked her to "vitalize" the Orange, New Jersey, branch, which had fallen victim to apathy.[39]

Protest meetings were held in at least a few colleges. The NAACP had been trying to recruit students to join its ranks for some time. Now, with the federal Jim Crow issue a hot topic nationally, the NAACP had a dual purpose: recruitment and protest. In mid-November Villard addressed students at Cornell University and stressed the work the association was doing to combat federal Jim Crow, among other things. A college chapter of the NAACP was formed shortly thereafter. Federal Jim Crow also contributed to swelling the ranks of the Howard University chapter of the NAACP as scores of students there, dismayed over the growing discrimination in Washington, signed up for battle and eagerly protested against racial caste in the federal government. "Never in the history of the University [Howard] had there been such an outpouring of students for such a cause," noted DuBois. And at Union College in Schenectady, New York, Villard addressed a "large and appreciative audience" on Jim Crow in Washington, and some students and faculty forcefully expressed their opposition in letters to President Wilson.[40]

VILLARD, THE NAACP, AND THE MEGARALLIES IN WASHINGTON AND BALTIMORE

Villard addressed overflowing mass meetings in Washington and Baltimore after his letters and talks to Wilson and McAdoo had convinced him that the two politicos had no desire to halt federal discrimination. In fact, McAdoo was still claiming there was no segregation issue in the Treasury Department. Instead, he tactfully admitted there had been an effort to remove causes of complaint and irritation in cases in which white women had been forced to sit at desks with black men. After denying that black women in the Bureau of Printing and Engraving were forced to eat in the toilet rooms, McAdoo declared, "I shall not be a party to the enforced and unwelcome juxtaposition of white and negro employees when it is unnecessary and avoidable without injustice to anybody."[41]

Wilson's attitude at that point was more confusing. He had earlier admitted that he approved of segregating blacks and whites in the departments. On October 7, 1913, after avoiding Villard for some time and in the face of mounting public pressure, the president finally met with the editor and gave a slightly different spin on the issue from that of his earlier comments.

Wilson appeared more concerned than previously and shifted the responsibility for the Jim Crow policy to Congress and his Cabinet officials. Only two weeks earlier, the president had written Villard asking that he keep things "at a just and cool equipoise."[42] Now, realizing that the issue could no longer be brushed aside, Wilson allowed the editor to "speak with the utmost frankness" regarding where the NAACP stood. The president's open attitude was a sure sign that the pressure was being felt in Washington. He told Villard that he "hoped . . . to accomplish something" for the colored people but was "absolutely blocked" by "not only Senators from the South . . . but Senators from various parts of the country." Wilson reiterated that for the time being it was virtually impossible to do anything on the matter without jeopardizing "any accomplishments" in his legislative agenda. Furthermore, white men had been chosen instead of the "customary colored men" as ministers of Haiti and Santo Domingo because they were "peculiarly fitted" for "certain specifics which [Secretary of State William Jennings] Bryan wanted accomplished." Yet Wilson assured Villard that they would soon be recalled, and colored men would be appointed to the positions. On the other hand, he emphasized again that he would "never appoint any colored man in the South, because that would be a social blunder of the worst kind." In response, Villard stressed that Wilson's subordinates were going about segregation in a "high-handed way" and read parts of Nerney's Jim Crow report made only a week earlier, the details of which would not be made public for over a month. He further expressed the concerns of African Americans nationwide regarding the long-term consequences of executive-approved Jim Crow. The president acted surprised by the specifics in Nerney's report and declared that he would "draw the teeth" and "put a stop to that sort of thing."[43]

It was obvious to Villard that Wilson was trying to downplay the Jim Crow issue and minimize his own role only to avoid more public scrutiny. Joseph Tumulty, the president's front man for the onslaught of complaints from Villard and other protestors, had been sending danger signals to his boss for months. Wilson seemed to have finally gotten the hint, and he met with Villard in an attempt to take the heat off himself by appeasing the liberal press via Villard's *Evening Post*. In doing so, he hoped to accomplish his pressing legislative objectives unencumbered and then deal with the low-priority Jim Crow problem later. The interview ended with his seeming inability to face the problem at all. "I see no way out," expressed the leader in a tone of defeat. "[I]t will take a very big man to solve this thing."[44]

Taken aback by Wilson's alleged powerlessness—he had been to the young editor, after all, a dignified symbol of intellectual strength in the rough-and-tumble world of politics—Villard was now utterly discouraged by Wilson's attitude. If reformers had entertained any hopes that the "New Freedom" president would or could contribute to alleviating the race problem in the country, by now they had no such illusions.

For many, a potential friend had become a foe, and African Americans found themselves in a battle for their dignity and survival. They were opposed to being branded inferior by the highest office in the land and were ready for a fight to hold on to the gains earned as men and women irrespective of color in the federal government. Pain and experience had schooled African Americans in the incontrovertible lesson that "injustice once started is bound to spread apace," and now in the executive branch injustice was rapidly spreading as individual merit was eclipsed by color in department after department, office after office, and the president seemed unable or unwilling to do anything about the situation. These events did not bode well for the future of African Americans in federal service. And Villard clearly understood that there was no chance the administration would abate its efforts unless more pressure was applied. The NAACP was far from backing down.

On October 27, 1913, while protest meetings continued across the country, Villard—armed with the details of Nerney's visit to the federal departments, which would not be published for almost three more weeks—along with other speakers, addressed a hall packed with thousands of protestors at the Metropolitan African Methodist Episcopal Church in Washington, D.C. It was reported that among those attending were a "great number" of African American clerks who had been Jim Crowed.[45]

"The meeting was advertised for 8 o'clock," said Villard in the NAACP's Fourth Annual Report, "but at 7:30 the doors were ordered closed by the police" because the church was unable to hold any more of the "dense" crowd trying to squeeze in from outside. The number in attendance at this "epoch-making meeting," wrote an ecstatic DuBois in Crisis, was "estimated at from 8,000 to 10,000 people," although the NAACP Fourth Annual Report one month later revised that number to "from 5,000 to 6,000 people." Yet DuBois's estimates may not be that far off, since there was a reported "overflow" of "4,000 outside" whom the speakers, including Villard, addressed afterward.[46] The press was at the NAACP rally that October night in 1913 as well. A week and a half before the protest meeting in Washington, Nerney and Grimke had collaborated to get as much publicity as possible, which included the local and national press.[47]

Villard was still reluctant to hang his friend out to dry during the mass rallies in Washington and Baltimore. Although he criticized President Wilson because he "most wrongly and needlessly antagonized one-ninth of the population . . . and its white sympathizers," a week earlier he had told a Baltimore audience of 1,500 jammed in the Bethlehem African Methodist Episcopal Church that he still had "complete respect" for the president's sincerity and that Wilson would eventually "do something big and fine for the colored people." Even in perhaps his most critical comments against "Mr. Wilson," who, he declared, "may go down in history as the man who set in motion terrible forces for evil," Villard gave an apologetic explanation on the president's behalf: he was "without adequate conception or provision of the dangers he was inviting."[48]

After the chairman wrapped up his speech by blaming McAdoo and those like him for establishing "two kinds of government employees," resolutions of protest were adopted and wired to Wilson. Frank Cardozo, president of the Baltimore NAACP branch, made it clear in the wire that the attendees objected to the storm of racial discrimination "gathering forth" since Wilson became president. He called attention to the fact that Jim Crow, in statutes and law and in the federal departments, was going to severely limit "economic opportunities for nine million American citizens."[49]

Villard could not bring himself to abandon all hope in Wilson. In his mind, there was still time for his friend in the White House to take a stand against Jim Crow. During their October 7 meeting, the president had sent him mixed signals regarding Jim Crow in the federal departments. Although he claimed he was presently faced with insurmountable obstacles in regard to the race issue, Wilson disarmed the usually bold Villard with ambiguous platitudes regarding his intentions to help African Americans in some way, as well as to "put a stop" to the worst manifestations of Jim Crow in the federal departments.[50]

Villard, in what he would call one of "the most remarkable interviews in my entire journalistic career," seemed dazzled by the fact that the leader had invited him for lunch and spent an hour talking about the issue. He was even more taken aback by the president's openness in admitting that he felt "shame and humiliation" about Jim Crow in the government. Wilson, in fact, had been disarming Villard from the very first time the chairman confronted him about the policy, even explaining his refusal to meet with him on one occasion as an understanding between two intimate friends seeing eye to eye: "I would not venture to do this with anyone who I knew would not instantly comprehend the situation."[51]

The president handled Villard with success. During the mass meetings in Washington and Baltimore, the chairman went full force after McAdoo

ANTI-SEGREGATION PETITIONS

Cut This Out of Paper

ATTENTION!

COLORED CITIZENS --- PETITION

National Petition Against Jim Crow and Color Segregation by Federal Government

Read Citizens, sign your name and address and mail to the editor of this paper. Have several sign. Return at once

PETITION

To the President of the United States, Hon. Woodrow Wilson, White House, Washington, D. C.

Sir:

This is to certify that we, the undersigned, are surprised and indignant, that under your administration there should be any rules made by members of your cabinet to segregate employees of the national government by race or color. We protest against this as a plain insult, public degradation, and insufferable injury to Colored Americans, the establishment of caste in this free republic. We petition you to reverse, prevent and forbid any such movement by your bureau chiefs, in accord with your promise of fair, friendly, just and Christian treatment of your Colored fellow-citizens.

Name ....

Address ....

Name ....

Address ....

Name ....

Address ....

N. B.—By pasting on sheet of paper any number of names can be put on, can be used in churches, lodges, societies—Sign on one side only, don't sign for others.

RETURN TO GUARDIAN OFFICE, 21 CORNHILL, BOSTON

Protest petition as it appeared in the Boston Guardian. *Moorfield Storey Papers,* courtesy *Library of Congress.*

instead. This may have been influenced to a degree by Wilson's implication during the meeting of McAdoo's involvement with Jim Crow activities in Washington. It certainly had much to do with McAdoo's clear-cut refusal to admit there was a segregation issue at all. In addition, Villard was dismayed by McAdoo's denial a few days before the Washington mass meeting of racist statements made by the collector of internal revenue in Atlanta that there were "no government positions for Negros in the South" and "a Negroe's place is in the cornfield." As it turned out, the NAACP's fears were realized one month later when the collector discharged six black men with good service records and replaced them with unqualified white men from his own district.[52]

At any rate, during the well-organized and publicized mass meeting at Washington, Villard criticized McAdoo once again for his role in federal Jim Crow. Following the eloquent and impassioned antisegregation addresses by Archibald Grimke, president of the Washington, D.C., NAACP branch; the Rev. John Haynes Holmes, well-known minister and advocate for social equality; and the Rev. Walter H. Brooks, NAACP national director and popular black religious orator and scholar, Villard read verbatim the remarks McAdoo had made to him avowing that there was no segregation issue in the federal departments. The large audience "laughed derisively" at the treasury secretary's comments. Villard then criticized McAdoo. After explaining how he had been "urged by those in high authority" not to stir things up, the chairman had his audience squirming in their seats and interrupting with applause when he declared at the top of his voice, "I shall lose no opportunity to preach the doctrine of peaceful rebellion and revolution against discrimination of every kind."[53]

Shortly after the speech, the "Battle Hymn of the Republic" brought the energized audience to its feet. Following the benediction by the Rev. Holmes, the thousands of people in attendance sent a "vigorous protest" to President Wilson, Treasury Secretary McAdoo, and Postmaster Burleson. "BE IT THEREFORE RESOLVED," declared the protestors, "that it is the sense of this mass meeting of citizens of Washington, D.C., and of many states within the Union, that we express our unqualified abhorrence and condemnation of such reactionary and un-Democratic practices." The protest ended by making it clear that federal Jim Crow was an "insult to the colored people of the country."[54]

In all fairness to McAdoo, although he wanted to create an all-black division at Treasury and segregate black workers wherever feasible, it appears he wanted this arrangement to be gradually and cautiously phased in, not imprudently enforced as the Democratic Fair Play Association and some of his subordinates had wished. The day after the Washington mass meeting, a distressed Villard wrote the treasury secretary that segregation was "being perfected" in the office of the auditor of the Post Office Department, an adjunct of Treasury, and that it had already been hastily implemented in "every other division." Feeling the heat of the protests and alarmed that things were spinning out of control, McAdoo immediately sent a memorandum to James Wilmeth, chief clerk and superintendent of treasury, asking for all of the details regarding Jim Crow in the auditor's office.[55]

McAdoo was probably sorry he asked. If he had hoped to find a shred of defense to fire back at Villard and take the focus off his department, he was disappointed. Although Wilmeth responded that "it was a segregation or grouping of work rather than a segregation of employees" in the office of the auditor of the Post Office Department, the figures he offered the secretary clearly showed a pattern of racial segregation throughout the department. An exclusive workforce that was either black or white occupied almost all the "rooms," "corners," and "alcoves." The only area that had an integrated workforce was the highest grade of clerical work, known as "Room 629," and even here Wilmeth never mentioned whether the employees were grouped together by race. He did admit, however, that Robert Woolley, chief auditor, had recently "transferred four colored men" into this one room to keep them together, and included in his response to McAdoo was a curious tabulation of all "colored" employees in the room made by Woolley two days before the treasury secretary's memorandum. Wilmeth never brought up the subject of toilet or lunchroom segregation, an arrangement Woolley had personally enforced in his department by a written order back in July. With the obvious in hand, it appears that McAdoo dropped the inquiry.[56]

THE COMMITTEE OF FIFTY AND MORE

During fall 1913, the Committee of Fifty and More—acting under the auspices of the NAACP—was formed to organize protests, challenge Jim Crow in the nation's capital, and solicit contributions for the local and national branches. Described as "nothing short of a miracle," it succeeded in creating an amazing solidarity among the Washington African American community and lifted people out of their hopelessness by empowering them with a mechanism for change. The committee was largely instigated by the city's religious leaders and included many black government employees who used the organization to conceal their activities in reporting and working against Jim Crow in federal departments. After praising the committee's efforts in the Fourth Annual Report, the organization informed readers that it could not publish the names of the committee members.[57] The NAACP's reputation as an agitator for black equality was growing, particularly in the departments at Washington, and being openly associated with it put federal employees in danger of being harassed at work or dismissed from their positions altogether. Black federal employees active in the protest, such as Lafayette Hershaw, an executive in the civil service and a reputable Washington attorney, had much to lose.

The stream of information coming from black federal employees was indispensable to the NAACP. Black preachers used this material to stir up their congregations and ambivalent ministers in protest and to acquire members for the NAACP. The Committee of Fifty and More organized a speakers' bureau, often utilizing the oratorical talents of the city's ministers who visited churches, lodges, and schools "to arouse the colored people . . . and at the same time to make them willing to make sacrifices for the cause." These meetings—held all over Washington and in the surrounding suburbs—regularly flooded the offices of President Wilson, Cabinet members, and members of Congress with resolutions of protest.[58]

The speakers appealed to their audiences in terms of a moral crusade, not uncommon in other NAACP meetings, and equated racial uplift with Christian duty. In a letter to the Rev. W. H. Dean asking for permission to hold a protest meeting at Ebeneezer Church in southeast Washington, a committee member concluded by writing in capital letters, "IS NOT THIS CAUSE YOUR CAUSE? WILL NOT CHRISTIAN EBENEEZER OPEN HER DOORS TO THESE MILITANT CHRISTIANS WHOSE ONLY PURPOSE IS BY BETTER SERVING THEMSELVES TO RENDER BETTER SERVICE TO GOD?" Permission was promptly granted.[59]

RELIGION, PROTEST, AND GENDER

This is a good place to highlight the fact, touched upon earlier, that much of the federal Jim Crow protest effort was launched from church pulpits all over the country. Several NAACP leaders and officers were ministers and laymen. Even many of the social reformers without ministerial status tended to be Christians who spoke with religious fervor in denouncing racial injustice, whereas others who lacked a confident belief in God retained a commitment to Christian ethics. NAACP leader Mary Wilson, for example, often combined the rhetoric and symbols of Christianity with NAACP principles when addressing audiences.

Most of these liberal-minded Christians were caught in the swirl of the popular social gospel movement, with its emphasis on social reform—works as well as faith as espoused by those such as Walter Rauschenbusch—and its pursuit of a "brotherhood" for races and in some ways a unification of Jew and Gentile, that was sweeping northern cities during the Progressive Era. These Christians, black and white, opened their pulpits and organizations to Jews as well, and social reformers from both faiths protested together in rallies, as seen earlier with Rabbi Eichler of Boston. And Jewish reformers, such as Joel and Arthur Spingarn, were prominent in the founding and early leadership of the NAACP and worked incessantly for black equality.[60]

Unlike many of their religious white counterparts, black Christians and social gospel whites interpreted their religious precepts as antithetical to the intolerant, exclusive, and divisive Jim Crow. "Race prejudice is contrary to every known principle of Christianity," declared the Rev. Francis Grimke to his congregation at the Fifteenth Street Presbyterian Church in Washington, D.C. "There is absolutely nothing in the Christian religion upon which it can rest—nothing which even the bitterest Negro hater can find in it, if he is truthful."[61] Bessie Garrison, field secretary of "colored conferences" for the Women's Home Missionary Society of the M. E. Church, admonished Wilson for his "cognizance to the vilest sin the human race is heir to—race prejudice," as manifested in the "segregation of Negroes from other races at work in government buildings in Washington."[62]

In addition, numerous churches, ministers, and religious organizations from various Protestant and Jewish denominations sent letters and resolutions of protest to the president—including the National Council of Congregational Churches of the United States, a denomination in which Wilson's maternal grandfather had served as minister for several years in Carlisle, England, before finally crossing the Atlantic. Its denominational organ in the United States, the *Congregationalist and Christian World*, as well, was one of the most vociferous press critics of the Wilson administration in regard to federal Jim Crow. White female Unitarian minister and president of the Frederick Douglass Center in Chicago Celia Parker Woolley, although cautious in her opposition to the Wilson administration, nevertheless sent "many" letters of protest on behalf of the Douglass Center and tried to enlist several white government officials in federal departments to "make a personal appeal to the president." "No religious group," said Kathleen Wolgemuth, "appears to have written Wilson in favor of the federal segregation policy."[63]

However, it must be admitted that of the white churches, only the progressive ones strongly influenced by the social gospel—such as the Unitarians, Episcopalians, and Congregationalists—along with Jewish synagogues, voiced their opposition. The many more conservative Protestant churches in the North and especially those in the South remained mute on the subject and probably supported or were ambivalent in regard to Jim Crow in government departments.[64]

Religion also played an important role in weakening the gender barriers to female participation and leadership in protest activities and organizations. This was accomplished mostly through the efforts of black women. Perhaps in no other reform movement of the Progressive Era did women, particularly black women, work collectively with men in such large numbers as they did in the struggle for racial equality and justice. Black leaders such as Francis Grimke, Oscar de Priest, Benjamin Brawley, Robert Terrell, W.E.B. DuBois, and William Monroe Trotter were forthright in their opinions favoring women's suffrage. Modifying the position of Kevin Gaines, who believed race progress was equated with male dominance during this time, racial reformers actually tended to be more fluid in their views regarding the role of women in social and political activism compared with most of their white contemporaries who dogmatically held to the traditional notions of female subordination. Here African Americans did not quite replicate the white gender patriarchal structure to the degree that has been supposed.[65]

From a religious perspective, black women racial reformers challenged, in their activism and rhetoric, the conservative interpretation of Christian doctrine used to hold women in a perpetual state of intense subordination within the white male hierarchy, as well as the often parallel but more precarious black male hierarchy. "Black women reinterpreted the churches' social teaching," explained Evelyn Higginbotham, "so that human equality embraced gender as well." Their successful demands within the church for the inclusion of women in the black church's long-held commitment to the social teaching of human equality under God—a commitment that justified and motivated all endeavors for racial advancement and survival, including protest, and one that had been a part of the black church long before the social gospel movement—helped to sharply distinguish black churches and progressive interracial and white churches from their more conservative white counterparts during the early twentieth century. Although there were always instances of male chauvinism and racial paternalism in the racial reform movement, the former existing in the black church as well, black women had much more mobility to develop and use their skills and leadership in protesting racial injustice.[66]

Ironically, Christianity may have been the reason some African Americans supported Wilson in the first place. Strongly influenced by his Protestant upbringing, Wilson's personal religious beliefs permeated his public speeches, as he often used moral imagery to describe political issues. In one speech entitled "The Bible and Progress," reprinted more than any of his career speeches except his major wartime addresses, Wilson proclaimed that "the man whose faith is rooted in the Bible knows that reform cannot be stayed, that the finger of God that moves upon the face of the nations is against every man that plots the nation's downfall or the people's deceit." Such sentiments led J. Milton Waldron to tell African Americans during the 1912 campaign that Wilson "will take his religion into the Presidency and follow the teachings of Christ in the performance of his duty."[67] After reading Wilson's remarks about the importance of Bible study, the Rev. Francis Grimke was inspired to write a letter to the newly elected president: "No American citizen, white or black, need have any reasonable grounds of fear from the Administration of a man who . . . believes . . . in the Word of God, and who accepts . . . the great, eternal, and immutable principles of righteousness for which that Word stands."[68] Wilson responded by reassuring Grimke that he intended "to treat every man like a Christian gentleman."[69] Shortly after William Monroe Trotter met with the Democratic presidential nominee in Sea Girt, he felt confident that he could tell "Colored men" that Wilson would endeavor to work "in the spirit of the Christian religion . . . according even-handed justice and equal rights to all regardless of race, color or nativity."[70] And National Independent Political League president Byron Gunner, campaigning for the Democratic candidate, emphasized in a series of pamphlets that "Governor Wilson" was "a good man and [a] Christian gentleman."[71]

To a beleaguered and isolated people excluded from participation in the white man's world and whose political and social roots were deeply embedded in the freedom and equality of their segregated churches, the Christian Democrat's religiosity offered a hope that perhaps the time was at hand for African Americans to finally become part of the American nation.[72] "The simple fact is," wrote Grimke to Wilson in speaking for so many downtrodden people, "the only hope which the colored man has of fair treatment in this country, is to be found in men . . . like yourself."[73]

NOTES

1. Form Letter to Friends from Oswald Garrison Villard, August 18, 1913, and numerous letters responding to the NAACP's call to protest, Administrative Files, Box C-403, NAACP Papers, Manuscript Division, Library of Congress, Washington, DC [hereafter NAACP Papers].

2. Ibid.

3. Oswald Garrison Villard to Darwin J. Meserole, August 25, 1913, Box C-403, NAACP Papers.

4. Form letter to newspapers from Oswald Garrison Villard, August 19, 1913, newspaper listing, August 22, 1913, Box C-403, NAACP Papers; NAACP Fourth Annual Report, January 1914, 12, Box 9, Moorfield Storey Papers, Manuscript Division, Library of Congress, Washington, DC [hereafter Storey Papers].

5. W. B. Windsor, Greensboro *Herald,* to Oswald Villard, September 1, 1913, in Box C-403, NAACP Papers; NAACP Fourth Annual Report, 12; Emma Lou Thornbrough,

"American Negro Newspapers, 1880–1914," *Business History Review* 40 (Winter 1966): 469, 476, 486. Although it would be difficult to determine a precise number of those who joined in the protest, it seems likely that the number eventually reached in the tens of thousands, evidenced by newspaper accounts, mass meetings, organizations, and the thousands of individual protest letters sent to the NAACP, the NIPL, and President Wilson, among others. Kathleen Wolgemuth notes as well that "private letters of protest appear in the *Wilson Papers* from over thirty-four states"; Kathleen Wolgemuth, "Woodrow Wilson and Federal Segregation," *Journal of Negro History* 44 (April 1959): 165 note 20.

6. Form letter to newspapers from Oswald Garrison Villard, August 19, 1913, newspaper listing, August 22, 1913, Box C-403, NAACP Papers; W. B. Windsor, Greensboro *Herald,* to Oswald Villard, September 1, 1913, in Box C-403, NAACP Papers; NAACP Fourth Annual Report, 12; Thornbrough, 469, 476, 486.

7. NAACP Fourth Annual Report, 12; Thornbrough, 469, 476, 486.

8. Oswald Garrison Villard to Senator Elihu Root, August 20, 1913, Box C-403, NAACP Papers.

9. Ruth Worthy, "A Negro in Our History: William Monroe Trotter, 1872–1934" (M.A. thesis, Columbia University, 1952), 54; August Meier, *Negro Thought in America, 1880–1915: Racial Ideologies in the Age of Booker T. Washington* (Ann Arbor: University of Michigan Press, 1963), 167–170.

10. NAACP Third Annual Report, January 1913, 29, and Fourth Annual Report, 18.

11. Nettie J. Asbury to Washington, September 13, 1913, in Louis R. Harlan and Raymond W. Smock, eds., *The Booker T. Washington Papers,* vol. 12, *1912–1914* (Urbana: University of Illinois Press, 1982), 279, original emphasis.

12. DuBois to Miss Force, 1910, quoted in Herbert Aptheker, ed., *A Documentary History of the Negro People in the United States: From Reconstruction to the Founding of the NAACP,* vol. 2 (New York: Citadel, 1990), 883.

13. Trotter quoted in Worthy, 54.

14. Villard quoted in August Meier, "Booker T. Washington and the Rise of the NAACP," *Crisis,* February 1954, 120.

15. Ibid., 69–76, 117–123; Villard to Root, August 20, 1913, Administrative Files, Box C-403, NAACP Papers; Lewis, 275; *New York Times,* August 18, 1913.

16. Washington to Villard, August 8, 1913, and Washington to Villard, August 10, 1913, in Harlan and Smock; James M. McPherson, *The Abolitionist Legacy: From Reconstruction to the NAACP* (Princeton: Princeton University Press, 1975), 378.

17. Washington to Villard, August 8, 1913, Villard to Washington, August 8, 1913, Washington to Villard, August 10, 1913, and Washington to Frank Fox, October 6, 1913, all in Harlan and Smock; Francis Garrison to Villard, August 11, 1913, Folder 1451, 7, Oswald Villard Papers, Houghton Library, Harvard University, Cambridge, MA.

18. Bruce to Fred R. Moore, March 20, 1914, quoted in Charles Flint Kellogg, *NAACP: A History of the National Association for the Advancement of Colored People,* vol. 1, *1909–1920* (Baltimore: Johns Hopkins University Press, 1967), 173. Bruce was the son of Blanche K. Bruce, United States senator from Mississippi during the Reconstruction period.

19. National Negro Press Association to Wilson, October 13, 1913, Series 4, Reel 230, Woodrow Wilson Papers, Manuscript Division, Library of Congress, Washington, DC; for

the National Negro Press Association, see Wolgemuth, "Woodrow Wilson and Federal Seg-regation," 161 note 7. Also, it is not unthinkable that Washington may have secretly sup-ported protest activities to a greater extent than is known during the Wilson years. August Meier points out that "while publicly he [Washington] defended the disfranchisement amendments to the state constitutions . . . he personally spent thousands of dollars to test their constitutionality in the federal courts"; in "Booker T. Washington and the Negro Press," *Journal of Negro History* 38 (Janaury 1953): 77 note. And in an article written by Washing-ton published in the *New Republic* shortly after his death, along with an excerpt and commentary appearing in *Crisis*, the Tuskegeen said federal racial segregation was "unjust" and created nothing other than more "injustice. . . . [It has] widened the breach between the two races." *Crisis*, February 1916, 176–177.

20. May Childs Nerney to Archibald Grimke, September 4, 1913, Box 39-25, Archibald Grimke Papers, Moorland-Spingarn Research Center, Howard University, Wash-ington, DC.

21. Wolgemuth, "Woodrow Wilson and Federal Segregation," 165.

22. Cicely Gunner to Oswald Villard, August 23, 1913, Box C-403, NAACP Papers.

23. *Savannah Tribune*, October 10, 1913, and numerous news clippings in Box C-432, NAACP Papers; several newspapers quoted in *Crisis*, October, November, and December 1913.

24. Coretta Scott King, *My Life With Martin Luther King Jr.* (New York: Penguin, 1994), 29.

25. NAACP Fourth Annual Report, 59; Meier, *Negro Thought in America*, 218–224.

26. Mason to NAACP, Administrative Files, Box C-403, NAACP Papers.

27. NAACP Fourth Annual Report, 35.

28. *Crisis*, December 1913, 90.

29. Senator Clapp quoted in *Crisis*, December 1913, 69, 89. Also "Wilson and Segre-gation," *Philadelphia Public Ledger*, October 21, 1913, in Box C-432, NAACP Papers.

30. NAACP Minutes, December 2, 1913, in Box 39-30, Archibald Grimke Papers, Moorland-Spingarn Research Center, Howard University, Washington, DC; Adam Fairclough, *Better Day Coming: Blacks and Equality, 1890–2000* (New York: Penguin Putnam, 2001), 72.

31. *Crisis*, January 1914, 140–141; NAACP Fourth Annual Report, 45; "Strong Protest Against Segregation Voiced by White Voters for Wilson," *Guardian*, undated, Box 6, Storey Papers.

32. *Crisis*, January 1914, 140–141; NAACP Fourth Annual Report, 45.

33. Quoted in "Strong Protest Against Segregation Voiced by White Voters for Wil-son," *Guardian*, undated, Box 6, Storey Papers.

34. "Far Western outpost" quote in *Crisis*, November 1913, 342; "Jim Crowism Scorned," September 27, 1913, newspaper excerpt in Box C-432, NAACP Papers; NAACP Fourth Annual Report, 58–59.

35. *Crisis*, December 1913, 89, 90; NAACP Fourth Annual Report, 48.

36. *Crisis*, November 1913, 342.

37. *Crisis*, March 1914, 249; Trotter to Spingarn, January 2, 1914, and January 28, 1914, Correspondences, Box 95-11, Joel E. Spingarn Papers, Moorland-Spingarn Research Center, Howard University, Washington, DC.

38. NAACP Fourth Annual Report, 52, 54, 57.

39. Dorothy Salem, *To Better Our World: Black Women and Organized Reform, 1890–1920* (New York: Carlson, 1990), 160, 164.

40. *Crisis,* January 1914, 140–141.

41. McAdoo to Villard, Folder 2369, Oswald Villard Papers, Houghton Library, Harvard University, Cambridge, MA.

42. Wilson to Villard, September 22, 1913, quoted in Kellogg, 166 and note 43.

43. Villard to Garrison, October 10, 1913, Folder 1451, Oswald Villard Papers, Houghton Library, Harvard University, Cambridge, MA; Kellogg, 169; Villard/Wilson meeting described in Oswald Villard, *Fighting Years: Memoirs of a Liberal Editor* (New York: Harcourt, Brace, 1939), 238–240.

44. Villard, *Fighting Years,* 238–240.

45. Wolgemuth, "Woodrow Wilson and Federal Segregation," 167 and note 24.

46. NAACP Fourth Annual Report, 15; *Crisis,* December 1913, 89–90.

47. Nerney to Grimke, October 16, 1913, Box 39-25, Archibald Grimke Papers, Moorland-Spingarn Research Center, Howard University, Washington, DC.

48. *Crisis,* December 1913, 67, 89; F. M. Cardozo to President Woodrow Wilson, Night Letter, Western Union, October 20, 1913, Series 4, 152, Reel 230, Woodrow Wilson Papers, Manuscript Division, Library of Congress, Washington, DC; Sosna, 34; Oswald Garrison Villard, *Segregation,* quoted in Hayes, 42–43.

49. F. M. Cardozo to President Woodrow Wilson, Night Letter, Western Union, October 20, 1913, Series 4, 152, Reel 230, Woodrow Wilson Papers, Manuscript Division, Library of Congress, Washington, DC.

50. Villard, *Fighting Years,* 239.

51. "Most remarkable interviews" quote in ibid.; "not instantly comprehend the situation" quote in Wilson to Villard, August 19, 1913, quoted in Kellogg, 165.

52. McAdoo to Villard, October 22, 1913, in Kellogg, 170, 171; *Congregationalist and Christian World,* undated, Box 10, Storey Papers.

53. Moorland-Spingarn Research Center, Howard University, Washington, DC; Kellogg, 171; *Crisis,* December 1913, 89–90.

54. Mass Meeting Programme of the District of Columbia Branch of the NAACP, October 27, 1913, Box 39-25, and Segregation Protest, October 27, 1913, Box 39-33, Archibald Grimke Papers.

55. Oswald Villard to McAdoo, October 28, 1913, and McAdoo to Wilmeth, October 29, 1913, Box 97, Negro Employees File, Records Group 56, General Records of the Department of Treasury, National Archives II, College Park, MD.

56. Memorandum from the Chief Clerk for the Secretary, 1–3, October 30, 1913, and Room 629 tabulation of black employees made by Robert Woolley, October 27, 1913, Box 97, Negro Employees File, Records Group 56, General Records of the Department of Treasury, National Archives II, College Park, MD.

57. NAACP Fourth Annual Report, 36–37; *Crisis,* May 1914, 32; Constance McLaughlin Green, *Washington: Capital City, 1879–1950* (Princeton: Princeton University Press, 1963), 224–225.

58. *Crisis,* May 1914, 32; Green, 224–225.

59. Committee member to Rev. W. H. Dean, December 19, 1913, Box 39-25, Archibald Grimke Papers, Moorland-Spingarn Research Center, Howard University, Washington, DC; *Crisis,* January 1914, 142.

60. Egal Feldman, "The Social Gospel and the Jews," *American Jewish Historical Quarterly* 58 (March 1969): 312–316, 322; J. A. Thompson, *Progressivism* (London: British Association for American Studies Pamphlet 2, 1979), 18; Salem, 161; Ross, 4, 21–22.

61. "Christianity and Race Prejudice," Two Discourses Delivered in the Fifteenth Street Presbyterian Church, Washington DC, May 29 and June 5, 1910: "It is a wonder that colored people have a faith in religion at all . . . in the ever recurring exhibition of race on the part of so many so-called Christians"; Widener Library, Harvard University, Cambridge, MA. Twenty years later, Kelly Miller would write: "If Christ should next Sunday come to America and seek to worship in any Nordic church which he died to ordain, in the guise of a Negro, he would be ushered to the back seat or invited to take the door." *Washington Tribune,* February 5, 1934.

62. Bessie Garrison to President Woodrow Wilson, September 18, 1913, Series 4, Reel 230, Woodrow Wilson Papers, Manuscript Division, Library of Congress, Washington, DC.

63. Wolgemuth, "Woodrow Wilson and Federal Segregation," 166 and note 21; Celia Parker Woolley to Oswald Villard, August 29, 1913, C-403, NAACP Papers.

64. Thompson, 18.

65. Kevin Gaines, *Uplifting the Race: Black Leadership, Politics, and Culture in the Twentieth Century* (Chapel Hill: University of North Carolina Press, 1996), xvii.

66. Evelyn Brooks Higginbotham, *Righteous Discontent: The Women's Movement in the Black Baptist Church, 1880–1920* (Cambridge: Harvard University Press, 1993), quote on 121; see also 17, 129–136, 234 note 29. For an illuminating synthesis of the gender, race, and religious issues black women dealt with in the Progressive Era, see chapter 5 of her book, entitled "Feminist Theology, 1880–1900."

67. August Heckscher, *Woodrow Wilson: A Biography* (New York: Collier, Macmillan, 1991), 234; J. M. Waldron and J. D. Harkless, *The Political Situation in a Nut-Shell: Some Un-colored Truths for Colored Voters* (Washington, DC: Trades Allied Printing Council, 1912), 10.

68. Francis Grimke to Woodrow Wilson, November 20, 1912, in Leslie S. Fishel Jr., and Benjamin Quarles, *The Negro American: A Documentary History* (Glenview, IL: Scott, Foresman, 1967), 390.

69. Wilson quote in article entitled "For Colored Only," in Thomas H.R. Clarke Papers, Moorland-Spingarn Research Center, Howard University, Washington, DC.

70. Trotter to Wilson, July 18, 1912, Woodrow Wilson Papers, Seeley G. Mudd Library, Princeton University, Princeton, NJ.

71. National Independent Political League, Pamphlet 3, 1912, quoted in Meier, "The Negro and the Democratic Party," 189.

72. In *The Negro Church in America* (Liverpool: University of Liverpool, 1963), E. Franklin Frazier deals with the critical importance of religion and church for black social structure. Frazier calls the church a "nation within a nation." 35ff.

73. Grimke to Wilson, November 20, 1912, quoted in Fishel and Quarles, 390.

Plate 1. Rare picture of Woodrow Wilson, previously unpublished. Courtesy Library of Congress.

Plate 2. Ellen Axson Wilson. Courtesy Library of Congress.

Plate 3. Albert Burleson. Courtesy Library of Congress.

Plate 4. John Skelton Williams, left, *and William Gibbs McAdoo,* right, *previously unpublished. Courtesy John Skelton Williams Papers (#10040), Special Collections, University of Virginia Library.*

Plate 5. Rare picture of William Monroe Trotter. Courtesy Harvard University Archives.

Plate 6. Rare picture of W.E.B. DuBois, Harvard entrance photograph. Courtesy Harvard University Archives.

Plate 7. Senator Edwin Moses Clapp. Photo by Charles Zimmerman, courtesy Minnesota Historical Society.

Plate 8. Booker T. Washington. Courtesy Photography Collection, Miriam and Ira D. Wallach Division of Art, Prints and Photographs, The New York Public Library, Astor, Lenox, and Tilden Foundations.

Plate 9. Oswald Garrison Villard. From "Mass Meeting of the District of Columbia Branch of the NAACP" pamphlet, in Joel Spingarn Papers, Box 94-14, file 543, courtesy Moorland-Spingarn Research Center, Howard University.

Plate 10. Ida Wells-Barnett. Courtesy University of Chicago Library.

Plate 11. Archibald Grimke. Courtesy Moorland-Spingarn Research Center, Howard University.

5

"MEETING FOES IN HUMAN FORM"
William Monroe Trotter, the NIPL, and the Crusade for Freedom

PERHAPS FEW INDIVIDUALS IN HISTORY have attempted to change the world by sheer force of personality, as did William Monroe Trotter. His roots and life experiences were an extraordinary admixture of wealth, poverty, fame, tragedy, and determination; and they deserve special consideration to understand Trotter's unique historical capacity as a protest leader during the Wilson years, his life as an outspoken black agitator during the strongly antiblack Progressive Era, and perhaps most significant, his important influence on modern protest—an influence that has been sorely neglected. Thus, more time is spent here on Trotter's background and personality than on the other protestors.

TROTTER BEFORE THE WILSON PROTEST: SETTING THE STAGE

With fewer financial resources and staff members than the National Association for the Advancement of Colored People (NAACP) and far fewer members, the National Independent Political League (NIPL), formerly the Negro

American Political League, would rely on raw determination and unwavering persistence to challenge Jim Crow in federal departments. The NIPL's slate of national officers read like a who's who of some of the most prominent black professionals in the country. They included such notables and outspoken advocates for racial equality as Francis H. Warren and Dr. Charles Bentley. Warren, a Detroit lawyer, represented the local branch of the NAACP and became famous by challenging racial discrimination and exposing police brutality in his city.[1] Bentley was a dentist who pioneered the concept of dental examinations in public schools and the dissemination of preventative dental health information to the public, and as a staunch proponent of integration he opposed "any forms of segregation."[2]

Yet for the most part, the NIPL's crusade against federal Jim Crow was driven by the fiery militancy of its founder and editor of the Boston *Guardian,* William Monroe Trotter. Described by Lerone Bennett Jr. as "a singularly neglected figure in Negro history," Trotter has been utterly forgotten by most contemporary social historians who either overlook him altogether or briefly interject him on the pages of protest history as some obscure black figure who opposed racial injustice in the early twentieth century.[3] Even leadership in the modern civil rights movement—vocal about its inspiration from black protest leaders of the past such as Harriet Tubman, Frederick Douglass, and even W.E.B. DuBois—appears to have been oblivious to Trotter.

Perhaps this historical neglect resulted in part from the fact that Trotter's influence was discounted when he lived because of his reluctance to unconditionally join forces with the NAACP. In addition, the spotty contemporary historicism that has dealt with Trotter has minimized the worth of his historical contribution to the struggle of African Americans. Although he did work indirectly with the NAACP and at times even lavished praise, Trotter remained at a distance, suspicious of, in his view, the NAACP's white paternalistic membership that, he believed, watered down its militancy in fighting for black equality. Missing from his lifelong equal rights campaign as well were the powerful symbolism and pageantry Marcus Garvey so adeptly employed to attract followers to his United Negro Improvement Association.

With Trotter, however, for good or bad, what you saw was what you got. A robust man of short stature and habitually disheveled, nothing in his appearance struck one as impressive and regal. He often slept in his clothes at the *Guardian* office and ate on the run. In his later years it was not unusual to see Trotter walking the wintry streets of Boston, clothes wrinkled and seldom wearing an overcoat, with copies of his newspaper stuffed in his pockets. And although DuBois eulogized him as "a man of heroic proportions," he also echoed the sentiments of many others when he described the

Bostonian as a "fanatic"—a widely held perception during the time that alienated even some of his friends.[4]

But Trotter is extraordinarily important to understanding the transition in methodology and approach to seeking racial justice and uplift—a transition from the quiet hope in gradual equality through economic and moral achievement to a militant emphasis on aggressive protest and struggle as the best means for acquiring black political and civil rights—that occurred after the Booker T. Washington years. Yet several years before the scales had tilted from economic uplift to protest, Trotter relentlessly drove home to African Americans the crucial necessity of agitation. Even many racial reformers who found his methods and personality disagreeable watched with a sense of awe as he boldly challenged the world of racial injustice. It also appears that many of these racial reformers began to move closer to Trotter's radicalism, particularly in language directed toward the white establishment, as the first decade of the twentieth century came to a close.

A powerful and vociferous personality in a time before the arrival of powerful black leadership, the Boston editor's dogged determination and singleness of purpose grip the imagination as he defied obstacles and survived the ever-looming threat of impoverishment. As he was perceived as somewhat of an enigma by his generation, Trotter's eccentric life perhaps reflected signs of genius. He was intellectually brilliant, always out of step with his contemporaries, neglectful of his health, careless in manner and dress, and he had a lifelong obsession with an idea that was way ahead of its time.

Remarkably, early on Trotter gave up the possibility for a comfortable and prestigious bourgeois life as a Boston black elite, one that in reality was already his, to pursue the risky business of full-time agitation—and this at a time when accommodation seemed the wisest as well as the safest policy. "I have given my life to this work of trying to relieve the lot of our people," Trotter told President Wilson in 1914. "God knows I want to relieve it."[5] Even toward the end of his tragic life, broken in spirit, health, and capital and in the face of what he perceived as failure, he seemed to have had no regrets in pursuing what he felt was his destiny.

In Trotter's scheme of things there was no room for compromise—absolutely none—so long as African Americans were maliciously "labeled and branded as inferior." Thus, the system of Jim Crow, despite some popular arguments as to the benefits for black growth along independent lines, was an impossible consideration for him. "It is preposterous to plead benevolence for such a policy," argued Trotter to President Wilson. "Oppressors from time immemorial have declared oppression good for its victims. The world is no longer thus deceived. As there is no benevolence in despotism and tyranny and subjugation, so there is none in segregation and caste." The equal rights warrior, along with Ida Wells-Barnett and others, decided there was a need for an organization and focused efforts that took an uncompromising view in demanding complete and immediate equality for African Americans.[6]

Although social historians have not seriously considered the relationship between the NIPL and the NAACP, those who have touched upon the subject usually attribute the NIPL's inability to work more closely with the NAACP in fighting racial injustice to Trotter who, they maintain, refused to work with any organization he could not control. This view is somewhat misleading and has been taken at face value, more than likely out of context, from the words of W.E.B. DuBois.[7] When white sympathizers such as Mary White Ovington—one of the original founders of the NAACP and a tireless advocate for the poor and the oppressed—and the Kentucky-born socialist William English Walling issued a call for the creation of a broader-based organization for black equality one year after the Niagara Movement disbanded, Trotter, Wells-Barnett, and DuBois were among those who attended the founding conference of what would shortly become the NAACP. As the conference seemed to move toward a moderate platform on "racial agitation," Trotter and Wells-Barnett raised objections and fervently emphasized (to the annoyance of Villard and others) that aggressive action was needed most if there was any chance for obtaining equal rights. With midnight approaching, DuBois read the names of the Committee of Forty, the appointed governing body that would be responsible for breathing life into the NAACP. Even though they were successful in helping to put a sting into several important resolutions—a fact almost always overlooked in the founding of the NAACP—Trotter and Wells-Barnett were nevertheless excluded from the list.[8]

Whether Trotter and Wells-Barnett would have been able to compromise with the other, more moderate members of the NAACP had they been included in the committee will never be known. Though they were stunned and angry by the proceedings, rejection seemed to solidify their commitment to aggressive action and, in a sense, freed them forever from the restraints of moderation in advocating black equality. Shortly after the conference, Trotter made it clear that his then Negro American Political League was "an organization OF colored people, and FOR the colored people, and LED BY the colored people." Yet despite hurt feelings, not to mention differences in approach, Trotter and Wells-Barnett did agree to serve on the Advisory Committee of the NAACP—if for nothing else than to at least remain in touch with an organization that was working along roughly parallel lines to theirs.[9] Thus, Trotter did not walk away from the NAACP, at least initially, on his own accord. The organization, rather, purposefully excluded him and the more aggressive proponents of equal rights for African Americans.

Black consciousness during the first decade of the twentieth century was beginning to awaken to the prospect that aggressive action might be the only means to achieve equality for the race following on the heels of what Rayford Logan described as the all-time lowest point for blacks in America. During this time African Americans were shamelessly robbed as sharecroppers, tricked or forced into peonage, denied the right to vote, insulted by Jim Crow, branded as inferior by science and history, and committed to jail for menial offenses; most frightening of all, they were becoming vulnerable to ferocious violence at the hands of white mobs.[10] Accomplishments such as the tremendous increase in literacy and the gradual accumulation of property and holdings seemed only to intensify the prejudice many whites felt toward blacks. The striking presence of successful African Americans, often garbed in the symbols of their success, presented a threat to white supremacy and the racist order that was being ushered in. They had to be forced into an inferior status, or white control could not easily be justified. Expressing the most extreme viewpoint in the South, but with far-reaching implications as a reflection of the general racist white sentiment there, David Lewis Dorroh wrote, "It is only as a convict that the South finds the free-born negro a satisfactory laborer." In any other capacity, stressed the writer, he is utterly worthless.[11]

Even in Trotter's hometown during this time, once described by him as "the most liberal city on the color line" and often referred to as freedom's birthplace, the status of African Americans was deteriorating. In 1908 Ray Stannard Baker observed that a "few years ago, no hotel or restaurant in Boston refused Negro guests; now several hotels, restaurants, and especially confectionary stores will not serve Negroes, even the best of them." With southern racial demagogues such as James Vardaman, Hoke Smith, and Tom Watson nurturing white prejudice against blacks in the South and as anti-intermarriage and Jim Crow public transportation bills flooded northern legislatures, things seemed like they were only going to get worse.[12]

Trotter has been described as a man "fifty years ahead of his time," but he could just as easily be depicted as a throwback to the turbulent era of fiery abolitionists. Born in Boston in 1872, the young Monroe grew up as a black elite in the well-to-do and mostly white neighborhood of Hyde Park, the son of a classical musician and politically active Democrat who had been a federal appointee under President Cleveland and had religiously urged African

Americans to be independent in choosing their elected officials instead of blindly following the Republican Party. Although insulated by his privileged environment from the worst aspects of antiblack racism, Monroe lived in a household where at the dinner table and social gatherings it was not uncommon for his father to passionately thrash out the problems facing African Americans, including the racial climate of the day. Father James seems to have passed this fire on to his son. Later, the family recounted how the adolescent and young adult Monroe, after the premature death of his father, would also argue feverishly at the dinner table about the injustices facing his people.[13]

The Trotter family's upward climb from slavery to prosperity was nothing short of remarkable. Trotter's father, James, born in Mississippi in 1842, was the son of a slave named Letitia and her white slave owner. A decade or so later, Letitia, James, and her two other children were free and living in Cincinnati. In 1868, after serving as one of the few black commissioned officers in the northern army during the Civil War where he led a mass protest for equal pay, James met and married Trotter's mother, Virginia Issacs, the daughter of a slave, in her hometown of Chillicothe, Ohio. This is interesting because Chillicothe is where Woodrow Wilson's mother, Jessie Woodrow, had grown up as well and where his parents had met and married almost two decades earlier in 1849. Thus, it was here in tiny Chillicothe, a former Shawnee Indian village, where one of those strange intersections in history occurred. Here was destiny presenting the origins of the two men who would one day face off at the White House—one white and one black; one trying to maintain the old social order between the races, the other trying to usher in a new age of racial progress.[14]

To add even more significance to the Chillicothe connection, this southeastern Ohio town and surrounding area so close to the cotton kingdom were where many slaves traveled the underground railroad to finally emerge in freedom and where Lewis Woodson, a black abolitionist and resident, started one of the early black benevolent societies to take care of the poor black residents living in the area. In the midst of such a haven to free and help prosper those who had lived in demoralizing bondage, one wonders what effect, if any, this local activity may have had on the Woodrows.[15]

More than likely, Wilson's maternal relatives were at best aloof to the events swirling about them. Wilson's grandfather, Thomas Woodrow, served as pastor of the Presbyterian Church in Chillicothe for twelve years and resigned, according to most Wilson biographers, because of poor health. Yet historian August Heckscher points out that the resignation had more to do with the "unpopularity of his conservative theology and narrow Calvinistic views," emphasizing life in the hereafter while ignoring the need for social reform. The world for a strict Calvinist such as Thomas Woodrow was one of utter hopelessness and depravity and one in which human affairs should be pursued in a careful and legalistic way so as not to fall prey to evil. This view must have been out of step with the progressive atmosphere that engulfed much of Chillicothe and the surrounding area. Thus, the conservative Thomas Woodrow, with his strict conformity to rules and regulations and otherworldly focus, probably relegated the working out of the slavery problem to divine destiny rather than to the efforts of abolitionists who often broke the law to achieve their objectives.[16]

There is a Monticello connection in this story as well. Trotter's great-grandfather on his mother's side, Joseph Fossett, was a biracial slave on Thomas Jefferson's Monticello plantation and was rumored to have been fathered by the third president. Jefferson's slave records do show the birth of Joseph Fossett in 1780, several years before the children of Sally Hemings were born, and in light of the controversy surrounding the latter, the truth of such a rumor is not improbable. The son of Mary Hemings, sister of Sally Hemings, Joe Fossett was first a privileged Monticello house servant, as were most of the light-skinned Hemingses, and later the chief metal crafter at Monticello. Joe appears to have had a very close relationship with Jefferson who eventually freed him in his will at the same time he freed Sally Hemings's sons, Madison and Eston; her younger brother John; and her cousin Burwell (of the approximately 200 slaves Jefferson owned, the only ones he ever freed were members of the Hemings family). The sage of Monticello seems to have only had grace sufficient for the bloodline that may have crossed directly with his—Joe's wife and family, including Trotter's grandmother, Elizabeth Ann Fossett, were sold to different bidders. Several years before being granted his freedom, however, Fossett ran off to Washington, D.C., in pursuit of a woman he had fallen in love with, and Jefferson seems to have taken his fleeing from Monticello personally. His distress, curiously, seemed based not in the financial or economic loss of a slave but more in a father's shock and disappointment by the rejection and disobedience of his child.[17]

It is difficult to determine what impact the Fossett-Jefferson rumor may have had on Trotter or whether he took it seriously. His grandmother seems to have passed it on as fact to the young Monroe, and Fossett's descendants, as late as the 1950s, still believed it to be true. But interestingly, Trotter seldom referred to his questionable Jefferson lineage and was much more proud of his black heritage and race. His only biographer, Stephen P. Fox, illustrated this point in a comparison between the two greatest advocates for racial advancement of the early twentieth century operating at opposite ends of the spectrum: "Washington came up from the black mass and Trotter was from a favored 'white' background, and yet Trotter seemed to have more outward pride in his color and in Negroes."[18]

In 1891 Trotter, an exceptionally bright young man, graduated from an all-white high school at the top of his class, having served as student body president and valedictorian—a mind-boggling feat for an African American in racist nineteenth-century America. He went on to Harvard College where in his freshman year he earned the Deturs award for academic achievement, and in his junior year he became the first African American to earn the academic honorary distinction of membership in Phi Beta Kappa. The highly accomplished student graduated in 1895 magna cum laude and stayed on for a year to complete a master's degree. Shortly after leaving Harvard, Trotter became disheartened by what he felt was a subservient attitude by Booker T. Washington in the face of rampant Jim Crow, particularly after Washington declared in front of an audience in Atlanta made up mostly of white southerners that the "wisest of my race understand that agitation on questions of social equality is of the extremist folly." From then on Trotter became more and more involved in equal rights agitation. He would later describe this turning point in his life as something that was thrust upon him: "I did not seek a career of agitation and organization for equality for my race. It was dropped upon me by the desertion of others and I would not desert the duty."[19]

But it should be emphasized that the Washington speech in Atlanta coincided with the conclusion of Trotter's years at "dear old Harvard." There he experienced little overt racial prejudice and discrimination and was treated like any other student, white or black. The most distinguished university in the country had shown Trotter how fair American society could be. This made a deep impression on him that he would never forget and served as a sort of catalyst for his crusade. With this utopian experience under his belt, the black Bostonian—perhaps a little naive and a lot idealistic—walked out of the ivy gates into a world that was anything but fair to people of his color; and to make matters worse, he was aghast by what he saw as the most popular black leader in the country helping to maintain such inequity.[20]

The degree to which Trotter despised the message he believed Booker T. Washington was sending to the white world cannot be overemphasized. The last thing black people needed to hear from a leader was that they should forget about their rights and allow Jim Crow to walk all over them. Professor George Towns of Atlanta University, a Trotter loyalist even to the point on one occasion of jeopardizing his tenure, summed up the problem with Washington's leadership in a letter to the fiery advocate: "[W]hite people select and set up our leaders before whom we should all fall down and wor-ship without a question or any suggestion of dissent."[21]

Such criticisms in regard to Washington's leadership were not unfounded. He was, as Trotter complained, an apologist to the white world for what he perceived to be the deficiencies of his race. No black leader had so eloquently defended Jim Crow as Washington did in his Atlanta speech. Worse still, the leader from Tuskegee often warmed up his white audiences with "darky" stories and jokes and habitually conjured up images of an immoral and use-less urban black American. Moreover, Trotter felt such "race ridicule and belittlement" were an unpardonable "crime" on Washington's part, since he was a black man echoing the sentiments of white racists and thus exploiting their racial fears with all their dangerous manifestations.[22]

But Washington could also show enormous pride in his race. At a time when scientific consensus had proclaimed African Americans inferior, he proudly declared to a Harvard audience, "If I could be born again and the Great Spirit should say to me: 'In what skin do you wish to be clothed,' I should answer, 'make me an American Negro!'" Washington at times even took a stand against racial injustice. He publicly opposed federal segregation efforts; he secretly fought Jim Crow transportation laws, disfranchisement, and peonage; he opposed the exclusion of blacks from juries; and he strongly condemned black lynching in speeches and in a letter to the Associated Press.[23]

Such utterances of racial pride mattered little to the Moses-warrior Trotter who felt the Tuskegeen did far more harm than good. Washington's later candor in regard to racial injustice, believed Trotter, was too little too late. He always believed African Americans needed a deliverer rather than what he felt was an overly cautious doublespeak spokesman. The self-appointed black messiah dedicated his life to seeking full equality for his people, inspired largely by William Lloyd Garrison's relentless agitation through the press and public speeches. This had given Garrison "real power" in his crusade to abolish slavery, believed Trotter. With a bust of the great abolitionist staring at him from the top of his desk and in the same Cornhill office—indeed, on the same floor—where Garrison had published the abolitionist organ the *Liberator* and the first edition of *Uncle Tom's Cabin* made its revolutionary debut, the Boston editor, sensing that these ghosts were reaching from the past and pushing him forward, utterly devoted himself to ending the caste slavery that now enveloped his people.

Like Villard, Trotter thought of himself as a modern-day Garrison and seemed to have been perhaps more passionately committed to the grandfather's militancy than the grandson was. This resulted from the fact that the Boston editor had a one-track mind that was focused on black equality, whereas

Villard was a man of many causes.[24] The latter's color, wealth, and prominence—but mostly his color—afforded him a luxury that Trotter's obsessive sense of urgency could never allow.

It is also interesting that the equal rights advocate identified so strongly with Garrison. The famous abolitionist was really quite conservative in regard to black political rights, reflecting more of a position that Trotter's nemesis, Booker T. Washington, would take several decades later. Although he passionately fought against the institution of slavery and incessantly called for its immediate abolition, Garrison believed "social, civil, and political equality" would gradually come through "industrial and educational development, and not by any arbitrary mandate." Although he eventually felt universal suffrage should be granted, his advocacy of such was at best lukewarm.[25]

In 1901 Trotter started the *Guardian* "to voice intelligently the needs and aspirations of the colored American," and its masthead summed up what would become the fiery advocate's personal trademark: "For Every Right With All Thy Might." "As editor," reminisced close friend the Rev. Leroy Ferguson, "Trotter wrote not in ink that was black, so much as with blood that was red." Trotter also fits within the framework of the Progressive Era as one of the crusading journalists who led the way in calling for a more equitable democracy. Yet he differed with most by including in the term equitable African Americans. As Charles Puttkammer remarked, "[S]eldom has any Colored U.S. publication stressed being an American and possessing full American citizenship and equality as [strongly as] the Boston *Guardian*."[26]

Most striking and unlike other white reform-spirited newspapers, the *Guardian* marked the revival of the press from antebellum days as a means of protest in the twentieth century, and its black editor was later credited as the "patriarch in the journalistic field" who, like other black journalists, was one of the driving forces behind racial progress. Reflecting black pride and a commitment to the beauty of those of African descent, Trotter refused to print advertisements in his paper for products to straighten hair or lighten skin. Early black journalists like Trotter, emphasized one historian, were soldiers without swords, fighting for the dignity of their people. By the time Wilson took office and federal Jim Crow was on the increase, Trotter, lukewarm toward the NAACP and leery of its predominantly white membership and as intensely critical as ever of Washington's passive philosophy, had turned his full attention to the *Guardian* and the NIPL and their protest efforts in what he dubbed a "crusade for freedom."[27]

The general assumption as reflected in the historical literature, including encyclopedic references, is that Booker T. Washington and W.E.B. DuBois represented—both symbolically and as active race leaders—the divergent philosophies for black progress during the early twentieth century. Washington is representative of the economic uplift approach for black advancement and passive in regard to equal rights as his critics have charged, whereas DuBois is seen as the leading agent for social change through his militant advocacy of black political and civil rights. Although technically these two assertions are valid, such broad strokes fail to consider an important factor that challenges DuBois's role as the most militant and important black leader in this early debate (besides ignoring the fact that many if not most adhered more or less to both approaches).

That factor is William Monroe Trotter, the first persistent and most radical proponent of black equality in the early twentieth century and the spark that helped ignite the struggle for black political and civil rights throughout the century. DuBois, by comparison, was quite conservative during the late nineteenth and early twentieth centuries and had remained aloof in the storm his Harvard classmate was creating with his unrestrained criticisms of Washington. In fact, DuBois on at least three different occasions had seriously considered joining Washington at Tuskegee—once in 1896, again in 1899, and even as late as 1902 he had considered an invitation to join the Tuskegee staff. In addition, he had taught there for a summer and had supportively attended a series of conferences at Hampton and Tuskegee.[28]

During the first few years of the new century, DuBois was sometimes critical of Trotter's strong anti-Washington language. Although it would be an overstatement to say that DuBois wholeheartedly embraced Washington's philosophy during these early years, the rising scholar was sympathetic to the conservative approach and had cautiously aligned himself with other Washington-type conservatives. In the last two or three years of the nineteenth century, he sometimes passionately joined other conservatives in their public defense of Washington against the growing attacks by such radicals as Reverdy Ransom, a prominent A.M.E. clergyman from Chicago who would play a part a few years later in the Niagara Movement, and the loud but relatively unknown B. T. Thornton of Indianapolis. In 1900 DuBois was the brainchild behind Washington's National Negro Business League—essentially a mechanism for Washington to exert his influence in "every city with a substantial black population." All this pro-Washington activity led Trotter to denounce his friend in July 1902: "Like all the others who are trying to get into the bandwagon of the Tuskegeen, he is no longer to be relied upon."[29]

But DuBois's association with the Tuskegee activities must be balanced with his scholarship during those early years that set out to revise the historical contributions of blacks in America, particularly during the Reconstruction period. His was a lone voice in a wilderness of racist historicism that blamed black inferiority and incompetence for the supposed failure of Reconstruction. Thus, although his adherence to the Washington approach may reflect a conservative DuBois during this time, his scholarship was nothing short of radical in its conclusion that black political leaders after the Civil War had largely accomplished what the previous all-white democracy would not: a universal (although precarious and temporary) application of democratic freedom for all races. And contrary to most white popular opinion of the times that declared the Freedmen's Bureau a disaster, DuBois wrote in the *Atlantic Monthly* in 1901 that it was actually "a great human institution" that "set going a system of free labor; it established the black peasant proprietor; it secured the recognition of black freemen before the courts of law; and it founded the free public school of the South."[30]

DuBois eventually embraced Trotter's position of protest and agitation in 1903 after the latter was jailed for starting an alleged riot during a meeting at which Washington was speaking in Boston. It appears the radicals simply but noisily wanted Washington to respond to a series of prepared questions regarding his stance on black equal rights (this will be discussed in more detail later). It was an awakening for DuBois who in the weeks that followed felt the Tuskegee Machine was determined to use its power to silence Trotter and its critics for good and prevent any open discourse in regard to alternative methods for racial advancement. But even after DuBois became a radical, Trotter remained in the forefront of the struggle for black equality as the loudest critic of racial injustice in the journalistic world and, most strikingly, in personal direct confrontation with those he believed were creating injustices for African Americans. DuBois remained more moderate or low-key and eventually aligned himself with the more reserved but active NAACP, which was made up of leaders "young enough to be militant yet conservative enough [to] use their militancy in a lawful and discreet manner."[31] Moreover, he confined most of his criticisms regarding Jim Crow, stinging as they were, to its organ, the *Crisis.*

Trotter, by comparison, was never discreet and was sometimes unlawful. During the first two and a half decades of the twentieth century, he created an uproar with his disobedience of society's norms and laws—something most racial reformers were not bold enough to do—by aggressively confronting powerful individuals and institutions: Booker T. Washington, Woodrow Wilson, movie theaters showing the film *Birth of a Nation,* Harvard University, and segregated businesses and hospitals. He was arrested, jailed, fined, attacked, and driven to poverty, and he lost his wife and trusted "comrade" in the struggle to an influenza epidemic during his crusade to make a better world for blacks in America. Most leaders on both sides of the race issue during this time, white and black, had heard of or knew William Monroe Trotter and respected or despised him; but few could remain indifferent to his shocking behavior, which drew the bitter consternation of prominent figures—including Washington and President Wilson—and made him the object of enmity among many more moderate racial reformers.

The black and white press nationwide took notice of him as well, particularly after his second meeting with President Wilson. The equal rights advocate held mass meetings and sent numerous petitions, telegrams, and letters protesting racial injustice (often badgering those who did not respond to the written missives with more of the same). He not only managed to become known in the South as well as in the North and West but also acquired international recognition in his crusade for black equality after his spat with Wilson, not to mention his incredible journey to France to plead for justice for African Americans during the Paris Peace Conference in 1919. DuBois, in contrast, was relatively unknown during this time outside the small world of racial reformers and academics in the East and the elite black community, although he did reach fairly substantial audiences with his classic *The Souls of Black Folk* and his editorial mouthpiece, *Crisis*. He was admittedly not an active reformer in the sense that Trotter was, confining most of his opposition to philosophical protest in the form of scholarship and articles.

With all considered, it appears that Trotter essentially eclipsed DuBois as the most prominent and assertive African American leader of the early twentieth century. Indeed, the profound currents he released into the stream of black protest—his tenacious use of confrontational protest with its emphasis on the procurement of equal rights and integration—would become widely accepted by racial reformers, particularly after the 1920s, and became the hallmark of the modern civil rights movement. Trotter not only planted the seeds of the modern civil rights movement, but he tried over and over to fertilize them long before they were ready to germinate. Thus, the divergent philosophies for racial advancement during the first few decades of the twentieth century, when considered within a context of juxtaposition, can be more accurately represented, it seems, by the views and actions of Washington and Trotter than by those of Washington and DuBois.

A UNITED FRONT: TROTTER AND THE NAACP

When complaints of segregation in federal departments began to grow, Trotter deployed Freeman Murray and Maurice Spencer to Washington to find out the details. Lacking the organizational base of the NAACP, the Boston editor was completely reliant on Murray and Spencer, with little account-ability. In the beginning the NIPL's investigation made virtually no progress. Weeks after the NAACP's August letter of protest was released, Trotter was still groping for details about Jim Crow from his two men. "I am sorry you and Spencer cannot find out better the specific facts," Trotter disappointedly wrote to Murray. "I have not been kept informed well of the actual increases and changes of Jim Crow." The information he was receiving was second-hand: "I asked Spencer to send me one of the Jim Crow orders. . . . I had to copy it out of the *Amsterdam News*." To make matters worse, Trotter had to learn some of the details of Jim Crow under Burleson from a "white editor" in Boston. And the *New York Age* beat the NIPL to the punch by first pub-lishing details about segregated "toilets."[32]

Although Trotter would have preferred to get the details of Jim Crow in government departments from his own men, it was not his highest priority. He was an agitator above all else, not so preoccupied with getting proof of one more instance of racial injustice in a Jim Crow world. "The Jim Crow now is so bad that . . . we cannot afford to be explaining where it originated," Trotter declared. "If we as a race are to be saved, we have got to stop federal Jim Crow no matter who started it." African Americans had been treated unfairly during their entire history in the United States, and Jim Crow in Washington was for Trotter an anticipated extenuation of that prejudice into the one area in which the race had made some of its greatest progress. Con-frontation was the key for the young equal rights activist who was powerfully driven by an unquenchable passion. Even Trotter's correspondence, both personal and professional, seems to have been written in haste, often reflect-ing shoddy grammar and poor spelling—not something one would expect from a Harvard honors graduate. But he was a man on a mission with no time to be concerned with trivial formalities. As a man of action, Puttkammer has pointed out, Trotter had no patience for "long table discussions" that considered every angle and shred of evidence and yet failed to take "strong or bold" action to get things done.[33]

For years, Trotter had been clamoring for equal rights in the pages of the *Guardian* and through participation in the Boston Suffrage League, the Niagara Movement, and the NIPL. He was the first of the "radical" black leaders to publicly censure, and the only one to directly and aggressively confront, Booker T. Washington for "undermining the rights of colored Americans." On July 30, 1903, in what is known as the Boston Riot, Trotter, along with some of his followers, disrupted the Tuskegeen as he was speaking to a crowd at the Columbus Avenue A.M.E. Zion Church. Some accounts claim his supporters shouted and threw eggs at Washington and that chairs were upset in a shoving and shouting match in the fight that ensued. Others maintained that audience members pulled out knives. And yet some concluded that it was nothing more than a high-pitched barrage of sincere questions from Trotter and others directed to the guest of honor and that most of the disruption was caused by Washington supporters shouting to have his inquisitors thrown out. Prior to the chaos, however, Trotter loyalist Granville Martin stood up and shouted, "In your letter to the Montgomery *Advertiser* on November 27th, you said: 'Every revised constitution throughout the Southern states has put a premium upon intelligence, ownership of property, thrift, and character.' Did you not thereby endorse the disfranchising of our race?"[34]

Although most accounts of the explosive meeting portrayed Trotter as the main instigator, others claimed the leader was inconspicuous during the confusion that erupted at the A.M.E. Church. Whatever happened that night, Trotter was arrested and jailed for instigating a riot and became a local and, to a lesser extent, a national hero. After thirty days of confinement in the Charles Street jail, where he seems to have developed a bit of a martyr complex and where he pumped out scathing editorials on Washington for the *Guardian,* the hero walked out of his cell among a throng of cheers and was greeted with affectionate embraces and handshakes from friends and admirers.[35]

A decade later he wrote Joel Spingarn that "had others taken the same position then, instead of upholding Booker T. Washington and denouncing me for opposing Washington, the colored race would not be where" it is today. Trotter's belief in effecting change meant a ceaseless campaign through appeals in the press, petitions to public officials, and, most important, direct confrontation or "meeting foes in human form," as he described it, with those responsible for denying African Americans their rights.[36]

Another reason Trotter did not push harder for his own investigation of federal Jim Crow was his relationship with the NAACP. Although it can never be said that Trotter was on intimate terms with the organization, he was on its advisory board and considered himself a member—even referring to it in one correspondence as "our association"—and his name appeared on NAACP stationery as one of six Bostonians on the General Committee. In 1911, while fretting over "the wide-open-door policy of membership," Trotter nonetheless praised the "Association" as a "great, important and noble movement" and told his *Guardian* readers, "we should all . . . take part in making it of great benefit to race and country." Several members of the NIPL were also members of the NAACP, and others regularly corresponded with national officers. Although Trotter, as mentioned, was leery of an organization dominated by whites, he kept in touch with the group's efforts against Jim

Crow and believed it was doing a "good" service for African Americans. In friendly correspondence with NAACP firebrand Joel Spingarn, Trotter explained that he was unable to attend an upcoming NAACP meeting but that he was sending copies of the *Guardian* for those attending. In addition, he told Spingarn that he had printed his "article in full on page 2" of the equal rights organ. Thus, as the January 1913 letter seems to demonstrate, Trotter's presence at some NAACP meetings, particularly national ones, was welcome and expected; and at least in this case he had given a high-ranking NAACP member a voice in the *Guardian*. Later, as federal Jim Crow was at its zenith, the Boston editor printed in the *Guardian* speeches condemning racial caste in Washington from other NAACP officers as well, including Moorfield Storey and Oswald Villard.[37]

Factional disputes between the NAACP and the NIPL, Trotter wholeheartedly believed, must be put aside for the good of the race. Although he believed the NAACP protest letter was wrong in claiming federal Jim Crow was new, he felt it would be a mistake to make a public spectacle about it. The NIPL must "pocket unselfishly any partisan advantages." When Freeman Murray, the Washington press correspondent for the NIPL and a federal employee, publicly castigated the NAACP over the statement, Trotter made it clear to his friend that it was an "error . . . to attack the circular letter of the NAACP in your public correspondence." "The circular is a great help to the cause of the race," he continued. "[W]e must show a more or less united front by fighters on our side." This exchange preceded a plea from NAACP president Moorfield Storey to Trotter in which he echoed the latter's sentiment for unity: "Personal ambitions, personal hostilities, differences of opinion on minor points should all be sunk for the race as a whole."[38]

Thus, for Trotter the NAACP was doing a service, and its report verified for him the Jim Crow hearsay that had been coming out of the federal departments for months. His dislike of certain members, and his disagreement with the organization's more moderate approach, was overshadowed by his commitment to help his race.

Despite Trotter's volatile reputation in the arena of racial agitation, in private he has been described as a kind and unselfish man; and, as most of his private correspondence demonstrates, he was willing to sacrifice the recognition he desired (and deserved) if it meant saving his race. The pugnacious Murray perhaps more than anything felt personally slighted by the NAACP protest letter, since he believed he was "authorized and expected" to "speak" for the Washington NAACP branch, as well as for the NIPL. The letter seemed to show that the NAACP disregarded his position by not consulting him and by ignoring his investigative efforts. The possibility cannot be overlooked, however, that his investigation of federal Jim Crow may have been compromised by his employment with the federal government. It may have been asking too much to have a federal employee working in such a high-profile position as press correspondent for a protest organization. With or without the NAACP protest letter and despite any fallout between Murray and the NAACP, Trotter, putting factional disputes aside, began making preparations to protest against federal Jim Crow and to directly confront the person at the apex of power who he believed was responsible.[39]

THE NIPL'S NATIONAL PETITION CRUSADE

In early August 1913 Trotter wired Wilson's secretary, Joseph Tumulty, asking him to speak with his boss over the alarming spread of Jim Crow in the federal government. Around the same time he appealed to a fellow Bostonian serving in Congress, future mayor James M. Curley, who, like Trotter, always seemed to generate controversy. The editor lobbied Curley to pressure the Wilson administration to end federal Jim Crow and pleaded with him to protest the president's recent selection of a white man to the traditionally black post of minister to Haiti. And on August 25 Trotter and the NIPL sent Wilson official "resolutions" protesting against the loss of black federal appointments in the offices of register of the treasury and minister to Haiti and strongly condemned the president for segregating African Americans in the federal departments at Washington. They ended by asking for an "immediate change of policy."[40]

In mid-September, after several letters to McAdoo and Burleson protesting Jim Crow in their departments went unanswered and with no response from Wilson in regard to the August 25 protest resolution, the NIPL endorsed a strongly worded appeal entitled "Memorial to President Wilson," which was signed by seven people including a woman, "Mrs. A. Truitt" of Pennsylvania. After appealing to the president's "honor" and campaign pledges of "justice and fair treatment" and warning the Democrat of the negative historical perception federal Jim Crow would render his presidency, the equal rights leader asked Wilson in "good faith" to reconsider the Jim Crow policy being enforced under his administration: "We know the President has been absorbed over the schedules of his tariff bill. But we think it not impertinent to remind him that free wool, etc., is vastly less important than the interests of free men."[41]

Although these efforts stirred up opposition among African Americans, the Democratic administration continued to downplay federal Jim Crow. When the issue was forced upon him, Wilson repeated his belief that segregation was an act of compassion, since it would make colored people "safe" from discrimination and allow them to develop along independent lines. McAdoo, however, either flat-out denied that there was a segregation issue in the Treasury Department—calling the charge "erroneous" that some black women in his department were forced to eat in "toilet" rooms while the evidence, including testimony, pointed to the contrary—or invoked the doctrine of separate but equal in justifying federal Jim Crow in work and eating places. In addition, Trotter's letters to Wilson, McAdoo, and Burleson—including the NIPL resolution and memorial—and the results of a segregation inquiry sent directly to all three men at the end of October went unanswered.[42]

An out-of-patience NIPL soon launched a massive national campaign to acquire signatures on a petition protesting federal Jim Crow to be presented directly to President Wilson. The "National Petition Against Jim Crow and Color Segregation by the Federal Government" was sent to black and liberal white newspapers across the country. It instructed those concerned to "sign" their "name and address and mail to the editor of this paper" or to "Committee" headquarters in Washington or to the *Guardian*'s Cornhill office in Boston. "Get several names," the petition continued, "any number of names can be put on, can be used in churches, lodges, societies, etc."[43]

The *Guardian*, which sponsored the petition drive, printed copies of the petition daily in its pages and called on citizens to do their part. "Have you, dear reader, done a thing against segregation," asked the newspaper in an effort to strike a sense of responsibility in its readers. "Don't be satisfied to deplore and condemn in private conversation, but do something," it demanded.[44] One of the most unlikely publications that printed the NIPL petition was the *Odd Fellows Journal*. A few years earlier, that journal had been persuaded directly by Booker T. Washington to support and promote his more "tactful approach" to racial advancement.[45]

On the NIPL petition was a statement of protest to President Wilson. The wording is worth looking at because the tone was militant, and unlike the NAACP August protest letter, it did not offer a rational and moral argument against federal Jim Crow or acknowledge the reasons put forth by the Wilson administration for the policy. Instead, the NIPL protest got straight to the point. "[W]e, the undersigned are surprised and indignant," began the protest,

> that under your administration there should be any rules made by members of your cabinet to segregate employees of the national government by race or color. We protest against this as a plain insult, public degradation, and insufferable

injury to Colored Americans, the establishment of caste in this free republic. We petition you to reverse, prevent, and forbid any such movement by your bureau chiefs, in accord with your promise of fair, friendly, just, and Christian treatment of your Colored fellow citizens.[46]

The petition was also signed at numerous mass meetings during fall 1913. Although NIPL petitions were circulated and signed at protest meetings sponsored by the NAACP—in fact, almost all of the signed NAACP petitions in the Wilson Papers at the Library of Congress used verbatim the NIPL protest statement quoted here—the league also held its own mass meetings protesting against federal Jim Crow. Most of these meetings appeared to have taken place at churches in the Northeast, particularly in Boston and Washington. In addition, the NIPL aggressively targeted churches and ministers. The protest petition was widely circulated at churches in Connecticut, Massachusetts, New Jersey, New York, North Carolina, Virginia, and Washington, D.C.[47]

Interestingly, newspaper accounts claimed that around half of the signatures on the petition came from African Americans living in the South.[48] It does appear that the protest petition was printed in numerous black southern newspapers such as the Richmond *Planet,* the Richmond St. Luke *Herald,* and the Piedmont *Advocate.* In Mound Bayou, Mississippi, most of the residents in an entirely black town signed the NIPL protest petition and sent it to "Petition Committee" headquarters in Washington, D.C. And many of the individual protest letters sent to Wilson "bitterly denouncing" the policy were from African Americans living below the Mason-Dixon line, although a few expressed submission to Wilson's judgment and opposition to Trotter—including one interesting letter from the "Supreme President" of the "American Colonization Association."[49] Putting aside these few exceptions, utterly disempowered southern blacks were active participants in protesting against federal Jim Crow.

All over the nation, numerous literary societies; suffrage leagues; religious organizations; local, state, and national politicians; political organizations; college presidents and faculty; and others—all encompassing citizens of both races—signed the NIPL petition of protest. Once all the petitions were gathered, they contained an astonishing 20,000 signatures from thirty-six states. As the petitions were coming in, Trotter collaborated with Rep. Thomas Thacher and Rep. Andrew Peters, both Democrats from Massachusetts and the latter a classmate of Trotter's at Harvard, and Rep. John Rogers, a Massachusetts Republican,[50] to arrange a meeting to present the NIPL with signed petitions and to protest directly to President Wilson. The three congressmen, courted by both the NIPL and the NAACP to assist protest efforts in Washington because of their outspoken support or sympathy for black equal rights, arranged for the NIPL delegation a thirty-five-minute meeting with the president.[51]

With the meeting set, the protestors had yet another obstacle to overcome. The NIPL and the *Guardian* were too strapped financially to sponsor such a delegation to the nation's capital. Trotter had been trying desperately to keep both his newspaper and equal rights organization afloat by pleading for contributions from NIPL members and *Guardian* subscribers. Anything other than these two enterprises was a luxury he could not afford. Trotter was not lacking in resourcefulness and creativity, however. To raise money for the trip to Washington, he sponsored a dance in Boston and promoted it in the *Guardian*. It was a big success, and through the admission fee charged at the door and with an enthusiastic response from hundreds of black Bostonians who danced the Turkey Trot and were entertained by a ragtime band, he was able to defray much of the cost. Thus, on November 6 at 12 noon, an NIPL delegation made up of Trotter, the outspoken antilynching crusader Ida Wells-Barnett, intense advocate for racial equality Dr. William Sinclair, NIPL president and fiery black minister the Rev. Byron Gunner, and Washington NIPL local branch officers Freeman Murray, Maurice Spencer and Thomas Walker, accompanied by Rep. Thacher, met with President Wilson at the White House.[52]

The autumn air was cool that day, the sky was overcast, and the well-groomed trees on the north White House lawn were almost barren except for a few leaves that clung to the stiff branches. Inside the mansion crystal chandeliers sparkled, and the electric lights along the corridors—which twenty-five years earlier had been gas lamps—lit the grayish interior. The urbane ebony guests, escorted by Joseph Tumulty, made their way down one corridor and then another until they arrived at the Oval Office. Newly built by Wilson's predecessor, William Howard Taft, the room was impressive, regal, and painted an unusual olive-green color.

Representative Thacher proudly told the president that he had come all the way from Massachusetts to present this distinguished delegation of "American citizens" and then introduced each by name. A smiling President Wilson welcomed them and shook hands with each of his visitors. Trotter presented to the president letters from political leaders in his state endorsing the delegation and protesting against federal Jim Crow. These letters—some militant in tone—were from Rep. Andrew Peters, Deputy Governor-elect William Barry, and Secretary of State Frank J. Donahue. Outgoing Governor Eugene Foss and Governor-elect David Walsh, both Massachusetts Democrats, had sent their letters of protest directly to the president.[53]

One interesting letter came from Boston mayor John F. Fitzgerald, or Honey Fitz as he was known to his constituents, the grandfather of future president John F. Kennedy. The first mayor in America to have been born of Irish immigrants and, as an Irish Catholic, all too familiar with ethnic and religious discrimination, Honey Fitz wrote Trotter that he was "heartily in sympathy with the protest" and emphasized the importance of the editor's "mission" in ending federal Jim Crow.[54]

Trotter also gave the chief executive letters and copies of speeches and editorials by many "prominent men, newspapers, religious bodies, meetings, etc.," condemning Jim Crow practices in the federal government. Last but not least, the NIPL leader presented to the president of the United States the "National Petition Against Jim Crow and Color Segregation in the Federal Government," rolling out the impressive list bearing the signatures of 20,000 of his fellow countrymen in thirty-six states until it draped over the edge of Wilson's long desk and rolled onto the floor.[55]

Feeling the burden of an entire race bearing the crushing weight of Jim Crow and with the other members of the delegation looking on, Trotter began his speech without a single page of notes to assist him—amazing considering that his remarks extended to almost five eloquent single-spaced typed pages. What the passionate race leader had to say, however, was etched in his heart. "There can be no equality, freedom, or respect from others in segregation by the very nature of the case," began an astonishingly confident and controlled Trotter, described by his entourage as looking impressive as he faced the most powerful man in America. Interestingly, throughout his speech to the president, Trotter repeatedly used the term *African American*—a term not commonly used at the time but one that was finding its way into the vernacular of the more radical proponents for racial justice.

Not since Frederick Douglass came to Washington to lobby President Johnson for black suffrage in 1866 had such a bold and demanding black figure stood in the White House face-to-face with a president. Now, almost fifty years later, Trotter wasted no time getting to the crux of the problem.

First and foremost, segregation is a humiliation, explained Trotter. It is an "indignity" and an "insult" that implies that "African Americans are unclean, diseased or indecent as to their persons, or inferior beings of a lower order." He derided the government for distinguishing between its citizens by denying equality to African Americans in "violation of the Constitution" with no basis other than racial prejudice.[56]

A few weeks before the meeting, Trotter had come to Washington to help arrange the appointment with the president. He stayed for a few days to find out as much detail as possible regarding federal Jim Crow. Thus, when Trotter met with the president he was armed with fresh details of Jim Crow in the departments, most of which he had already sent to McAdoo and Burleson. After mentioning the "already notorious" segregation in the departments much publicized by the NAACP, he emphasized the fact that the policy was in effect more than ever. He gave the president a copy of the report made by "those in position to know from the inside," which contained previously unreported efforts to segregate, downgrade, dismiss, and harass black employees in new government buildings in southern cities, the Fourth Auditor Division of the Treasury Department, the Supply Division of the Post Office Department, the City Post Office Annex, the new City Post Office, and the Interior Department. The Boston editor went on to debunk the "unwelcome juxtaposition" excuse given for segregating black and white employees: "African-Americans and other American employees have been working together, eating at the same tables, and using the same lavatories and toilets for two generations." This policy, Trotter continued, "can be attributed to no cause but the personal prejudice of your appointees in the Executive Branch of the Government." "Race prejudice" has now been "incorporated in a National Government policy," he declared. He emphasized further that a precedent was being set that made the rights of African Americans in federal employment precarious and open to arbitrary abuse, and he predicted that their opportunities there would be severely curtailed.[57]

There was nothing perfunctory about Trotter's manner of speech or body language as he spoke to the president. Some moments he gestured with his hands in an animated fashion, whereas at others he leaned over and pressed his palms on the leader's desk to stress a point.

The articulate guest, in a variable tone, explained that "thousands upon thousands of African Americans" had voted for Wilson and did not deserve such "a blow" from his administration. Exemplifying the growing race pride among African Americans, Trotter educated the president as to the historical contributions blacks had made to their country through blood, toil, and struggle. He reminded the Democrat verbatim of his "pre-election pledge" to "see justice done them in every matter, and not mere grudging justice, but justice executed with liberality and cordial good feeling." Trotter continued by reasoning that "[n]o fair man would say that African-Americans could find these words of promise consistent with . . . separate toilets, separate eating tables, separate working desks, separate washrooms." The ebony leader then eloquently yet forcefully summed up the meaning of the protest that was now before the president of the United States:

We confidently believe that the protest of African-Americans from east, west, north and south, from laborers, artisans, clerks, businessmen, professional men, from lodges, from churches, from men and women of high and low degree, such a protest as they have never made on any Federal policy, a protest only just begun, convinces you that Colored Americans did not interpret your words to mean segregation; convinces you that they regard it as unjust, un-Constitutional, un-Christian and an undeserved limitation, degradation, a terrible injury, and by virtue of its influence for contempt, for maltreatment, for race discrimination . . . a calamity.

Segregation is a "wrong and an injustice" that cannot and will not ever be tolerated. "It compels resistance forever," declared Trotter in a militant tone. He concluded his address by calling on the "apostle of the 'New Freedom'" to "wipe out this blot" and end racial segregation in federal departments, and he prophesied the historical repercussions for Wilson's legacy if he did not do so. "We cannot believe that you would stain your honor or the record of your administration in history to satisfy sectional prejudice," ended the leader of the NIPL delegation (interesting in light of the fact that during this time it would have seemed absurd to most whites that a president's attitude toward African Americans, regarded as the lowest social group in society, would in any way negatively influence historical perception).[58]

President Wilson seemed impressed by Trotter's protest. He pointed to the petition lying before him and said that no president could ignore such a protest but that he doubted segregation was implemented with official sanction. Trotter read a segregation order from the Virginian Robert Woolley, chief auditor of the Treasury, dated July 16, 1913—which implicated Secretary McAdoo—and handed it to the president. "To the Chiefs of Divisions and the other officers" began the notice:

This toilet is exclusively for the White employees of the Office of the Auditor of the Interior Department. The toilet on the third floor is for the exclusive use of the Colored employees of the Office of the Auditor of the Interior Department. Any violation of this rule will be promptly dealt with. By order of the Secretary of the Treasury. R. W. Woolley, Auditor.[59]

Wilson played dumb and responded that this was the first he had known of any official action. The president had conveniently forgotten about Williams's order segregating toilets in the Treasury Department that had been brought to his attention by the NAACP, not to mention splashed throughout the liberal press, three months earlier. The Burleson proposal to segregate black employees in the Post Office Department, brought up in a Cabinet meeting, must have slipped his mind as well. And on several occasions

Wilson had admitted to and endorsed the Jim Crow policy in letters to such polar opposites as Oswald Villard and Thomas Dixon, as well as in at least one newspaper interview. The know-nothing president now made a curiously ardent attempt to convince his skeptical audience that his "colleagues" were not prejudiced toward African Americans, perhaps attempting to avert the daily negative coverage his administration was receiving in the liberal press, particularly in the widely circulated and influential *New York Evening Post*. In any case, a seemingly concerned President Wilson assured the delegation that, although he still believed the matter had been exaggerated, he hoped to "do the right thing."[60]

But Trotter was not finished. He reiterated that federal Jim Crow was unjust. Irritated by the president's refusal to admit that anyone in his Cabinet had given the go-ahead to segregation while in general downplaying the whole issue, Trotter brought up the fact that McAdoo had "announced" what amounted to a policy based on color. "Never has any person announced this policy," Wilson shot back. "He said separate tables," countered Trotter. "I beg your pardon," snapped President Wilson, appearing slighted by his guest's bravado. "If a newspaper has made what we regard as a gross misrepresentation" of a policy that was never "announced," it was an "inexcusable" distortion of the facts. "I assure you it will be worked out," concluded the evasive president—a curious statement in light of the fact that he had just said in so many words that the whole unjust segregation matter did not really exist.[61]

The only other delegate to speak before the meeting came to a close was the tenacious Ida Wells-Barnett. A petite and attractive woman, her eyes had an intense, almost defiant expression. The presence of this fighting spirit in the delegation signaled that federal Jim Crow was a very serious matter that demanded immediate action to be stopped. Wells-Barnett had been born to slave parents in Mississippi six months before Lincoln signed the Emancipation Proclamation. She committed her life to "fighting racial oppression" and leading antilynching campaigns through public speeches and journalism, and she was a tireless advocate for women's suffrage. Evelyn Brooks Higginbotham has pointed out that many of Wells-Barnett's female contemporaries in the black Baptist Church compared her to the Old Testament heroine Queen Esther who essentially prevented the genocide of the Jewish people living in the Persian Empire around 485 B.C. "We have found in our race a Queen Esther," trumpeted the *National Baptist World*, "a woman of high talent, that has sounded a bugle for a defenseless race."[62]

More than seventy years before Rosa Parks, Wells-Barnett started the battle that challenged Jim Crow transportation in Tennessee. Black women who had purchased first-class tickets were often humiliated while traveling through the South by being ordered to the smoking car. Fearing violent reprisals by whites, most quietly moved without incident. But on March 4, 1884, Wells-Barnett, while traveling her routine ten-mile stretch from Memphis to her teaching job in Shelby County, Tennessee, refused to give in to a conductor's demand that she move to the second-class coach. Realizing that the defiant little black woman had no intention of budging even an inch, the "irate" conductor first attempted to move her himself and was abruptly stopped by the pain of teeth in the back of his hand as she attempted to secure her position by gripping the back of her seat and bracing her feet against the seat in front of her. He got help from two other bullying white men who dragged a kicking and fighting Wells-Barnett from the train as white passengers cheered her forced exodus. She immediately sued the railroad.[63]

A circuit court ruled in her favor, awarding $500 in damages. But the victory was short. The case went all the way to the Tennessee Supreme Court, dominated by former Confederates, where she lost in 1887 on the grounds that her "persistence was not in good faith" while the court invoked the separate but equal doctrine.[64]

Over twenty-five years later Wells-Barnett was still resistant to being treated as anything other than an equal American with respect and dignity. What a paradoxical scene it must have been at the White House as the only woman of the delegation, the most disempowered person in a country that refused her a voice because she was both black and a woman, and who could not even sit in the section of the train she desired without being forcibly removed, now stood before the president of the United States in protest. Making this scene even more incongruous was the fact that Wilson, not unlike most southern white men, personally idealized the traditional white Victorian woman and at the time scorned suffragettes like Wells-Barnett who only eight months earlier had marched in a female suffrage parade in Washington during his inauguration.[65]

Ida Wells-Barnett did not say a lot to President Wilson that day, but what she did say summed up the core issues involved in the battle against racial injustice in America and signaled the shift from accommodation to agitation. She told the president, "no one could so well represent . . . the feelings of Colored people" toward federal Jim Crow in particular and racial injustice in general as "members of this race." The equal rights delegation now standing before the president, Wells-Barnett emphasized, comprised the real leaders of the race. White sympathizers, for all their sincerity, could not completely understand the dilemmas facing blacks because they were white. Leadership, Wells-Barnett seemed to imply, must come from within the race; thus she indirectly attacked the paternalistic views of Wilson and others while distancing the delegation of black leaders from the white-endorsed Booker T. Washington. The tiny crusader ended by putting the persistent injustice of racial prejudice in sharp perspective and summarizing the chronic inability of most whites to relate: "[T]he only way by which we could even convince our best friends who can't see how we suffer would be [for them] to suffer . . . a black or brown face, as we do, and they would see this democracy in a new light in which they have never seen, in a light in which they could well see the difference . . . those who suffer know best."[66]

The delegation left the White House feeling a tremendous sense of accomplishment and immediately had a group picture taken (excluding Wells-Barnett, who had to dash off to fulfill other obligations) to commemorate the occasion. "I think you men should feel very proud," remarked Trotter's encouraging and politically astute wife, Geraldine, or Deenie as close friends knew her, a tireless equal rights advocate herself. "You have certainly done your duty."[67] Described as an extremely attractive and strong-willed woman of African and European ancestry, Deenie wrote editorials for her husband's paper and spoke at ceremonies commemorating past heroes who had struggled for freedom, and she had the enormous task of keeping afloat the always financially unstable *Guardian*. But to Monroe she was more than a comrade and adviser in the struggle for black equality; she was also his soulmate whom he had deeply loved throughout his life and romanced until her premature death.[68]

Deenie had reason to be proud after the White House meeting. It was a victory for African Americans that a black delegation had been granted a private meeting with the country's most powerful leader to express a grievance, especially since most of the race could not vote for him. Although Booker T. Washington had been meeting with presidents for years, he had more or less done so without challenging the status quo, and he really represented the political establishment; whereas the Trotter delegation represented a growing mode of thinking among independent African Americans who sought changes in their status through nonpolitical channels such as confrontation, protest, and petition. The National Association of Colored Women (NACW) and the NIPL, along with a handful of black newspapers and some in the NAACP, even went so far as to publicly urge "boycott movement[s]" of white-owned businesses—dependent on black patronage—that discriminated against African Americans. These rising leaders were not so much interested in a few black political appointees as they were in freeing the whole race from the fetters of racial discrimination. This meant nothing less than an end to racial injustice and the beginning of black equality.[69]

On its own stationery, the NIPL described its "Mission" as "The Political Emancipation of the Colored Man in America."[70] For black leaders such as Trotter and even white sympathizers like Villard, confronting federal Jim Crow in protest was to challenge the entire caste structure of society. The color line in Washington provided a convenient target to expose the injustice and hypocrisy Jim Crow was for blacks in so-called democratic America. In short, these new race leaders wholeheartedly viewed their efforts as working for the second emancipation, a feat they perceived to be as historically significant as the first.

The black and liberal white press hailed the meeting as a positive step toward ending Jim Crow in the federal civil service. Trotter immediately mailed out a "condensed account" of what he described as a "historic event" to black newspapers across the country. Much like the NAACP's protest letter in August, the Trotter delegation succeeded in focusing attention on federal Jim Crow and heightening awareness in regard to the injustice. Newspapers reported that the meeting was a success because Wilson promised to launch an inquiry into conditions in the federal government. The *Boston Recorder* represented the sentiments of many newspapers when it declared, "Colored folks are now more hopeful." Even the socially moderate *Washington Post* reported on the meeting and told readers the "petition bearing 20,000 names" had persuaded the president to institute "an investigation to determine whether Negro employees in the federal government are being segregated." The *New York Herald* assured its readers that "President Wilson is now facing the negro problem in a more serious form." And it is no surprise that the *Guardian* devoted several issues to the meeting and praised Wilson for his "courteous attitude" and his promise to start an "inquiry." "This proves that protest pays," trumpeted the newspaper.[71]

In the pages of the *Guardian*, Trotter urged readers to continue the protest and informed them of every newly reported case of Jim Crow in the federal government. He was on a roll after the Wilson meeting, and he unmercifully pounced on anything that even reeked of racial injustice in Washington. Determined to keep the pressure on the Wilson administration, the incessant editor told readers that "now is the crucial time to push forward with appeals." He also asked that "everyone" send a protest letter to the president and other political leaders and encouraged them to "write to someone else to do the same . . . in an endless chain letter fashion." "Do it now," demanded a persistent Trotter. In another article the editor asked readers to write letters to "both Postmaster-General Burleson and President Wilson" protesting "the reported 'Colored' and 'White' railway postal clerk crews as ordered by the General Superintendent of the Railway Mail Service at Little Rock."[72]

The plans for Jim Crow in this service were more ambitious than just color segregation in Little Rock, however. In calling on President Wilson to "interdict," Trotter forwarded to him an Associated Press article in which Alexander H. Stephens, general superintendent in charge of the Railway Mail Service and one of the highest appointees in the Post Office Department, declared, "Negro and white mail clerks will be absolutely separated. The Department, in fact, has taken steps already toward that end."[73]

The battle in this service was formidable. Its official organ, the *Railway Mail,* had made it clear that "it is useless for the Negro to speak of his qualifications, his progress, his ambition; that does not remove our instinctive racial dislike." Black employees were not only segregated from whites and regularly transferred from one line to the next, but they were harassed with threats of dismissal; and almost any reason—trumped up or not—was sufficient to terminate them from the service altogether. With the southern sentiment under the Burleson regime prevailing, threats of violence against black employees whose runs happened to cross into certain southern localities where whites were offended by their presence and status became commonplace. And some all-black crews were being downgraded in pay while their white counterparts' salaries remained the same—thus fixing separate pay scales for the same work determined not by performance but by color. Even Mary White Ovington, in *Crisis,* castigated the Railway Mail Service in the South for having "two scales of wages—one for its white and one for its colored workers." "The latter," she continued, "when doing the same work, receive only two-thirds of the amount received by the white employee."[74]

Trotter let no injustice or potential injustice go unopposed. After John Lorance of the *Boston Record* reported that racial segregation existed in part of the Department of Commerce's new "11-story office building," the NIPL promptly wired a protest to Commerce Secretary Redfield, which was also printed in the *Guardian*: "We petition you in the name of justice to countermand this segregation if it is true." Shortly after the telegraph was sent, the NIPL began to routinely mail out summary articles to "white and colored newspapers" of every instance of federal Jim Crow it had uncovered and challenged.[75]

The *Guardian* also reported that Assistant Secretary of the Treasury John S. Williams not only continued to push Jim Crow policies in his department but, like the RMS, denied salary increases for black employees because he believed "no more Colored men should have more than a thousand dollars['] salary." Theoretically, employees with federal civil service status—white or black—should have made the same amount when performing the same functions. However, it does appear that African Americans in the RMS were routinely the victims of salary discrimination and were the first affected when departments experienced cutbacks. Also, there were complaints and reports that African Americans were regularly passed over for promotion in federal departments in Washington, particularly the Treasury Department. In other cases it appears that attempts were made to reduce their salaries at Treasury. Whereas in the past, excuses such as "reduction in work" were given for dismissals or salary freezes, these new attempts to reduce or eliminate black federal workers were more brazen, as the public statements of Secretary Williams in Treasury and General Superintendent Stephens of the RMS demonstrated by trumpeting their true motive.[76]

Mass meetings followed the White House visit as well. Trotter and members of the delegation addressed many of these meetings, which included members of the NAACP, the National Association of Colored Women, suffrage leagues, and people from all walks of life who squeezed into packed churches and halls to hear the details. In late November, at the Columbus Avenue A.M.E. Zion Church in Boston where Trotter had protested against Booker T. Washington ten years earlier in what had come to be known as the Boston Riot (discussed earlier), a mass meeting of a "thousand colored people" convened to continue the protest against federal Jim Crow. The meeting was sponsored and led by the city's religious leaders and featured, among others, William Monroe Trotter, who drew thunderous applause and a standing ovation as he stood to speak. Following several other speeches by some of the city's most prominent black leaders, protestors "signed a petition to President Wilson asking him" to end federal Jim Crow.[77]

In Washington, a "packed" mass meeting led by Trotter was held at the Nineteenth Street Baptist Church under the "auspices" of the NIPL. In this meeting, which showcased all of the protest delegation, Trotter emphasized the need for a continual protest to President Wilson and other congressmen by "Colored citizens everywhere," and he filled the attendees in on the details of the White House meeting. From the audience, sporadic shouts of "amen" and "tell the truth, brother" seemed to punctuate his every sentence. The church erupted with applause after Trotter proclaimed, "We must fight for our own rights and organize for our own defense!" Following Trotter's speech, Dr. William Sinclair, Maurice Spencer, Ida Wells-Barnett, and others spoke on the need for race organization and rebuked those who promoted race prejudice.[78]

A "mass meeting and rally" was held in Salisbury, North Carolina, to raise money for Livingston College. The theme of the meeting was federal Jim Crow, led by Trotter friend Bishop Alexander Walters, who criticized the policy and "emphatically" denied the popular rumor that he "advocated or approved" of federal segregation. Those present unanimously condemned the practice as well and sent a protest to President Wilson. Other NIPL officers spoke to various groups and associations. R. R. Horner and Freeman Murray, for example, addressed the Hillsdale Citizens Association about the segregation in Washington and stressed the need for continued protest. Interestingly, NAACP opponent Murray gave the organization credit for its efforts, and when the Hillsdale Association voted to give the NIPL a financial contribution, both speakers suggested that the money be divided between the NIPL and the NAACP.[79]

The NIPL-Wilson meeting seems to have also sparked protest from various individuals, organizations, and groups. Former Atlanta University president and Trotter critic during the 1903 Washington riot, Dr. Horace Bumstead, now had nothing but praise for Trotter and the NIPL's "righteous cause" in demanding an end to federal Jim Crow. The Young Men's Hebrew Association of Chelsea, Massachusetts, "unanimously" agreed to send a stream of protests to President Wilson and all their state leaders. At the state conference held on November 12, the Congregational Churches of Connecticut sent strong resolutions of protest to the president. One day earlier, the Unitarian Conference of Middle States and Canada had sent a petition to President Wilson demanding an end to the "injustice" of federal Jim Crow. During the November meeting of the "Executive Committee of the Illinois Commission on Half Century Anniversary of Freedom," which included Governor Edward F. Dunne, an "appeal" was sent to the president asking him to "use his authority" to "prevent this public degradation and humiliation of Afro-American employees of the National Government." The Men's Sunday Forum of Colorado Springs sent resolutions of protest to the chief executive and blamed him for encouraging "injustice of all kinds."[80]

A few days after the delegation met with Wilson, Representative Rogers sponsored a resolution in the House to inquire into federal Jim Crow, and on December 9, Representative Thacher went to the White House once again to urge the president to take seriously the recent protest from the black delegation after Trotter's two follow-up inquiries went unanswered. The NACW, which had many members serving in all sorts of capacities in the NAACP and to a lesser extent in the NIPL as well, "resolved" during its national conference held during summer 1914 in Wilberforce, Ohio, to donate fifty dollars to the NAACP and strongly protested against the "wholesale segregation of colored people at the National capitol and other parts of the country." And although the proposal to send an official protest to the president failed to gain unanimous approval, the Northeast Washington Citizen's Association "refused to adopt resolutions favoring segregation" following several speeches rallying against such by some vocal members—amazing considering that this group was an all-white community-based organization in a city where most whites favored drawing the color line.[81]

NOTES

1. J. Clay Smith Jr., *Emancipation: The Making of a Black Lawyer, 1844–1944* (Philadelphia: University of Pennsylvania Press, 1993), 457.

2. Clifton O. Dummett, "Prevention Began Early: Charles Edwin Bentley, DDS, 1859–1929," *Journal of the National Medical Association* 75 (1983): 1235, and a presentation made by Dr. Dummett to the annual convention of the National Dental Association, Washington, DC, July 30, 1978, quoted in *Crisis*, April 1979, 134. Dr. Bentley was also one of the original founding members of the Niagara Movement and later a director of the NAACP.

3. Lerone Bennett Jr., *Before the Mayflower: A History of the Negro in America, 1619–1964* (Baltimore: Penguin, 1970), 285.

4. Stephen Fox, *The Guardian of Boston: William Monroe Trotter* (New York: Atheneum, 1970), 140; Ruth Worthy, "A Negro in Our History: William Monroe Trotter, 1872–1934" (M.A. thesis, Columbia University, 1952), unnumbered preface, 18, 39–40; DuBois quoted in Robert C. Hayden, "William Monroe Trotter: A One Man Protestor for Civil Rights," *Trotter Institute Review* 2 (Winter 1988): 7.

5. Christine Lunardini, "Standing Firm: William Monroe Trotter's Meetings With Woodrow Wilson, 1913–1914," *Journal of Negro History* 64 (Summer 1979): 261.

6. "It is preposterous to plead benevolence" quote in ibid., 248; also Hayden, 7; William Harrison, "William Monroe Trotter—Fighter," *Phylon* 7 (July 1946): 238, 240–241; Werner Sollors, Caldwell Titcomb, and Thomas A. Underwood, eds., *Blacks at Harvard: A Documentary History of African-American Experience at Harvard and Radcliffe* (New York: New York University Press, 1993), 97; *Guardian* excerpt entitled "Address to Delegation by N.I.P.L.," in Box 6, Moorfield Storey Papers, Manuscript Division, Library of Congress, Washington, DC [hereafter Storey Papers].

7. W.E.B. DuBois, *The Autobiography of W.E.B. DuBois* (New York: International Publishers, 1968), 254.

8. Mary White Ovington, "How the National Association for the Advancement of Colored People Began," *Crisis*, August 1914, 184; *Crisis*, July 1932, 225.

9. Trotter quoted in Fox, 140; Fourth Annual Report of the NAACP, 6, Box 9, Storey Papers.

10. Rayford Logan, *The Negro in American Thought and Life: The Nadir, 1877–1901* (New York: Dial Press, 1954); Warren D. St. James, *The National Association for the Advancement of Colored People: A Case Study in Pressure Groups* (New York: Exposition, 1958), 35.

11. David Lewis Dorrah, "President Taft and the Solid South," *Nineteenth Century* 72 (November 1912): 1019.

12. Baker quoted in Fox, 34–35.

13. "Monroe would also argue feverishly" quote taken from recollections shared with the author by Monroe Trotter's grandniece, Peggy Trotter Dammond Preacely, in which she

recounts these episodes as described by her mother, Ellen Craft Dammond, and her aunt, Virginia Trotter Craft Rose.

14. Fox, 3–5, 8–9; Hayden, 7; Ray Stannard Baker, *Woodrow Wilson Life and Letters: Youth, 1856–1890* (New York: Doubleday, Page, 1927), 13–17.

15. "A Trip Back in Time on the Underground Railroad," Akron (Ohio) *Beacon Journal,* April 4, 1998; Benjamin Quarles, *Black Abolitionists* (New York: Da Capo, 1991), 6, 101.

16. August Heckscher, *Woodrow Wilson: A Biography* (New York: Collier, Macmillan, 1991), 8–9.

17. Annette Gordon-Reed, *Thomas Jefferson and Sally Hemings: An American Controversy* (Charlottesville: University of Virginia Press, 1997), 38–39; Jack McLaughlin, *Jefferson and Monticello* (New York: Henry Holt, 1988), 119; Lucia Stanton, "'Those Who Labor for My Happiness,' Thomas Jefferson and His Slaves," in Peter S. Onuf, ed., *Jeffersonian Legacies* (Charlottesville: University of Virginia Press, 1993), 143, 151–153, 161, 169, 173 note 6; Will and Codicil of Thomas Jefferson, March 16 and 17, 1826, in MSS 514, Thomas Jefferson Collection, University of Virginia, Charlottesville, VA; Fox, 8–9, 37.

18. Fox, 37. Jefferson-Fossett lineage discussed in Lerone Bennett Jr., "Thomas Jefferson's Negro Grandchildren," *Ebony* 10 (November 1954): 78–80; also Fox, 8–9.

19. Booker T. Washington, *Up From Slavery* (New York: Oxford University Press, 1995), 131; Trotter quoted in Worthy, 8 note 19, 9. Also Hayden, 7.

20. *Harvard College Class of 1895, 7th Class Report: Secretary's Report* (Boston: Harvard College, 1925), 303.

21. Horace Bumstead to George Towns, November 5, 1903, Towns to Bumstead, November 7, 1903, Towns to Trotter, November 1903, and Bumstead to Towns, December 5, 1903, all in Horace Bumstead and William Monroe Trotter Files, George A. Towns Papers, Robert W. Woodruff Library, Atlanta University, Atlanta, GA; Francis L. Broderick and August Meier, *Negro Protest Thought in the Twentieth Century* (New York: The Bobbs-Merrill Company, Inc., 1965), 25–30.

22. Fox, 37.

23. Washington quoted in Sollors, Titcomb, and Underwood, 110. Also Adam Fairclough, *Better Day Coming: Blacks and Equality, 1890–2000* (New York: Penguin Putnam, 2001), 62. For an interesting discussion of one black family's devotion to Booker T. Washington, see Douglas Brinkley, *Rosa Parks* (New York: Penguin Putnam, 2000), 17, 28–38.

24. Stephan Thernstrom, "Oswald Garrison Villard and the Politics of Pacifism." *Harvard Library Bulletin* 14 (Winter 1960): 127.

25. Quoted in James M. McPherson, *The Struggle for Equality* (Princeton: Princeton University Press, 1992), 297–298.

26. "William Monroe Trotter: 'For Every Right With All Thy Might,'" *Boston Globe,* February 11, 1973, article in William Monroe Trotter File, Boston Herald Traveler Library, Boston, MA; Rev. Leroy Ferguson, "William Monroe Trotter," eulogy in Thomas H.R. Clarke Papers, Moorland-Spingarn Research Center, Howard University, Washington, DC; Charles Puttkammer to Stephen Fox, September 4, 1965, Guardian of Boston Collection, Mugar Memorial Library, Boston University, Boston, MA.

27. "William Monroe Trotter: 'For Every Right With All Thy Might.'" *Boston Globe,* February 11, 1973, article in William Monroe Trotter File, Boston Herald Traveler Library,

Boston, MA; William Monroe Trotter to Freeman Murray, September 23, 1913, Corre-spondences, Box 74-1, Freeman Murray Papers, Moorland-Spingarn Research Center, Howard University, Washington, DC [hereafter Murray Papers]; Charles Puttkammer to Stephen Fox, September 4, 1965, Guardian of Boston Collection, Mugar Memorial Library, Boston University, Boston, MA; Worthy, 38.

28. August Meier, *Negro Thought in America, 1880–1915: Racial Ideologies in the Age of Booker T. Washington* (Ann Arbor: University of Michigan Press, 1963), 198.

29. Trotter quoted in ibid., 198; "substantial black population" quote in Louis R. Harlan, *Booker T. Washington: The Making of a Black Leader, 1856–1901* (Oxford: Oxford University Press, 1972), 266.

30. W.E.B. DuBois, "The Freedmen's Bureau," *Atlantic Monthly* (March 1901).

31. St. James, 41.

32. William Monroe Trotter to Freeman Murray, September 7, 1913, Box 74-1, Murray Papers.

33. Trotter quote in Trotter to Murray, September 7, 1913, also Trotter to Murray, September 23, 1913, Correspondence, Box 74-1, Murray Papers; Puttkammer to Fox, September 4, 1965, Guardian of Boston Collection, Mugar Memorial Library, Boston University, Boston, MA; Worthy, 34, 68.

34. Trotter to Murray, September 7, 1913, Trotter to Murray, September 23, 1913, Correspondence, Box 74-1, Murray Papers; "In your letter" quote in Worthy, 65. For Worthy's depiction of the Boston Riot, see 63–67.

35. Fox, 49–54; Hayden, 8; Worthy, 67–69.

36. Trotter to Spingarn, January 28, 1914, Box 95-11, Joel Spingarn Papers, Howard University, Washington, DC; Hayden, 7; Worthy, 65.

37. *Guardian,* April 1, 1911; William Monroe Trotter to Joel Spingarn, January 2, 1913, Correspondence, Box 95-11, Joel Spingarn Papers, Howard University, Washington, DC; Fox, 131.

38. William Monroe Trotter to Freeman Murray, September 7, 1913, Freeman Murray to Trotter, September 22, 1913, Correspondences, Box 74-1, Murray Papers; Moorfield Storey to Trotter, September 16, 1913, Storey Papers.

39. Insight into Trotter's personality from interview with Robert Bonner II, a writer for the *Guardian* in 1926 whose father had served as associate editor in its early years, by Ruth Worthy, March 22, 1948, in Worthy, 35.

40. Trotter to Joseph Tumulty, August 15, 1913, Trotter to James M. Curley, August 11, 1913, Woodrow Wilson Papers, cited in Charles LeBron Ballew, "Woodrow Wilson and the Negro" (M.A. thesis, University of Maryland, 1965), 58; Trotter and the NIPL to Wilson, August 25, 1913, Trotter File, Woodrow Wilson Papers, Seeley G. Mudd Library, Princeton University, Princeton, NJ.

41. Trotter to McAdoo, July 29, August 21, 1913, McAdoo Papers, Manuscript Division, Library of Congress, Washington, DC; Trotter to Burleson, May 23, 1912, quoted in Fox, 173; Trotter and delegates to Wilson, September 22, 1913, enclosing "Memorial to President Wilson," Trotter File, Woodrow Wilson Papers, Seeley G. Mudd Library, Princeton University, Princeton, NJ; Fox, 171–172.

42. Wilson to Villard, July 23, 1913, August 19, 1913, August 29, 1913, McAdoo to Villard, October 22, 1913, October 27, 1913, Folder 2362, Oswald Villard Papers,

Houghton Library, Harvard University, Cambridge, MA, and also partially quoted in Charles Flint Kellogg, *NAACP: A History of the National Association for the Advancement of Colored People,* vol. l, *1909–1920* (Baltimore: Johns Hopkins University Press, 1967), 163, 165, 170–171; "McAdoo's Statement to Villard of No Segregation a Big Joke," *Guardian,* December 13, 1913, Box 6, Storey Papers; newspaper article entitled "Segregation Charges Submitted to Pres. Wilson . . . Secy. McAdoo and Postmaster General Burleson," November 6, 1913, Trotter File, Woodrow Wilson Papers, Seeley G. Mudd Library, Princeton University, Princeton, NJ.

43. Jim Crow Petition in Murray Papers; various *Guardian* extracts in Box 6, Storey Papers.

44. *Guardian* excerpt, untitled, indecipherable date, Box 6, Storey Papers.

45. Meier, "Booker T. Washington and the Negro Press," 76; unauthored, "Protest Against Race Discrimination," *Odd Fellows Journal,* October 30, 1913, in Box C-432, NAACP Papers, Manuscript Division, Library of Congress, Washington, DC.

46. Jim Crow Petition in Murray Papers.

47. *Guardian* extract entitled "Anti-segregation National Protest Petition Goes to Pres. Wilson Next Week," indecipherable date, in Box 6, Storey Papers; Trotter to Freeman Murray, October 25, 1913, Box 74-1, Murray Papers; Woodrow Wilson Papers, Manuscript Division, Library of Congress, Washington, DC.

48. *Guardian,* "Anti-segregation National Protest Petition Goes to Pres. Wilson Early Next Week," indecipherable date, "President Hears Colored Delegation With National Anti-segregation Petition," November 8, 1913, and "Petition Starts Presidential Inquiry," November 15, 1913, all in Box 6, Storey Papers.

49. *Guardian,* "Anti-segregation National Protest Petition Goes to Pres. Wilson Early Next Week," indecipherable date, "President Hears Colored Delegation With National Anti-segregation Petition," November 8, 1913, and "Petition Starts Presidential Inquiry," November 15, 1913, all in in Box 6, Storey Papers; Kellogg, 165–166 note 40. In this note Kellogg derives his opinion from a "recent analysis" on the subject of black government workers by George Osborn, "The Problem of the Negro in Government, 1913," *Historian* 23 (1960–1961): 344, and Series 4, Reels 230 and 231, Woodrow Wilson Papers, Manuscript Division, Library of Congress, Washington, DC. A biography that mentions one southern woman's letter-writing campaign to Wilson protesting federal segregation can be found in Carrie Allen McCray, *Freedom's Child: The Life of a Confederate General's Black Daughter* (Chapel Hill, NC: Algonquin, 1998), 132–133.

50. It appears that Republicans by and large did not seize on the issue of federal segregation until around election time, especially during the campaigns of 1916, 1920, and 1924. Even then, however, most of the criticism was confined primarily to the Republican Campaign Textbooks. Republican leaders had been, in fact, some of the most vocal proponents of immigration restriction, including Senator Henry Cabot Lodge of Massachusetts. Referring to efforts aimed at immigration control during the second decade of the twentieth century, Morton Sosna remarked, "[T]he omnipresence of color consciousness during the progressive years was a veritable fact of American life"; Morton Sosna, "The South in the Saddle: Racial Politics During the Wilson Years," *Wisconsin Magazine of History* 54 (Autumn 1970): 30. Dewey Grantham said, "In reality Northerners and Republicans—and

Progressives as well—had adopted attitudes towards Negroes and other colored races not unlike those of the South"; Dewey W. Grantham Jr., "The Progressive Movement and the Negro," *South Atlantic Quarterly* 54 (October 1955): 476.

51. *Guardian* extract entitled "Delegation of Colored Americans Have Audience With President Wilson and Present Petition Against Segregation" and subtitle caption "From Congressman Peters," Box 6, Storey Papers.

52. Trotter to Freeman Murray, September 1913, Box 74-1, Murray Papers.

53. *Guardian* extracts with subtitle captions "Thacher Introduces" and "Letters From Mass. Democrats," Box 6, Storey Papers.

54. John F. Fitzgerald to William Monroe Trotter, October 11, 1913, quoted in Ballew, 62 and note 22.

55. Article entitled "Present Petition to President," November 15, 1913, Box 6, Storey Papers.

56. Trotter dialogue quoted in *Guardian* extract with subtitle caption "Spoke Without Notes" and article entitled "Full Authentic Statement of Federal Segregation to President Wilson," Box 6, Storey Papers; Lunardini, 246; McPherson, *The Struggle for Equality,* 345–346.

57. *Guardian* extract with subtitle caption "Spoke Without Notes," article entitled "Full Authentic Statement of Federal Segregation to President Wilson," newspaper extract entitled "Segregation Charges Submitted to Pres. Wilson," all in Box 6, Storey Papers; Lunardini, 246–247.

58. Trotter dialogue quoted in *Guardian* extract entitled "Full Authentic Statement of Federal Segregation to President Wilson," Box 6, Storey Papers; Lunardini, 247–249.

59. Lunardini, 249; "exclusively for the white employees" quote in *Guardian* extract entitled "Reads the Official Order," November 15, 1913, Box 6, Storey Papers.

60. *Guardian* extract entitled "Committee of Colored Men See President Wilson and Protest Against Race Segregation" and extracts with subtitle captions "Speaks of Petition in Response," "Reads the Official Order," and "Reading of This Order by Delegate Trotter Convinced President of Reality of Segregating," November 15, 1913, all in Box 6, Storey Papers; Lunardini, 249, 252.

61. Lunardini, 250.

62. David L. Lewis, *W.E.B. DuBois: Biography of a Race, 1868–1919* (New York: Henry Holt, 1993), 244; Evelyn Brooks Higginbotham, *Righteous Discontent: The Women's Movement in the Black Baptist Church, 1880–1920* (Cambridge: Harvard University Press, 1993), 143.

63. Lewis, 244; Linda O. McMurray, *To Keep the Waters Troubled: The Life of Ida B. Wells* (New York: Oxford University Press, 1998), 22–31; Christopher Waldrep, "Ida B. Wells, Higher Law, and Community Justice," in Ballard C. Campbell, ed., *The Human Tradition in the Gilded Age and Progressive Era* (Wilmington, DE: Scholarly Resources, 2000), 31–50.

64. McMurray, 29. Ironically, Wells-Barnett's loss in the Tennessee Supreme Court gave a precedent to the nationalization of the separate but equal doctrine in *Plessy* almost nine years later.

65. Heckscher, 74–75, 80, 234. Wilson tried to sidestep the issue of women's suffrage for as long as he could, but he eventually did an about-face when he found it politically inexpedient not to do so.

66. Wells-Barnett dialogue quoted in *Guardian* extracts with subtitle captions "Mrs. Barnett Speaks" and "'Shoe Now Pinches Washington Negro,' Says Mrs. Barnett," Box 6, Storey Papers; also dialogue of meeting included in Link, *Papers* 25: 491–498. *Papers* mistakenly treats the dialogue of Wells-Barnett as part of the Trotter address. This may be because the "official" transcript from this meeting, published by Christine Lunardini in the *Journal of Negro History* (64 [Summer 1979]: 244–264), also makes an error in attributing Wells-Barnett's dialogue with the president to Trotter. However, Trotter's own *Guardian* newspaper, as seen earlier, cites her as making these remarks.

67. Geraldine L. Trotter to Freeman H.M. Murray, November 13, 1913, in Fox, 175; Worthy, 17.

68. Worthy, 16–18.

69. National Conference at Wilberforce, 1914, 42, Reel 1, Records of the NACW, 1895–1992, Manuscript Division, Library of Congress, Washington, DC.

70. NIPL Stationery in Box 95-11, Joel Spingarn Papers, Moorland-Spingarn Research Center, Howard University, Washington, DC.

71. *Boston Recorder,* November 10, 1913, reprinted in *Guardian,* November 22, 1913; *Washington Post,* November 9, 1913, reprinted in *Guardian,* November 15, 1913; *Guardian* front-page headlines entitled "Delegation of Colored Americans Have Audience With President Wilson and Present Petition Against Segregation" and "Committee of Colored Men See President Wilson and Protest Against Race Segregation," November 15, 1913; *New York Herald,* November 9, 1913, reprinted in *Guardian,* undated, all in Box 6, Storey Papers.

72. *Guardian* extract "push forward with appeals" appears at the end of an article under the caption "New York State News, etc.," undated; "The Segregation Situation," November 22, 1913, undated, Box 6, Storey Papers; *Railway Mail,* quoted in *Crisis,* August 1913, 184.

73. "Some More Segregation," *Boston Record,* November 12, 1913, reprinted in *Guardian,* November 15, 1913; "NIPL Protests by Telegraph," undated, Box 6, Storey Papers.

74. *Railway Mail* quoted in "Burleson," *Crisis,* August 1913, 184; also Trotter to Murray, November 17, 1913, Box 74-1, Murray Papers; Trotter to Wilson, December 5, 1913, Trotter File, Woodrow Wilson Papers, Seeley G. Mudd Library, Princeton University, Princeton, NJ. More segregation under John S. Williams, *Guardian,* untitled, undated; "Organization of the Department," *United States Official Postal Guide* 6 (July 1913); A. L. Glenn, *History of the National Alliance of Postal Employees, 1913–1955* (Cleveland: NAPE, 1956), 17, 24, 56–58; Mary White Ovington, "Segregation," *Crisis,* January 1915, 143.

75. John Lorance of the *Boston Record* and *Guardian* telegram printed in *Guardian,* November 15, 1913.

76. More Segregation Under John S. Williams, *Guardian,* untitled, undated; Laurence J.W. Hayes, "The Negro Federal Government Worker, 1883–1938" (M.A. thesis, Howard University Graduate School, 1941), 20, 25, 37.

77. *Guardian* extracts entitled "Protest Color Line to Wilson," undated, "Delegation Makes Report to Colored American Public," November 11, 1913; A. F. Jackson to the District of Columbia Branch of the NAACP, April 22, 1914, Box 39-25, Archibald Grimke Papers, Moorland-Spingarn Research Center, Howard University, Washington, DC.

78. *Guardian* extracts entitled "Protest Color Line to Wilson," undated, "Delegation Makes Report to Colored American Public," November 11, 1913; A. F. Jackson to the District of Columbia Branch of the NAACP, April 22, 1914, Box 39-25, Archibald Grimke Papers, Moorland-Spingarn Research Center, Howard University, Washington, DC.

79. *Guardian* extracts entitled "Protest Color Line to Wilson," undated, "Delegation Makes Report to Colored American Public," November 11, 1913, and "Walters Answers Villard," December 10, 1913. The controversy was over an alleged statement made by Walters to the president and McAdoo that he favored a black division in the Registry of the Treasury. In a letter to Trotter, a fuming Walters asked, "Do you think I have lost my senses and interest in my race? Why, [I] would die before I would betray my race." Walters to Trotter, November 10, 1913, reprinted in *Guardian,* undated, Box 6, Storey Papers; A. F. Jackson to the District of Columbia Branch of the NAACP, April 22, 1914, Box 39-25, Archibald Grimke Papers, Moorland-Spingarn Research Center, Howard University, Washington, DC.

80. *Guardian* extract entitled "Dr. Bumstead on NIPL Address to President Wilson," November 15, 1913; for criticisms of Trotter in 1903, see Horace Bumstead to George Towns, November 5 and November 14, 1903, Horace Bumstead File, George A. Towns Papers, Robert W. Woodruff Library, Atlanta University, Atlanta, GA; "Y. M. Hebrew Association Protest Segregation," undated; "Connecticut Ministers Assail Segregation" and "Unitarians Enter Lists Against Segregation," November 22, 1913; "Ill. Half Century Freedom Commission Sends Protest" and "Protest From Colorado," undated, all in Box 6, Storey Papers.

81. Thacher visit in *Christian Science Monitor,* December 9, 1913, and *Boston Advertiser,* December 10, 1913, short extracts reprinted in *Guardian,* undated; "Segregation Attacked by White People in D. of C.," *Washington Star,* December 9, 1913, reprinted in *Guardian,* December 13, 1913, Box 6, Storey Papers; National Convention in Wilberforce, 1914, 41, 48, Reel 1, Records of NACW, 1885–1992, Library of Congress, Washington, DC; *Guardian* excerpt in Fox, 173–174 note 42.

6

NERNEY GOES TO WASHINGTON,
GRIMKE TAKES ON JIM CROW

ENATOR EDWIN MOSES CLAPP OF MINNESOTA, an austere-looking man with
a bushy walrus mustache and a short robust frame, had the reputation
for being a dynamic advocate for black equality and the most persistent
opponent of racial injustice in the Senate during the first two decades of the
twentieth century. Described as a friend of the National Association for the
Advancement of Colored People (NAACP), he was often a featured speaker
at meetings and conferences sponsored by the organization or other groups
that sought to improve the lives of African Americans. Lambasting anything
that reeked of racial injustice, Senator Clapp frequently stirred audiences at
protest rallies with his impassioned speeches heightened by flailing arms
and animated gestures. The senator was also an advocate for the equitable
treatment of American Indians and had served on the Indian Affairs Committee. Although vastly out of step with most of his colleagues—with the
exception of the abolitionist-spirited Sen. Joseph Benson Foraker of Ohio
and the social reformer from Wisconsin, Sen. Robert M. LaFollette—and
always butting heads with the unanimous ambivalence or outright hostility

to black equality he encountered in the Senate, his goal nevertheless was clear: to achieve full political rights for black Americans and an end to lynching and segregation.[1]

In early September 1913, Senator Clapp had introduced a resolution in Congress calling for a committee to investigate Jim Crow in federal departments. The congressional committee was grudgingly approved and appears to have been authorized to investigate only the rumored signs designating separate lavatories in the Treasury Department. White officials in the department prepared for the visit by removing the signs before the committee arrived. As a result, the investigation was a flop. To make matters worse, several newspapers reported that once the investigators had left, white supervisors—either by "orders" from their superiors or on their own initiative—made it clear to black employees that the order was still in effect.[2] The New York *Evening Post* printed a "formal order" from the "Chief Clerk's Office" that notified "Superintendents and Chiefs of Divisions" in the Treasury Department that the segregation of black employees in "toilet rooms" was "still in force" and asked them to "please notify any of the employees . . . who may be affected."[3] Needless to say, the NAACP was displeased with the investigation and urged Senator Clapp to sponsor a bill calling for a larger investigation of federal Jim Crow.

Shortly after the committee's visit, the *Chicago Defender* released an article claiming that the Architect's Office of the Treasury Department had "received instructions to arrange for the installation of separate toilet rooms for Negro employees in all federal buildings south of the Mason-Dixon line." The article also informed readers that Assistant Secretary of the Treasury John Skelton Williams "gave orders" that a black assistant division chief in the Auditor's Office of the Navy Department be removed from his position for no other reason than the color of his skin. Around the same time, the Democratic Caucus, emboldened by the recent movement to segregate black federal employees and given impetus by the onslaught of proposed racist legislation from members of its own party, brazenly recommended that white men replace all black workers not under the civil service "in the Capitol and in the Senate and House office buildings." Although nothing seemed to have come from it, exasperated protestors feared this latest move signified that "there is no limit to the mean ends the new regime will resort to." This also underscored the recent anxiety of many administration critics that the secretive Democratic Caucus was scheming and formulating legislation behind closed doors, thus usurping power from committees in Congress to openly debate legislation.[4]

With opposition to federal Jim Crow mounting, particularly in regard to toilet segregation at Treasury, at the end of September President Wilson issued a curious executive order to "All Officers and Employees of the Treasury Department." In the order, titled "Prohibition of Use of Towels by More Than One Person," the president "ordered . . . that the use of roller towels and other towels intended for use by more than one person be discontinued in public buildings of the U.S."[5] Although this seems a trivial matter to require an executive order, Wilson may have issued such—probably at the request of William McAdoo who circulated the order—as an attempt to satisfy his subordinates in the executive branch whose plans to create segregated restroom facilities were being foiled by protestors. If McAdoo, Williams, and Robert Woolley, along with other white employees, were opposed to sharing toilet facilities with black coworkers, then perhaps removing roller towels—which were regularly touched by black as well as white hands ("more than one person")—at the powerful insistence of the president could serve as either an alternative or a temporary "executive" solution to a universal policy of Jim Crow restrooms.

In the meantime, the energetic secretary of the NAACP, May Childs Nerney, more determined than ever to catch Jim Crow red-handed, prepared a trip to Washington to tour the federal departments herself. On September 30, following the unanimous approval of the NAACP board of directors, she visited all of the federal departments where Jim Crow had been reported. The "special agent," as newspaper headlines called her, personally toured and inspected various bureaus and divisions within the Post Office and the Treasury departments.

Nerney would not willingly divulge any information about who she was and why she was there unless she had to, even being mistaken as a Jim Crow sympathizer by a supervisor in the Main Treasury Building. It is not clear whether she intentionally disguised her motives, as it appears she did with federal Jim Crow sympathizer Charlotte Hopkins, or she had revealed her affiliation with the NAACP when originally scheduling her visit. At least one of Nerney's guides during the tour, however, knew that his visitor was from the NAACP. Although it is uncertain how many guides escorted Nerney through the various bureaus and divisions, it appears that one was a superintendent in the Post Office Department and another was a clerk in the Treasury Department.[6]

When Nerney returned to NAACP headquarters in New York, she wrote a comprehensive report based on her observations and interviews while visiting the departments. The organization's protest campaign got the boost it needed when on November 17 the report was released to the public. *Segregation in the Government Departments at Washington* was the culmination of months of painstaking research, and it exposed Jim Crow like never before, leaving little doubt in the minds of Jim Crow opponents that this was an authorized policy by the Wilson administration. "The past few months of Democratic party control," maintained the report, "have given segregation impetus, and have been marked by more than a beginning of systematic enforcement. It is becoming known as a policy of the present government."[7]

Unlike the letter of protest released in August,[8] a 900-word abstract of Nerney's original seven-page report was prepared for the Associated Press (AP), which included only white news publications—thus reaching a much larger audience in the pages of major white newspapers across the country. It is significant that a nationwide general news agency picked up the report in the first place. This signaled a growing sympathy for the injustice being committed in Washington, not to mention the increasing success of the NAACP's protest campaign in swaying the press. In addition to the AP, the NAACP claimed the report was sent to "600 dailies, the colored press and secret societies [the AP would not admit black newspapers], 50 religious papers, the radical press, to all members of Congress, except southerners, magazines and to a list of individuals who might be interested." Nerney's segregation report, moreover, provided the greatest opportunity thus far to publicize the NAACP as a viable organization that was fighting to end federal Jim Crow.[9]

Much of Nerney's investigative reporting was concerned with the "facts" of segregation. During her visit, black federal employees, fearing retribution, shied away from talking to her. Thus Nerney, gathering facts strictly by observation and by whatever information she could get from her white escorts or department supervisors, was unable to incorporate for the most part the crucial human element in her report. Missing were the explicit harassment, threats, downgrading, and dismissals, not to mention humiliation, black employees were encountering on a daily basis.

The AP article began by stating that the "association," which had "twenty branches throughout the country, conducted the investigation." Since AP distribution meant, in effect, more white press coverage, as mentioned earlier, the NAACP made it a point to emphasize four of its most influential white members in its abstract: "Moorfield Storey of Boston is president, Oswald Garrison Villard is chairman of the board of directors, which includes, among others, Miss Jane Adams and Miss Lillian D. Wald." W.E.B. DuBois, who was almost always listed with the first two in official releases by the NAACP, was conspicuously absent from the list. Even a headline in Villard's New York *Evening Post*, "Friends of Negro Report on Washington Condition," seemed to verify the NAACP's desire to publicly portray the organization as controlled by whites to gain support from a white public that might be persuaded to join in a protest led by white "friends" rather than a fringe movement driven by a growing black assertiveness.[10]

After the NAACP's brief introduction, the abstract attempted to grab the reader's attention by announcing that "the effect of segregation is startling"; before taking up specific instances of segregation, it explained that Jim Crow had eliminated competition for black workers by relegating them to the least desirable jobs while often forcing them to endure the most unpleasant working conditions. "Those segregated are regarded as lepers and get what no one else wants," said the article. Although some criticized the report as vague—with some justification since the short abstract was, compared with the original detailed seven-page report, just a "brief summary"— the investigation verified for Nerney and the public the validity of the Jim Crow reports that had been coming from Washington since the summer.[11]

"In the miscellaneous and examining division of the Bureau of Engraving and Printing," the AP article informed its readers, "workers have been paired according to race." A white guide, unaware that Nerney was from the NAACP, told her "it was the future policy of the bureau to segregate all colored employees." Nerney also saw firsthand that black federal employees in the Dead Letter Office of the Post Office Department were, in fact, "segregated back of a row of lockers in the corner of the room"—a complaint that had come to her attention months earlier. In the Registry Division of the Treasury Building, which had the largest concentration of black employees at Treasury and which Wilson and McAdoo had wanted to make into an all-black division, another guide had explained to Nerney that "as many colored clerks as possible are to be segregated."[12]

In the office of the auditor of the Post Office Department, an adjunct to the Treasury Department, "segregation seems to have been most skillfully worked out," as employees were grouped and paired by race, continued the article. "In one room colored men operate what is known as the 'gang punch' and in another room, the force working at the 'assorting machines' is entirely colored." The chief of that office, Charles Kram, a northerner notorious for his outspoken advocacy of federal Jim Crow, informed Nerney that he "would not lose an opportunity to increase" segregation in the two main divisions of his department, which included the Postmaster's Accounts and Warrant Payments.[13]

"In the Bureau of Engraving and Printing," continued the report, "the lunch room assigned to the colored women is unsanitary." "These [conditions] are most unpleasant," since the "wash rooms, lavatories and lunch rooms" are "all in one." The Post Office Department did not provide a lunchroom for black employees but offered the "white employees a very attractive room." Nerney's guide gave the excuse that "as no restaurants in Washington were open to colored people, the government could not be expected to furnish one." And black workers in the office of the auditor and the Dead Letter Office of the Post Office were "taken from light and airy rooms" and placed together in the most "unpleasant" and "least desirable" work spaces, whereas white workers were given the best work environments.[14]

Interestingly, the report mentions in its concluding paragraph that "one official has given the colored people an opportunity to express their opinion on the policy of segregation." In the Pension Bureau, the chief of the division permitted its black employees to vote as to whether they wanted a segregated division. They unanimously voted against it. However, that democratic decision was soon overturned. Shortly after the vote, all employees in the Pension Office were moved into the corridor for reasons that were unclear. The white employees were soon moved back into the office, but the black employees were left in the corridor. And the New York *Evening Post,* one of a handful of periodicals quoting more of Nerney's report than the average AP article, claimed that "many white employees" in the federal departments support segregation only because they fear they will lose their positions "if they do not put themselves on record as approving this policy."[15]

In her report, Nerney mentioned several times that her guides and various department supervisors told her directly or implied, sometimes unintentionally, that the policy of segregating the races, wherever practicable, would continue to be carried out as far as possible. One department supervisor in the Treasury Building, mistaking Nerney for a "sympathizer," "confidingly remarked that they wanted to inaugurate segregation everywhere in the Treasury Department" but was quickly interrupted by the guide who "warned" him of Nerney's affiliation with the NAACP. The secretary ended her seven-page report in a pessimistic tone: "More dangerous to the colored people than the segregation itself, is the subtle" and "sinister" method by which its justification is being skillfully spread, which not only arouses "latent prejudice" but "create[s] it where it does not exist." The prevailing belief is, "We cannot have colored men working in the same room with white women or colored men in charge of the departments employing white women."[16]

Although Nerney investigated the federal departments on September 30, the results were not released to the public for over a month and a half. It was decided that a better option would be to wait and release the report in November so as not to be lost in the shuffle of election press coverage. Since the congressional midterm elections were still a year away, that coverage must have pertained to local or state elections—probably in New York where,

159

according to one NAACP report, the segregation abstract was sent to every newspaper.

By the time the Jim Crow report was published on November 17, Nerney felt parts of the report were out of date. Villard had let out quotes from some of the unpublished findings at mass meetings at Washington and Baltimore in October and in talks with Wilson and McAdoo. In addition, some of the material had been used in an article criticizing federal Jim Crow. Regardless, Nerney's report was widely published as an AP article and received "unexpected publicity." In addition, copies of the report were sent to all NAACP branches and to religious newspapers, and they were mailed "first class" to "every senator and representative in Washington from the North, East, and West." Shortly thereafter, an avalanche of requests for copies began to pour into NAACP headquarters and branches from politicians, libraries, organizations, and individuals from all over the nation.[17]

ARCHIBALD GRIMKE, NERNEY, AND THE WASHINGTON NAACP BRANCH

After Nerney's investigation, the president of the Washington NAACP branch, Archibald Grimke, "kept in touch with the local situation" and continued to gather reports from black employees in the federal departments. Grimke had been eagerly sought after by the national office during the summer to take over a branch in crisis. The dismissal of the former president, J. Milton Waldron, for soft-pedaling in regard to the spread of federal Jim Crow, allegedly to obtain an appointed office in the Wilson administration, had created a vacuum in the most "current strategic point" for battling federal Jim Crow. Nerney had filled this role to a degree, but her demanding duties as national secretary, not to mention the fact that her role required spending much time at the New York headquarters, meant the District of Columbia—a city that was busily creating problems for its black citizens—was not getting the focused day-to-day attention it demanded. The NAACP wanted someone who was a committed organization man but independent enough to take matters into his own hands and battle vigorously against Jim Crow in the nation's capital. Grimke was that man.[18]

The son of a strong-willed slave mother of mixed ancestry and a white planter from one of the most famous and distinguished families in South Carolina, Archibald Grimke overcame nearly insuperable odds to become one of the first of Harvard Law School's black graduates and the American consul to Santo Domingo under President Cleveland. Before taking over the NAACP in the Capital City, he had been working there and in Boston, his established home, as a successful writer and journalist. Friends with the Trotter family for years, the Grimkes lived in the same elite Hyde Park neighborhood of Boston during Monroe's childhood.[19]

Grimke was considered one of the radical leaders in Boston during the first few years of the twentieth century. Close friends with the boy he had watched grow into a man, William Monroe Trotter, the elder Grimke shared with the young newspaper editor a distrust of Booker T. Washington. By 1904, however, to the dismay of DuBois who had recently abandoned Washington, Grimke softened his posture toward the leader from Tuskegee. Hoping to work for what he believed was a broader platform of racial progress, he would attempt to straddle the fence between radicals and conservatives.[20]

By the time Grimke became the Washington NAACP branch president in 1913, he had inched back to a more radical posture. In his late fifties, Archibald Grimke was distinguished in appearance with a full head of snow-white hair outlining his sharp, angular facial features and penetrating eyes. Although he was very amiable, such a striking appearance made him seem dignified, almost ostentatious; and with his scholarly eloquence he seemed to command respect even from his bitterest opponents.

Grimke was one of the most respected and well-known advocates for black equal rights, and this distinction persuaded many of his suitability to lead the "cause of justice" in Jim Crow Washington. In one popular article in the *Atlantic Monthly* in 1904, which was printed separately in pamphlet form by the Tuskegee Institute (interesting, considering its militant tone), entitled "Why Disfranchisement Is Bad," Grimke portrayed disfranchised southern blacks not only as victims of white oppression but as future protestors who "will not consent to such a settlement," and he predicted an apocalypse of mass discontent erupting with "all the strength of rancor of centuries of accumulated outrages and oppressions." "The black American has tasted freedom," but more than that, "he knows his freedom" has "been written into the U.S. Constitution" and secured with his own "blood."[21]

WHILE IN WASHINGTON, May Childs Nerney did not acquire much information from black federal workers, in part because of the low profile she was trying to maintain. Thus, the facts she did gather, as mentioned earlier, came mostly from personal observation and from whatever her guides and the various supervisors in government departments leaked out. Even if black employees knew who she was, however, they almost certainly would have been reluctant to speak with her for fear of losing their jobs. "Please withhold my name as I am employed in the Govt. service," concluded a black federal informant in a letter to Villard. One southern black newspaper declared, "Any colored clerk who is so bold as to kick against the segregation or other humiliating regulations, soon finds himself without a job." Ralph Tyler, the former black auditor of the Navy Department and later an outspoken critic of the Wilson government, confirmed the reluctance of black federal employees to protest for "fear of dismissal" in an article appearing in the *Washington Star*. And the NAACP's Committee of Fifty and More served as a front for black federal workers who were protesting their employers' policies. Thus, pressure was put on Grimke to find out as many Jim Crow details as he could from black employees in the federal government.[22]

Grimke, not unlike Villard, Nerney, and Trotter, obtained most of his information regarding Jim Crow in federal departments from black employees, or "contacts," as he called them, within the various departments. Two of the contacts the NAACP relied on most were Lafayette Hershaw and Thomas Clarke. Trotter and the National Independent Political League (NIPL) had been pumping them for information as well. Both men were employed in the federal government and were active members of the NAACP.

Hershaw had quietly assumed the role of interim president of the Washington NAACP branch following Waldron's dismissal in July as the organization launched an aggressive campaign to recruit Grimke to fill the position. Classified as an executive in the civil service and a bitter opponent of Booker T. Washington, Hershaw had graduated from Howard University Law School in 1892 and had quickly built a reputation as one of the best attorneys in Washington. Clarke, a former lieutenant who served in the decorated 10th Calvary Regiment during the Spanish-American War, now served on another battleground as acting secretary of the Washington NAACP branch during the tumultuous summer of 1913 when the anti–Jim Crow campaign got under way. He was a talented journalist who kept the drumbeat rolling for black equality and against racial injustice—including federal Jim Crow— in the pages of newspapers such as the Boston *Guardian, Washington Star,* and Cincinnati *Union.* Although Hershaw and Clarke, along with others, provided invaluable information on some Jim Crow details, the "secret committee," as Nerney called them, maintained a low profile as far as their involvement with the NAACP and the NIPL was concerned, using the Committee of Fifty and More to conceal their activities so as not to "endanger" their positions.[23]

This last point should be emphasized. Not only were black federal employees the focus of widespread discrimination, but civil service rules prohibited most government employees from participating in political activities. This limitation extended to anything that smelled of political activity, direct or indirect, such as women's suffrage. In 1908 the all-white Seattle local of the National Federation of Post Office Clerks started a paper devoted to publicizing the removal of white civil servants for openly criticizing their department or the administration. Although it is unclear whether those bent on Jim Crowing blacks also abused the "political activity" restriction to remove or harass those believed to be affiliated with the NAACP, suffrage groups, or protest activities, the rule—in addition to skin color—reinforced in the minds of black federal employees the crucial necessity of concealing protest activities against their employer. Also, this threat of removal probably discouraged many hardworking blacks from participating in the protest altogether for fear of losing their jobs. For African Americans, overcoming the color barrier for employment in the private sector was difficult enough, but seeking employment there after being terminated from the federal civil service stigmatized them and created an almost insuperable barrier to finding a decent-paying job.[24]

Braving this dire threat of unemployment, however, many black federal employees still served as informants to Grimke and the NAACP and provided the branch president with a continual stream of Jim Crow details. With some of the latest information in hand, the Washington branch president reported to the NAACP that Jim Crow was increasing in the Main Treasury Building, including several floors of the auditor's office, and in the infamous Bureau of Engraving and Printing—known to black Washingtonians as the "old brick building"—where, it was reported, hundreds of black employees had been segregated from whites.

Grimke telegraphed the New York headquarters that "[i]n the Fourth Auditors five colored clerks segregated from whites in same room since you were here." "Also in Sixth Auditors Office," he continued, "colored are segregated on sixth floor . . . they must go either to eighth floor or basement for lavatory." Furthermore, "[W]hites have been seen to use colored lavatory. No such privilege allowed colored." The next day Grimke wired the office that a colored clerk in the Washington City Post Office "sat recently at same table in lunch room where he has been eating since May" and was ordered to eat only at "tables for colored clerks." The telegram ended by stating that "colored women" in the Main Treasury Building have been segregated in "lavatories and waiting rooms."[25]

A few days after Nerney's segregation report appeared in the press, Villard received a memorandum from a black female federal employee in the Bureau of Engraving and Printing. In it she informed him that a wooden partition with swinging doors had been built in the "colored girls'" dressing room, along with a table presumably for eating, making the "unsanitary" lunchroom they had been forced to use for months a permanent Jim Crow arrangement. In addition, continued the employee, the table "accommodates about 35 to 40 girls" out of a total of "300 colored girls who are assigned" to use it.[26]

Even though this information came too late to be included in Nerney's abstract, these complaints along with other reports made the secretary anxious to push protest activities to the limit. Nerney was like the engine of the NAACP, driving harder and faster than Villard (or most racial reformers) was willing to go. For all his passion and leadership in fighting Jim Crow in federal departments, Villard seemed unwilling to push things to extremes, adhering instead to a more moderate approach. He believed a protest should be "carefully planned in advance, should be perfect in its literary style, and moderate in its expression." Nerney had no such guidelines. She was frustrated that Villard seemed to almost stagnate, particularly after the release of the November 17 Jim Crow report.[27]

Nerney's frustration represented a crossroads the NAACP faced during those early years. Although the young organization leaned mostly toward litigation for achieving its objectives—as legal action soon became its definitive approach—in the early years it was open to, and experimented with, active protest. And although the ardent Nerney wanted to move in that direction, leadership as well as the masses were not ready for full-force direct action. At any rate, one week after the report was published, Nerney complained to Grimke that Villard seemed to think there was nothing else to do at that point. She was not convinced. The secretary believed the NAACP should "in some dramatic way" present the segregation injustice to the nation.[28]

Nerney confided in Grimke that she wanted to focus the protest in another direction. After three meetings with McAdoo she was convinced he was trying to "divert" protest efforts on behalf of the Wilson administration. The treasury secretary repeated the same old justification that segregation was implemented in his department not to do injustice to black workers but to reduce friction between blacks and whites and create a better work environment for both races. Private meetings with leaders in the executive branch, concluded Nerney, were not going to accomplish much. The secretary believed a grassroots effort might be the most effective way to protest against federal Jim Crow. "Would it be possible," Nerney eagerly asked Grimke, "to have our different branches . . . campaign hard in their respective localities, and put pressure upon their representatives in Congress to bring in a bill to have this thing investigated?" If enough people complained at the local level, she believed, it could prompt an official government investigation of Jim Crow in the federal departments and focus national attention on the matter like never before. She especially wanted NAACP members to canvass neighborhoods, go door to door, church to church, club to club in every town and city where the organization had a branch.[29]

Yet in 1913 America there was a real danger of knocking on the wrong door, one that could precipitate a violent reaction and endanger the lives of black and white protestors; understandably, many were reluctant to do so. Moreover, the success of such a campaign required a vast amount of organizational work on the grassroots level, and most NAACP branches in those early years were not prepared for such an undertaking. The persistent Nerney, discouraged by what seemed a no-win situation, settled for directing every NAACP branch to have "each member" write to his or her representative in Congress for "an official investigation of segregation."[30]

A local case of discrimination in the nation's capital also provoked a response from Grimke and the NAACP. On December 1, 1913, Wilson's daughter, Margaret, invited "fifty-six local civic organizations and others" to the White House for a special conference to discuss Washington's educational and recreational development. In a city with the largest black population in the United States, not a single black organization or church group was included on the guest list. Three years earlier, ten organized black neighborhood groups were openly excluded from the all-white Federation of Citizens Association in the city. The solution then was to form a separate civic association. But things had begun to change in such a short time. The NAACP had strongly emerged overnight in Washington, and the confrontational Grimke was there ready to clobber Jim Crow every time his head popped up. He hastily let the president's daughter know that African Americans in the nation's capital were "distressed and humiliated at their exclusion [from the conference]." "I take the liberty of submitting a most respectful protest against the exclusion of representatives of the colored civic organizations," wrote Grimke. "The local colored community is not undistinguished for its culture and its sense of responsibility for community betterment. No other element in the city's population is more deeply concerned than the colored people."[31]

The Washington branch president, in the same letter, also protested against the exclusion of black groups from a similar meeting held a few weeks earlier by Charlotte Hopkins, a close friend of both Margaret Wilson's and the First Lady's. "I am told by a good friend," explained Grimke, that the "accidental presence of one colored person" at the meeting drew many "looks of surprise."[32]

A response to his letter came almost immediately. Margaret Wilson's secretary, T. L. Haynes, wrote an apologetic explanation on Margaret's behalf, but, like her father as president, she shifted responsibility to someone else: "Miss Wilson did not herself personally issue any invitations for this meeting. The representatives of the different organizations were decided upon at an earlier meeting at Mrs. Hopkins's, so that Miss Wilson merely gave permission for the use of the room on Monday night."[33]

The total exclusion of the local black community in Washington during the Wilson years was a stark contrast to what African Americans had accomplished there. Besides having the largest black population in the country, the city had a significant and active black middle class that had made greater strides in advancing the race than was the case in any other city. In fact, since at least the 1890s, African Americans living and working in Washington, in addition to improving local and regional social services, had essentially laid the foundation and created precedents for black uplift that reverberated all over the nation (interestingly, black women led or contributed to many of these benchmarks of racial progress): the powerful National Association of Colored Women (NACW) had largely arisen from the Colored Women's League of Washington, D.C., and was organized there in 1896; Mary Church Terrell fought her way onto the all-white District of Columbia School Board, becoming the first black person ever to do so; Nanny Burroughs created the influential National Training School for Women and Girls; the Washington NAACP branch was quickly becoming one of the most powerful branches in the country, challenging Jim Crow and defeating racist legislation; black women, including Ida Wells-Barnett, marched as equals with white women in a controversial suffrage parade held in Washington during the inauguration of Woodrow Wilson in 1913; African Americans were working in practically every federal department throughout the city, including in supervisory and managerial positions; and black Washingtonians had numerous local and regional organizations, clubs, leagues, and associations and affiliates of organizations of national scope—including mutual benefit societies organized and run by lower-income blacks.[34]

But this mattered little to the new occupants of the White House who would raise the color barrier significantly higher in the nation's capital. Shortly after the 1912 election, the editors of *Current Literature* printed a picture of the Wilson women and the new president with the poignant caption "There will now be a new social revolution." With rumors swirling about Mrs. Wilson instigating racial segregation in federal departments and daughter Margaret's exclusion of the Washington black community in her plans for the city's social uplift, not to mention Woodrow's approval of federal Jim Crow, the prediction came true in perhaps a larger sense than the editors of *Current Literature* had imagined. The South had finally captured Washington.[35]

PURGING AFRICAN AMERICANS: THE CIVIL SERVICE PHOTOGRAPH POLICY

Sometime after the first of the year in 1914, rumors began to spread that the U.S. Civil Service Commission (USCSC) was requiring all applicants for civil service positions to include a photograph with their applications. The NAACP and the NIPL feared this measure was devised to discriminate against African Americans in the federal service. In addition, it revived alarm over the age-old civil service policy that required a list of the three highest-qualified candidates to be submitted for each position. Many believed those selecting personnel to fill vacancies more often than not abused their discretionary power by choosing whites over blacks when they could determine which candidates on the list were African American. The photograph requirement would ensure, many feared, that African Americans could be easily identified and thus discriminated against.

It was another major blow for African Americans, especially in light of the fact that the USCSC was considered an ally, having helped them obtain meritorious advancement in the past. It seems the USCSC was responding to the increasing southern influence in Washington and as part of the federal government was susceptible to political pressure. In contrast, the National Civil Service Commission (NCSC), although not willing to lift a finger to help black federal employees, was an independent agency that worked to distance itself from political influence and sought an end to corrupt hiring and placement practices in the federal government. The NCSC regularly conducted investigations into reported violations of civil service rules and regulations and lobbied for legal changes within the civil service itself.

Yet it appears the NCSC had been embroiled for several years in internal questions of how to increase its membership—particularly questions regarding the qualifications and recruiting strategies for admittance of state and municipal civil service reform leagues—and had been preoccupied with the appointment of officers to replace those lost in the high turnover within its ranks. Besides being out of touch and despite the fact that its membership included the liberal racial reformer Moorfield Storey, the NCSC was nevertheless in sympathy with Jim Crow in federal departments. NCSC president Charles Eliot believed in racial segregation across the board and expressed his conviction that "civilized white men" would not be comfortable beside "barbarous black men." Most racial reformers understood that Eliot's current stance was an unfortunate sign of the times, as many intelligent and liberal reformers, in the face of so much racist propaganda, gave credence to Jim Crow.[36]

With the civil service reportedly requiring photographs for some federal jobs, Grimke launched an investigation. He became quickly convinced that the civil service photograph policy was instigated by an official order and that its goal was to make the policy mandatory throughout the civil service. Laurence Todd of the Washington NAACP branch, at the request of Grimke, confronted the USCSC about the policy and the concerns of many blacks that photographs would be used to discriminate against them. The commission responded by vigorously defending its new policy as a "better means of identification for guarding against false personation than other precautions that have been taken."[37]

Grimke and the NAACP did not believe this defense. In the midst of all the federal Jim Crow and hostile legislation, they felt it was another "scheme . . . bent upon eliminating the negro from the government service." In addition, an "anonymous" black federal employee informed the NAACP in May that since examination photographs had become the norm in the "Philippine Service . . . there has not been one colored man appointed as a teacher in the Philippine School Service." Nerney pursued the matter further and wrote Grimke that there seemed to be no "specific rule or regulation" requiring photographs and that the only positions currently using such photos are those in the "Philippine . . . and Panama Canal Service." Frustrated, Nerney threw up her hands and declared that without "more information, I do not see what can be done."[38]

Nevertheless, the radical *Washington Bee* launched its own investigation and found that the requirement for civil service photographs was spreading. All confusion was laid to rest when, on May 27, 1914, the USCSC officially extended to all examinations the use of photographs for identification of competitors.[39] The NAACP's attorney, Chapin Brinsmade, sent a stream of letters to the commission during summer 1914 but was not satisfied with the commission's usual response that the photographs were to be used only for purposes of eliminating fraud. Although the president of the USCSC assured the NAACP attorney that the commission would take measures to prevent discrimination against black applicants, a despondent Brinsmade wrote to Grimke that "the photograph will result in discrimination against colored applicants." Brinsmade, like Nerney, did not know what to do next.[40]

The NAACP flooded the office of the USCSC and others with letters protesting the photograph policy, yet by fall 1914 Brinsmade felt any action on the matter—legal or otherwise—would be "futile," since the nation was becoming preoccupied with the war in Europe. It seemed that from the moment Archduke Franz Ferdinand was assassinated in Sarajevo on July 20, 1914, every major newspaper in the country was unable to talk about anything else. The great European powers were positioning themselves with lightning speed to enter an inevitable conflict on a grand scale never before seen. As the carnage began, the American press nervously debated if neutrality was possible and if not, how long it would be before the country would be pulled into war. During its 1914 national convention, the NACW, believing the "centers of civilization are on the threshold of a terrible war," resolved in an international moral protest to oppose the "horrible slaughter and frightful suffering of thousands of hopeless human beings." As the noise from the first large-scale modern war machine rolling across Europe drowned out everything else, the NAACP could not get its protest or its investigation of civil service photographs a hearing in the press or the nation.[41]

The NAACP's protest against federal Jim Crow also seems to have fizzled out after summer 1914 because of the war as well. The press was becoming increasingly inaccessible. Although by as late as November Nerney was scrambling to get the most recent "facts" on segregation into the press and was investigating the extent and abuse of the photograph policy, Grimke could no longer focus only on Jim Crow in government departments.[42]

Besides the controversy over civil service photographs, the Washington watchdog was "overworked" from challenging the onslaught of Jim Crow legislation as it came up before congressional committees. The three sessions of the Sixty-third Congress, which convened from April 7, 1913, through March 3, 1915, were loaded with discriminatory bills aimed at segregating blacks not only in the federal departments but on streetcars, as well as at forbidding intermarriage between the two races. This "Congress . . . had never so engrossed the attention of the NAACP as it had during the first two months of 1915," explained NAACP historian Charles Flint Kellogg.[43] With Democrats controlling Congress and southerners dominating most of its committees for the first time in fifty years, efforts to legislate blacks out of the white world were attempted with an intensity never before seen.

African Americans were also a point of indirect contention regarding proposed reform legislation in three other areas during Woodrow Wilson's first administration. The first, involving immigration restriction, mainly sought to curb the migration of Chinese, Japanese, and southern European immigrants into the country, but a rider to the bill was also introduced to exclude "[a]ll members of the African or black race." Next, in the debates over funding for federal-state educational agriculture programs in what is known as the Smith-Lever Bill, black colleges in the South were threatened with no funding because racist legislators such as James Vardaman and Hoke Smith—in an attempt to hoard all the money for southern white colleges— argued that African Americans were inferior, and thus "it [such funding] would be a waste of money." And with the women's suffrage amendment pending in Congress, white female suffrage leaders launched a "state-by-state" campaign to "convince Southerners that woman['s] suffrage would not result in additional Negro suffrage."[44]

Thus, Grimke had his hands full. The black equal rights advocate, who commanded the respect of the congressional committee members, made frequent appearances and debunked the rationale behind many of the discriminatory proposals being considered, and he was credited with squashing several of them. In one case, Grimke was informed that a committee hearing was in progress. He immediately ran to the chambers to protest against Jim Crow. Despite being late, the leader was admitted to the room, and his testimony was heard. Grimke's energies also appear to have been absorbed in relentless and amazingly successful efforts to obtain federal employment and promotions for African Americans and in getting those who had been dismissed or downgraded reinstated.[45]

Grimke caused such a commotion during spring and summer 1914 by badgering Cabinet members and department supervisors and chiefs regarding black federal employees unfairly terminated or reduced in position and salary that McAdoo, on July 13, 1914, ordered his chief clerk, James Wilmeth, to furnish him with a list of African Americans promoted and demoted in Treasury during the past year. The response came just two days later and included a brief summary tabulation that would have been almost impossible to come up with in such a short time for all the bureaus and offices of Treasury. The overnight figures showed a reasonable 220 black promotions, 8 reductions, and 34 dismissals.[46]

But these figures were either bad estimates or fraudulent numbers. Wilmeth had no way of knowing the numbers given to McAdoo, since most final figures regarding black employees did not come in from the many Treasury bureaus and offices until several months later. And most of the later tabulations were very sketchy not only in the number of black promotions, which do not even come close to Wilmeth's numbers, but in the dates of hire for the black employees supposedly promoted. One office, the Auditor for the Treasury run by Robert Woolley, who a year earlier had sent out a memorandum segregating toilets in the auditor's office in the Interior Department, stated bluntly that "no colored clerk or employee was promoted."[47]

With so much new Jim Crow legislation to combat at the local, state, and national levels, the NAACP was shifting its focus toward litigation. Legal "work has developed so rapidly and has increased so in volume and importance," wrote DuBois in the December 1913 issue of *Crisis*. One month later DuBois told readers that the NAACP would give victims of racial discrimination legal "assistance." Finally, the NAACP, like Brinsmade, realized that it had become "impossible to secure any publicity in the press" because of the fighting overseas. With the conflict in Europe heating up and commanding the attention of the media, the NAACP's noble cause was soon lost in the shuffle of war press coverage.[48]

NOTES

1. NAACP Fourth Annual Report, January 1914, 15–17, in Box 9, Moorfield Storey Papers, Manuscript Division, Library of Congress, Washington, DC; "Wilson and Segregation," Philadelphia *Public Ledger,* October 22, 1913, Correspondences, Box C-432, NAACP Papers, Manuscript Division, Library of Congress, Washington, DC [hereafter NAACP Papers]; Dickson D. Bruce Jr., *Archibald Grimke: Portrait of a Black Independent* (Baton Rouge: Louisiana State University Press, 1993), 189; Bruce A. Ragsdale and Kathryn A. Jacob, eds., "Clapp, Moses Edwin, 1851–1929," in *Biographical Directory of the United States Congress, 1774–1989* (Washington, DC: U.S. Government Printing Office, 1989); for sketch of Sen. Joseph Benson Foraker, see Stephen Fox, *The Guardian of Boston: William Monroe Trotter* (New York: Atheneum, 1970), 122, 153–157.

2. Baltimore *Afro-American,* October 25, 1913, January 17, 1914; *New York Age,* August 29, September 11, 1913; "Continues in Washington: Signs Down, but Order Lives," Louisville *Courier-Journal,* September 20, 1913, all in Administrative Files, Box C-432, NAACP Papers.

3. Ralph W. Tyler, "The Segregation in Washington Departments," New York *Evening Post,* September 9, 1913, Correspondences, Box C-403, NAACP Papers.

4. *Chicago Defender,* September 27, 1913, untitled, articles in Administrative Files, Box C-432, NAACP Papers; May Childs Nerney to Archibald Grimke, December 1, 1913, Box 39-25, Archibald Grimke Papers [hereafter Grimke Papers], and William Monroe Trotter to Freeman Murray, September 13, 1914, Box 74-1, Freeman Murray Papers, both in Moorland-Spingarn Research Center, Howard University, Washington, DC; "no limit to the mean ends" quote in "Continues in Washington: Signs Down, but Order Lives," Louisville *Courier-Journal,* September 20, 1913; *Republican Campaign Textbook, 1916* (Washington, DC: Republican National Committee, 1916), 383–384.

5. "Prohibition of Use of Towels by More Than One Person," September 29, 1913, issued by McAdoo on October 11, 1913, as Order no. 188331/2, Department Circular no. 9, *Circular Instructions of the Treasury Department, William G. McAdoo* (Washington, DC: U.S. Government Printing Office, 1915). This source was obtained from National Archives II, College Park, MD.

6. Various newspaper articles in Box C-432, NAACP Papers; *Segregation in the Government Departments at Washington,* 4, report by May Childs Nerney, September 30, 1913, Box C-403, NAACP Papers.

7. New York *Evening Post* clipping, November 17, 1913, and various newspaper clippings in Box C-432, NAACP Papers.

8. Although the NAACP Fourth Annual Report seems to imply that the August letter was sent to the Associated Press (12) and Kellogg mentions in the *History of the NAACP* that, in fact, it was (164), I have found no evidence that it was sent directly to the AP. Instead, it

appears the letter was sent directly to individual newspapers around the country. See Chapter 4.

9. NAACP Minutes of the Meeting of the Board of Directors, December 2, 1913, microfilm, and NAACP Fourth Annual Report, January 1914, 12, both in Box 9, Moorfield Storey Papers, Manuscript Division, Library of Congress, Washington, DC; various newspaper clippings in Box C-432, NAACP Papers.

10. *Boston Evening Herald, Boston Record, Boston Evening Transcript, Fall River* (MA) *Herald, Rochester* (NY) *Post Express,* and New York *Evening Post* are just some of the newspapers that carried the abstract of the investigation on November 17, 1913. These and many other similar newspaper clippings are in the Administrative Files, Box C-432, NAACP Papers.

11. *Segregation in the Government Departments at Washington,* report by May Childs Nerney, September 30, 1913, Box C-403, NAACP Papers; various newspaper clippings in Box C-432, NAACP Papers.

12. *Segregation in the Government Departments at Washington,* report by May Childs Nerney, September 30, 1913, Box C-403, NAACP Papers; various papers in Box C-432, NAACP Papers.

13. *Segregation in the Government Departments at Washington,* report by May Childs Nerney, September 30, 1913, Box C-403, NAACP Papers; various newspaper clippings in Box C-432, NAACP Papers; "Organization of the Department," *United States Official Postal Guide* 6 (July 1913): 4.

14. *Segregation in the Government Departments at Washington,* report by May Childs Nerney, September 30, 1913, Box C-403, NAACP Papers; various newspaper clippings in Box C-432, NAACP Papers.

15. New York *Evening Post,* November 17, 1913, article entitled "Segregation in the Civil Service," unknown source, and various newspaper clippings in Box C-432, NAACP Papers.

16. *Segregation in the Government Departments at Washington,* report by May Childs Nerney, September 30, 1913, Box C-403, NAACP Papers.

17. Nerney to Grimke, undated, Box 39-25, Grimke Papers.

18. David L. Lewis, *W.E.B. DuBois: Biography of a Race, 1868–1919* (New York: Henry Holt, 1993), 106; Bruce, 185–187.

19. Bruce, 1–7, 29, 42, 68.

20. Lewis, 106; Bruce, 97, 108–109.

21. Lewis, 106; Archibald Grimke, "Why Disfranchisement Is Bad," *Atlantic Monthly* (July 1904), reprinted in online collection "From Slavery to Freedom: The African-American Pamphlet Collection, 1824–1909," American Memory, Library of Congress, Washington, DC, http://memory.loc.gov/cgi-bin/query/r?ammem/rbaapc:@field(DOCID+@lit(11800) (accessed March 17, 2002).

22. "Kick against the segregation" quote in Louisville *News,* September 20, 1913, Box C-432, NAACP Papers; also *Washington Star,* August 9, 1913, quoted in Laurence J.W. Hayes, "The Negro Federal Government Worker, 1883–1938" (M.A. thesis, Howard University Graduate School, 1941), 39; Constance McLaughlin Green, *Washington: Capital City, 1879–1950* (Princeton: Princeton University Press, 1963), 224.

23. J. Clay Smith Jr., *Emancipation: The Making of a Black Lawyer, 1844–1944* (Philadelphia: University of Pennsylvania Press, 1993), 135, 173; various papers in Thomas H.R.

Clarke Papers, Moorland-Spingarn Research Center, Howard University, Washington, DC. Also, in the letters of protest sent directly to Wilson, says Kellogg, black "government employees showed the greatest opposition"; 166 note 40.

24. Sterling Spero, *The Labor Movement in a Government Industry: A Study of Employee Organization in the Postal Service* (New York: George H. Doran, 1924), 41–44, 122–123.

25. Grimke to Nerney, October 29 and October 30, 1913, Correspondences, Box C-403, NAACP Papers.

26. Dressing room segregation reported by James C. Walters, Esq., in Memorandum to Villard: James C. Walters to Villard, November 19, 1913, Correspondences, Box C-403, NAACP Papers.

27. Nerney to Grimke, November 25, 1913, Box 39-25, Grimke Papers.

28. Ibid.

29. Nerney to W. L. Stoddard, November 12, 1913, Administrative Files, Box C-403, NAACP Papers.

30. Ibid.

31. *Crisis,* January 1914, 142; Green, 217.

32. African Americans' exclusion at white conference, along with Archibald Grimke Correspondence, in *Crisis,* January 1914, 142.

33. T. L. Haynes to Archibald Grimke, December 3, 1913, Box 32-25, Grimke Papers.

34. In contrast to the community-in-action portrayal and significant national impact offered here, Green, in *Washington: Capital City, 1879–1950,* believes the black community as a whole was divided by petty squabbles and jealousy, cared little about community uplift, and was overall apathetic to the growing white racism in the city; 101–131.

35. *Current Literature* 53 (1912): 611.

36. Eliott H. Goodwin, Secretary of National Civil Service Reform League, to John A. Fairlie, March 3, 1911, John Fairlie Papers, Box 8, General Correspondence; Robert W. Belcher to Members of the Council, February 25, 1914, Robert W. Belcher to Members of the Council, April 22, 1914, and Richard H. Dana to Members of the Council, September 8, 1915, all in Box 10, Professional Correspondence, John A. Fairlie Papers, University Archives, University of Illinois at Urbana-Champaign; Charles Flint Kellogg, *NAACP: A History of the National Association for the Advancement of Colored People,* vol. 1, *1909–1920* (Baltimore: Johns Hopkins University Press, 1967), 172.

37. Nerney to Grimke, March 24, 1914, Box 39-25, Grimke Papers; Laurence Todd to Grimke, August 28, 1914, and United States Civil Service Commission to Chapin Brinsmade, July 28, 1914, Box C-272, NAACP Papers.

38. Todd to Grimke, August 28, 1914, Anonymous Federal Employee to Oswald Villard, May 11, 1914, and Nerney to Grimke, June 10, 1914, all in Box C-272, NAACP Papers.

39. *Thirty-First Annual Report of the U.S. Civil Service Commission,* 26–27, in Hayes, 54.

40. Wilson and Walters to U.S. Civil Service Commission, July 27, 1914, Box C-272, NAACP Papers; NAACP Minutes of Annual Board Meeting, September 1, 1914, NAACP Microfilm, Manuscript Division, Library of Congress, Washington, DC; Chapin Brinsmade to Grimke, September 23, 1914, Box 39-25, Grimke Papers.

41. Chapin Brinsmade to Grimke, September 23, 1914, Box 39-25, Grimke Papers; National Convention at Wilberforce, Ohio, 1914, 43, Reel 1, Records of the NACW, Manuscript Division, Library of Congress, Washington, DC.

42. Nerney to Grimke, November 13, 1914, Box 39-25, Grimke Papers.

43. Kellogg, 175.

44. Various transcripts from the Congressional Record, 63rd Congress, 2nd and 3rd Sessions, 1914–1915, quoted in Morton Sosna, "The South in the Saddle: Racial Politics During the Wilson Years," *Wisconsin Magazine of History* 54 (Autumn 1970): 39–49.

45. Grimke to Charles Hamlin, June 2, 1914, Hamlin to Grimke, June 2, 1914, Nerney to Grimke, July 14, 1914, Grimke to Hamlin, September 24, 1914, Hamlin to Grimke, September 25, 1914, all in Box 39-25, Grimke Papers.

46. McAdoo to Wilmeth, July 13, 1914, Chief Clerk (Wilmeth) to McAdoo, July 15, 1914, Box 97, Personnel—Negro Employees, Records Group 56, General Records of the Department of Treasury, National Archives II, College Park, MD.

47. Robert Woolley to Mr. Harper, November 17, 1914, W. E. Andrews to Mr. Harper, November 18, 1914, several pages entitled "Statement of Appointments and Promotions, March 4, 1913, to Date," and "Colored Employees Who Have Received Promotions During the Present Administration," from the Chief Clerk and Superintendent, Box 97, Personnel—Negro Employees, Records Group 56, General Records of the Department of Treasury, National Archives II, College Park, MD.

48. *Crisis,* December 1913, 88; *Crisis,* January 1914, 140; NAACP Minutes of Annual Board Meeting, September 1, 1914, NAACP Microfilm, Manuscript Division, Library of Congress, Washington, DC.

7

THE FINALE AT WASHINGTON
Mr. Trotter and Mr. Wilson

Even here in the Twentieth Century when if an Abraham Lincoln should
arise in the United States and if he should be a Jew in race or a Japanese in
color, or a Negro in descent . . . his soul would be pressed and shut out of
the republic of the civilized.

—W.E.B. DuBois

A LTHOUGH THE National Association for the Advancement of Colored
People (NAACP) ran out of steam by fall or winter 1914, the National Independent Political League (NIPL) still managed to bring
the protest to a heated climax. One year after Trotter and the NIPL presented to President Wilson the 20,000-signature petition protesting federal
Jim Crow, the group, in its most recent incarnation as the National Independent Equal Rights League (NIERL), made another trip to the nation's
capital to "renew" its protest against Jim Crow still being enforced in federal
departments.

On November 16, 1914, Trotter, along with the same NIERL delegation of 1913—with the exception of Ida Wells-Barnett and joined by the
Rev. E. E. Ricks, "race loyal minister" of the First Baptist Church of Washington, D.C.—met with President Wilson at the White House. The group
first presented to the president resolutions adopted by the Massachusetts
legislature and letters from three of the state's congressmen, all from Wilson's
party, protesting against Jim Crow in the federal government.[1]

Next, three NIERL delegates—the Rev. Byron Gunner, Maurice Spencer, and Thomas Walker—briefly took turns addressing the president as the Rev. Ricks looked on in silent protest. The first to speak was Gunner, the charismatic president of the NIERL and an Alabama native. Years earlier Gunner and his wife, Cicely, an active equal rights advocate for her race and gender and president of the Northeastern Federation of Women's Clubs, had been driven out of New Iberia, Louisiana, by a mob after their church was burned down. Described as hot-tempered and combative, Gunner was outspoken in his criticisms of racial segregation and disfranchisement, which did not go over well with some of the white citizens in his southern community. The exiled preacher now stood before the president of the United States as a spokesman for God: "Mr. President, there are now thousands and thousands of my race on bended knees in prayer to the Father of all men with faith. . . . If you wish to shed a halo of glory on your administration, be an instrument in the hands of the Almighty God in stopping this injustice by issuing an executive order to that effect."[2]

Maurice Spencer spoke next with an eloquent appeal that not only attempted to debunk the logic behind color segregation but also indirectly ridiculed the popular scientific racism myths of white superiority.

> Now Mr. President, has the peculiarity of the word color ever occurred to you? The master minds have been very careful in coining words, that each word shall convey the exact meaning—no more, no less—but as to the word COLOR as applied to the human being, I have yet to see a white or black man, for none are as white as your collar nor as black as your hat, all are between these two extremes, therefore all men are colored, so if the order for color segregation was consistently carried out there would be no segregation, it would neutralize itself.[3]

Thomas Walker, chairman of the Washington NIERL branch and the last to address the president before Trotter, spoke briefly about President Cleveland's refusal to "listen to any clamor for segregation" and pleaded with the leader to follow Cleveland's example: "We simply ask you to restore those conditions and maintain them."[4]

William Monroe Trotter, the final speaker, approached President Wilson not just with the grievances of those present but with an overwhelming sense of "great responsibility" in speaking for African Americans "in all parts of the country." What happened next would shock the sensibilities of white America and signal the beginning of a changing attitude among many African Americans that neither the federal government nor the president of the United States could be counted on to help acquire and protect their rights, regardless of laws and promises. The shelter provided by Uncle Sam in a Jim Crow world turned out to be nothing more than a weak prop at best. Trotter would become a hero for his people by "looking" white Jim Crow "full in the eye" at the apex of power and scoring a symbolic victory. He managed to publicize Wilson's views on federal Jim Crow like never before, leaving no doubt that the president was "in favor of race segregation," and he catapulted the issue into the national consciousness. Wilson was probably not up to such a confrontation either. He was very grieved and "broken in spirit" over the recent death of his wife, Ellen. The president had descended into a state of despair, sometimes blaming the pressures of his political ambitions for her premature death. Three days before the meeting with the NIERL, Wilson confided to a friend that he wanted to "run away, to escape something."[5]

Much of the dialogue during the meeting has been included in this chapter, since parts of it were widely published in the white as well as the black press, provoking much editorial comment from those on all sides of the race issue. In addition, it was perhaps the first time a black leader had aggressively confronted a president face-to-face over racial injustice.

Disregarding the customary deference given to a president, Trotter presented the anomaly of a black man challenging the most powerful white leader in America during a time when Jim Crow was at its zenith. Unlike a "stunned" Frederick Douglass who was cut off by an irritable President Johnson and ushered out of his office in 1866 before the black leader could make a case for black suffrage, Trotter stood his ground and boldly and passionately demanded that Wilson treat members of his race as equal American citizens.[6]

Moreover, in a period when groups used respectful requests and resolutions to communicate a grievance and ask for a change in policy, Trotter's actions anticipated the future of African American protest with his *demand* for change backed by a *threat* if unheeded. He also spoke not just for the delegation that was present that day but for the *masses,* and he communicated to Wilson their collective potential as a symbol of power.

THE MEETING

"Mr. President, we are here to renew our protest against the segregation of the colored employees in the departments of our National Government," began Trotter in front of a White House audience that included not only Wilson and the NIERL delegation but also the president's secretary, Joseph Tumulty. After recounting the last meeting from a year ago, the equal rights advocate named the various departments in which Jim Crow was still in force or had spread. He boldly appealed to the president to once and for all "abolish segregation of Afro-American employees in the executive department."[7]

The tension was thick in the White House that day. Unlike the meeting a year ago, this time Trotter had no doubt that the president supported federal Jim Crow. He was angry. Things had worsened since the last visit. President Wilson himself, having recently lost his wife, was in no mood for a confrontation over an issue he thought was cut-and-dry. Edgy and temperamental, he wished he were somewhere else.[8]

Trotter continued by rebuking Wilson for his failure to put an end to federal Jim Crow. He forcefully stressed that segregation was an absurd arrangement and a humiliation for African Americans. People "on the streets of the national capital" were free to use the "lavatories in government buildings," while African Americans employed in those buildings were "excluded." "We are entitled at your hands," demanded Trotter, "to freedom from discrimination, restriction, imputation and insult in government employ." The ebony leader summed up what was perhaps the essence of Wilsonian idealism for black Americans in a question to the president: "Have you a 'new freedom' for white Americans and a new slavery for your Afro-American fellow citizens? God forbid!"[9]

President Wilson, after expressing what must have seemed to the delegation like insincere platitudes regarding the progress of African Americans, responded that segregation, in his opinion as well as that of his "colleagues in the departments," was a practical solution to the inevitable friction that arises "when the two races are mixed." Such a policy, stressed the president, was "the best way to help the Negro." Unable to grasp the fact that segregation was discrimination against blacks, Wilson throughout the meeting seemed utterly perplexed that the delegation was so upset over the Jim Crow arrangement. Unmindful of the fact that he was speaking the language of accommodation to this delegation of militant equal rights advocates, the president reiterated over and over that his Cabinet had assured him that black employees were not at a disadvantage and that the separate but equal doctrine was rigidly adhered to.[10]

Trotter replied by cleverly challenging the president's remarks in the form of a loaded question that not only debunked the separate but equal doctrine in the federal departments but also emphasized the dire consequences of racial segregation:

> What do you think about the result of this present condition in the departments, where it has already operated to the detriment of so many of the employees, where some have been placed in a position where they are now

humiliated and indisposed . . . having to go far from their work to the toilet rooms . . . reduced from clerkships to laborers . . . forced right out of the departments entirely?

"I haven't known of such incidents," answered a defensive Wilson.[11] Of course, he had. More than a year's worth of letters, petitions, investigations, meetings, and newspaper articles had brought this policy to his attention numerous times. But Wilson's mind was set. Jim Crow would be implemented in the federal bureaucracy as it had been for years in his southern homeland. He blamed people like Trotter and the NIERL for stirring up resentment among the black masses against federal racial segregation and claimed this would only make things worse. After all, African Americans seemed to comply with the arrangement in the South. And both races there, Wilson believed, lived in mutual harmony and understanding. Why should it be any different in Washington?[12]

Frustrated by the president's lack of comprehension in regard to the injustice African Americans had to endure in federal departments, an out-of-patience Trotter became bold and forceful. "Mr. President," he said,

we did not come to the White House as delegates of the National Independent Equal Rights League protesting segregation in the attitude of dependent wards of the nation, but as full-fledged American citizens, absolutely equal with all others, to demand our equal rights under the Constitution. . . . It is untenable, in view of the established facts, to maintain that the segregation is simply to avoid race friction, for the simple reason that for fifty years white and colored clerks have been working together in peace and harmony and friendliness. . . . Soon after your inauguration segregation was drastically introduced in the Treasury and Postal departments by your appointees.[13]

Trotter slammed the hackneyed excuse that segregation was a benevolent policy instituted by white Cabinet leaders and subordinates who had the black employee's best interest at heart. The truth of the matter, he explained to Wilson, was that segregation was the result of nothing other than "race prejudice on the part of the official who puts it into operation." The eloquent spokesman then pointed the finger of blame at his host and stressed that African Americans were greatly disappointed in him for his lack of moral understanding in regard to Jim Crow. The Democrats, Trotter maintained, would be hard-pressed to get future support from black Americans—an implicit threat to the president and one which Wilson would later fume about.[14]

The offended president interrupted Trotter and snapped, "If this organization is ever to have another hearing before me it must have another spokesman. Your tone, sir, offends me." The equal rights advocate, shocked by the rebuke, asked in what way he was offensive, and the chief executive replied, "You are the only American citizen that has ever come into this office who has talked to me with a background of passion that was evident." "But I have no passion in me, Mr. President, you are entirely mistaken," Trotter fired back. "[Y]ou misinterpret my earnestness for passion."[15]

Trotter continued his rebuttal and was interrupted by President Wilson once again after he said he could not control the minds of black people and that even if he could, he would not do so on the segregation issue. The determined black speaker continued, saying, "Two years ago you were regarded as a second Abraham Lincoln" when Wilson stopped him and said he wanted "no personal references." Trotter told the president that if he were allowed to continue, his intent would become clear.[16]

The irritated president, perhaps caught off guard by the show of intellectual prowess and unabashed strength of character exhibited by his black visitor and feeling a loss of control, made it clear that he was "the one to do the interrupting."[17]

The fiery Trotter barreled on. "Now we colored leaders are denounced in the colored churches as traitors to our race." "What do you mean by traitors?" inquired the president, and the black leader replied, "[We are considered traitors] because we advised the colored people to support the [Democratic] ticket." Wilson claimed that bringing in the political issue was a form of blackmail, which he resented.[18]

Trotter was not ready to end his plea for justice. The chief executive felt slighted and perhaps embarrassed that his visitor had gotten the best of him, and the black leader knew this would be his last chance to ever address President Wilson personally. Although he gave up on trying to make Wilson "feel what this thing is like" for black federal employees, he fervently pleaded with the president to put an end to federal segregation. It was useless. Wilson repeated his unshakable belief that segregation was not "degradation."[19]

Emotionally drained by the meeting, Wilson wearily complained that his burdens as president were "more than the human spirit could carry." Trotter wrapped things up by taking "responsibility" if his tone had seemed offensive, but he made it clear that Wilson's snap judgment was a "mistake." The president smiled and said, "O[h], we'll call it all right."[20]

As the delegation began to leave, Trotter stopped and turned back toward Wilson. In a somber tone he said, "Just one more word, Mr. President. We were trying to bring about racial harmony throughout the country." And the black leader from Harvard turned and walked out the door.[21]

For Wilson, such a protest may have been a striking reminder, or perhaps even a revelation, that the intense political and social issues interwoven in the Civil War and its aftermath had not yet been settled. Growing up amid the disorder and turmoil of the war-torn South, he developed a strong conviction for national unity at all costs, even if it meant avoiding sensitive or even seemingly inoffensive issues altogether.

In expressing "regrets" for a holiday to decorate the graves of the Confederate dead, for example, a young Wilson wrote his cousin Hattie that "all the parade and speech-making, and sentimentality" are "exceedingly unwise." "I think that anything that tends to revive or perpetuate the bitter memories of the war is wicked folly." Now as president, Wilson could not so easily ignore the most sensitive and unsettled issue of the Reconstruction period—the social and political emancipation of the black man. Yet like the "wicked folly" of honoring the Confederate dead, Wilson believed only harm and friction would result if Trotter continued to tell his people that segregation was a "humiliation." He underestimated the legitimacy of deeply held beliefs and causes and desired to avoid controversy at all costs.[22]

Trotter and the chorus of protests from around the nation made it clear to the evasive president, however, that there was no avoiding "friction" by appeasing racial prejudice at the expense of black dignity. Trotter was the voice of the new abolitionist movement, and Wilson was caught off guard by his fiery protest and powerful presence. The meeting seems to have shattered the new president's youthful illusion—a weakness confirmed by his protégé Colonel House—that ignoring a sensitive problem would somehow make it go away, and unfortunately he was unprepared and unwilling to deal with such impassioned pleas for justice. Distraught by the heated exchange and ashamed that he had lost his temper, an exhausted Wilson could only complain that anyone who pursued the presidency was a "fool for his pains."[23]

After the chief executive dismissed the delegation, the protestors "caucused" in Tumulty's office to decide what should be said to the press waiting nearby. President Wilson had given the media unprecedented access to the White House during his administration, so it was natural for them to be there daily to catch the latest scoop from either Tumulty or the president himself. Trotter addressed the "newspapermen" as the spokesman for the delegation and described what had taken place in the president's office.

Once the interview was over, the group proceeded to leave the White House when Tumulty called the leader back in and said, "Mr. Trotter, you have violated every courtesy of the White House in quoting the President to the press." Surprised by the secretary's rebuke, Trotter explained that he had "done so in ignorance of the rules" and apologized. He then asked the newspapers, out of respect for White House custom, "not to publish" what he had said, and it appeared they agreed—at least for the moment.[24]

The clash of tempers nevertheless created what can only be described as a media frenzy. Over the course of the following weeks, newspapers and magazines of different political persuasions, representing all parts of the union, acquired the details of the Trotter-Wilson meeting and sharply expressed their opinions. It is unclear whether the press, which had consented not to publish Trotter's remarks, leaked them anyway or, as Trotter maintained, the White House hastily released its own statement regarding the meeting.[25]

Whatever the case, the NIERL leader was glad the meeting had made national news, since it generated more publicity for federal Jim Crow than had all the speeches, mass meetings, petition drives, and letter-writing campaigns combined. In one short meeting Trotter had violated three customs in front of the whole country. First, as a black man he had crossed the line, as far as most southern whites were concerned, by speaking in such a demanding and determined tone to a white man, particularly a southern-born white leader. The fact that it was the president magnified Trotter's "impudence." Next, he had violated White House custom by speaking to the press about the closed meeting, particularly in regard to such a volatile and sensitive subject and one over which the president had lost his composure. Finally, Trotter had boldly disregarded the accepted norm of his day that protestors should refrain from "protesting very loudly . . . in the presence of high authority," an unwritten rule of both black and white racial reformers.[26] "In an era when it was deemed a prodigious favor for a distinguished black leader to be granted an audience with the president of the United States," remarked an amazed David Levering Lewis, "Trotter's impertinence was almost beyond belief."[27]

THE PRESS AFTERMATH

The press response to Trotter's behavior at the White House was praiseworthy, critical, or a combination of both. The response to Wilson's handling of the affair, not to mention to his public approval of federal Jim Crow, followed closely along the same lines. It seemed everybody had something to say about the issue. Without a doubt, this was national news. For the first time in history a black protest had made its way from the obscure back pages of the *New York Times* (that is, if lucky enough to be included at all) to a front-page cover story under the headline "President Resents Negro's Criticism."[28] Much of the mainstream as well as the black press had, in fact, printed the meeting on its front pages. The *Savannah Tribune* noted what an "achievement" it was for a "Colored delegation" to surpass the "European war" in reader interest.[29]

Realizing that Trotter had accomplished more, in the words of NAACP officer Albert Pillsbury, by "insulting the President than all the polite words ever uttered on segregation could," a flustered May Childs Nerney was curious as to "what Mr. Trotter's next coup may be."[30] Oswald Villard wrote that if Trotter had not "riled" the president, the "question of segregation would not have figured in the newspapers save to the extent of perhaps three or four lines." "As it is," the chairman continued, "the cause of the colored federal employee has received a kind of publicity that could not have been bought for money."[31] Even Joseph Tumulty admitted to Villard that Trotter's speech to Wilson was one of the most eloquent he had ever heard, and it appears he urged his boss to heed some of the protestors' concerns.[32]

Although the spotlight was now focused on the segregation in Washington as never before (Tumulty assured Villard that the segregation issue was receiving the most earnest attention at the White House[33]), it was Trotter who became the focal point of a national controversy. The Bostonian had fired the imaginations of many African Americans. Newspapers from all around the country could not resist commenting on Trotter's grandstand act at the White House, and he became a sort of anomaly as curious audiences packed churches and halls to hear the black man who had stood up to the president.

Much of the northern liberal press backed Trotter and the NIERL while criticizing the president. "This delegation was within its rights in making its protest," declared the *Philadelphia Bulletin*. The issue was not whether Trotter and the NIERL were disrespectful to President Wilson, explained the *New York Express*. The issue was the fact that the "segregation of the colored clerks in the U.S. departments . . . is a shameful outrage." The *New Republic* severely faulted the president for condoning a policy that was "bitterly resented by colored people throughout the country." "Perhaps the language of the spokesman was not tactful," admitted the *Boston Traveler and Evening Herald*, but "the systematic denial of manhood rights to black men in America is the crying disgrace of the century." The president "would never have rebuked white callers in the superior way he did his black ones," maintained the *New Haven Register*. "We must screen you off," wrote the *Rochester Post-Express* in sarcasm, "but we will make things comfortable for you behind the screen." And Frank Cobb's *New York World*, an influential supporter of most Wilson policies, castigated the president's "Jim Crow government" as "a small, mean, petty discrimination" and "a reproach to his Administration and to the great political principles which he represents." In taking issue with Wilson's stated view of segregation, Cobb stressed, "Whether the President thinks so or not, the segregation rule was promulgated as a deliberate discrimination against Negro employees."[34]

Astonishingly, especially in light of the Trotter incident, some in the northern liberal press were still reluctant to hold Wilson responsible for Jim Crow in government departments and called on the progressive Democrat to take action against the "race-hatred fomenters." The president "has a chance . . . to be a second Abraham Lincoln by starting and leading a movement that will emancipate the race," wrote the irrepressible Wilson optimist Oswald Villard in the New York *Evening Post.* The *Springfield Republican* was careful not to even mention Wilson's name in response to the Trotter episode. Instead, the newspaper blamed the Jim Crow policy on "southern influence now dominating those departments." In the Midwest, the liberal Des Moines *Register Leader* explained to its readers that "segregation has been resorted to because the southern leaders in Congress are bound to have the Negro eliminated from the public service."[35]

Other northern newspapers echoed the sentiments of their counterparts further south. Black protestors should follow the example of leaders such as "Booker T. Washington" and live with segregation, advised the New York *Daily Eagle.* "Forced" integration in the workplace is "hurtful" to both blacks and whites, the paper continued. The *Syracuse Herald* chastised blacks who "insist upon thrusting themselves into white company." The segregation matter had been settled for the time being, believed the *Meriden* (Connecticut) *Journal* in echoing the views of the president: "Booker T. Washington answered the segregation question. . . . [A]s long as there is a clash of the races they should be kept apart."[36]

Many members of the southern white press, which had ignored the protest efforts altogether up to this point, were unable to contain themselves once they caught wind of the shocking incident at the White House. Not surprisingly, they were critical and mean-spirited in their attacks against Trotter and the NIERL. "The Tucker darky who tried to 'sass' the President is not a Booker T. Washington type of colored man," fumed the Beaumont (Texas) *Enterprise.* "He is merely a nigger." The *Macon* (Georgia) *Telegraph* blasted Trotter for regarding himself "as an equal." "The Negro will always grab an 'ell' if you grant him an inch," continued the newspaper. These "self-styled Negro leaders" are simply injuring their "cause" by such "offensive demands for racial social equality," barked the *New Orleans Times Picayune.* "There is some difference between the negro and the nigger," clarified the *Shreveport* (Louisiana) *Sunday Caucasian.* "Booker T. Washington is a negro." The "insolent William Trotter" is "a nigger." Another southern newspaper, angered that Trotter would have "Negro men work side by side with white women," blurted, "[f]oolish and disrespectful Negro!" "Trotter assumed a tone and an attitude in addressing the President that a Colored man from any other part of the country wouldn't have assumed," wrote the *Savannah Morning News* in boldface type. And the *El Paso Times* called Trotter a "Jamaica coon" who would be made to demonstrate that he was truly a "trotter" if he should visit "any representative southern community."[37]

Not all southern white opinion was prejudiced in its analysis of the Trotter-Wilson meeting, however. Two or three socially conscious southern editors from Kentucky were progressive on the race issue as well as on economic matters. DuBois referred to those enlightened newspapermen as part of the "new south." Kentucky, however, had a long history of breeding men and ideas that clashed with southern norms, the most famous being Abraham Lincoln and the border state's official neutrality during the Civil War. But the Bluegrass State also gave rise to such controversial men as Richard Mentor Johnson, vice president in the Martin Van Buren administration (1837–1841), who ceremonially married his slave and, to the dismay of southerners, treated her as an equal partner while making attempts to introduce their biracial children into polite Washington society. In 1896 Kentucky's own U.S. Supreme Court justice, John Marshall Harlan, one of only two southerners on the bench, vigorously dissented and rebuked his colleagues for approving racial segregation on public transportation in *Plessy v. Ferguson*. And nestled in the mountains of Kentucky, Berea College became the first academic institution in the South to transcend and, for many southerners, transgress racial and gender barriers by opening its doors for both students and faculty to blacks and whites, men and women.

Now Kentucky clashed once again with its southern brethren (and some in the North) over a controversial issue involving race. The *Lexington Herald,* edited by social reformer Desha Breckinridge, was one of those leading the charge below the Mason-Dixon line for a more universal application of equal rights extending to all races and creeds. The gutsy newspaper, aware that its outspoken racial views would be "condemned bitterly" in its section of the country, charged prejudiced white officials in the federal government with contributing to acts of violence and repression against African Americans in the South. "It is but a step in descent from the position taken by those public officials in Washington who segregate one race to the public official in a southern state who advocates lynch law," explained a distressed *Herald*. "The example of the higher official will be cited by the lower official as justification for his course." The outspoken critic of southern race policy, Col. Henry Waterson of the *Louisville Courier-Journal,* whose picture—accompanied by a favorable caption or article—was featured more than once on the front page of the pro-black *Guardian*, expressed anger at Trotter's "impudent" behavior in the "sanctity of the White House" but nevertheless declared that "the segregation order should be revoked." The article ended by calling on "Mr. Wilson" to "take matters . . . into his own hands, and restore the status quo."[38]

Black ministers in the South, although less open about their enthusiasm, praised Trotter for standing up to the president. It appears that several of the numerous "congratulation letters" that poured into the *Guardian* office after the meeting and were subsequently published in the paper came from black ministers living in the South.[39]

Although the black press expressed mixed feelings regarding Trotter's behavior, most were incensed by the president's treatment of him at the White House. Even many of the newspapers in the National Negro Press Association, reputed as mirroring the views of Booker T. Washington, lashed out at Wilson and the Democratic administration following the Trotter meeting. The *Guardian* credited the southern black press with taking the "high ground" in standing up for the NIERL and moving "a step far in advance for the race in that section." Although James Ross of the Buffalo *Informer* and Washington successor Robert Moton assured President Wilson that "Negroes, generally, do not in any way approve of Mr. Trotter's conduct at the White House," most, with the exception of his staunchest opponents, believed the equal rights advocate was "a brave man" for standing up to the president.[40] "There is not another Negro in the whole race who would have committed such a performance," trumpeted the *Birmingham Reporter*. The *Washington Bee* sarcastically remarked that Trotter's "inexcusable failure" was in forgetting his "place" when speaking in the presence of or to a "white man." The *Richmond St. Luke Herald* raked President Wilson over the coals for breaking his earlier promises to Trotter and miserably failing the black race. A cartoon in *Crisis* satirized Wilson as unwilling to hear the black delegation until his henchmen had utterly broken their spirits. Trotter's own newspaper used the episode at the White House as a rallying cry for African Americans to "realize the danger" and "exert pressure upon the federal government, both direct and through others." "We can win if we will work," concluded the article in a victorious tone.[41]

WILSON BASHING AT NIERL MASS MEETINGS

Trotter was elevated to celebrity status after the Wilson meeting. He was in demand as never before and toured the country speaking before ecstatic crowds. One black newspaper, in the midst of all the excitement surrounding the "incident," exaggerated Trotter's notoriety when it boasted that he now had a "world-wide reputation." There was no doubt, however, that he had managed to exceed Booker T. Washington, for the moment at least, as the most famous black leader in America. Most important, Trotter had become a symbol of black strength and fortitude in the face of a powerful white enemy. The episode had created an atmosphere of infectious optimism among many African Americans that an irrevocable step had been taken toward equality. For a moment, the future looked bright.[42]

Immediately following the Wilson meeting, Trotter and other NIERL delegates spoke at several churches, auditoriums, and clubs in the North. They used the opportunity to motivate people in protest and to recruit members for the NIERL. The speakers tended to be more emboldened in these mass meetings and lashed out at Wilson in more aggressive rhetoric than ever before, and the audiences were wildly excited. Yet the meetings were not as numerous or well organized as the ones held by the NAACP. Lacking resources and a strong organizational base, they appeared to have been more a sporadic response to the Trotter episode than strategic planning on the part of the NIERL.

The NIERL meetings were first held in the frenzied atmosphere of the nation's capital following the conference. A few days after the NIERL representatives met with the president, Trotter and some of the delegation members addressed a mass meeting at the Second Baptist Church in Washington, D.C. One newspaper, in describing the meeting, printed the inflammatory byline "W. M. Trotter Causes Riotous Scene, Describing White House Interview," a statement that was quickly denied the next day in the *Washington Evening Times*.[43]

Yet things did get a bit wild that night. Trotter was boiling over from his contentious exchange with the president. A Philadelphia friend described him as being "mad enough to eat nails." The crowd, along with the rest of Trotter's White House entourage, seemed ready to burst out of their skins as well. The delegates—including Thomas Walker, NIERL branch chairman in Washington, and Maurice Spencer—opened by brashly defending the race leader's behavior at the White House while castigating the president. Hardly a word could be uttered without the audience becoming aroused. Jeers and hissing echoed through the church whenever segregation or Wilson was mentioned.

When Trotter stood to speak, his voice was drowned out for five minutes by the cheers of an ecstatic audience clapping and stomping its feet, and he looked on "impressively" as if he were absorbing the energy of the moment. As he tried to describe the meeting with the president, he was continuously interrupted by people chanting his name, and every time Wilson was mentioned the crowd booed and yelled "put him out." Finally, with animated

THE WILSON PERFIDY OR PROMISE VS. PERFORMANCE

IF IT IS "POLITICAL BLACKMAIL TO MENTION NON-FULFILLMENT OF PLEDGES MADE BEFORE ELEC-TION AFTER ELECTED, WHY ARE NOT THOSE EXACTING PLEDGES BEFORE ELECTION SO NOTIFIED THEN?

Political cartoon of Trotter meetings with President Wilson, Boston Guardian. *Moorfield Storey Papers,* courtesy *Library of Congress.*

gestures, Trotter barreled on in describing the meeting while competing with a constant barrage of "laughter and hooting." With the audience quieting down to a murmur, Trotter yelled, "We carried out our mission. The main issue for us was to force from the President, after two years['] effort, an ex-pression of his views." "The President," continued the leader as the hum of the audience, anticipating a climax, began to grow louder, "declared in favor of race segregation," and the crowd let loose a roar of disapproval.[44]

After the meeting, resolutions of protest were adopted to the "American people" and printed in black and liberal white newspapers. The language here is unique, as it describes not only a political or a social problem but also a serious moral issue with a prophetic twang:

> We believe that the nation is passing through a physical and spiritual crisis, and that the issues of life and death will be decided ultimately when the people of the nation shall be called upon in the usual way to pronounce judgment for or against the responsible government at Washington in its unrighteous policy of discriminating against the citizens of the country on account of race and color.[45]

Another mass meeting was held at the Asbury M.E. Church the Sunday after the White House meeting. Although there is virtually no record of the proceedings, the meeting appears to have been addressed by delegates from the Trotter entourage, and it is not clear if Trotter was the principal speaker. The equal rights advocate also addressed the famous Washington-based Mu-So-Lit Club, an exclusive musical, social, and literary organization composed of men from the city's black middle class. Trotter once again described his meeting with the president and lambasted the leader for his attitude on federal Jim Crow. The club sent resolutions of protest to Wilson.[46]

Following on the heels of the Washington mass meetings, Trotter spoke to "enthusiastic" Boston audiences eager to hear the details of the White House meeting from their hometown hero. The Interdenominational Ministers' Union of Greater Boston sponsored a "mammoth" meeting of 900 people at the Twelfth Baptist Church in Roxbury. After describing the details of the heated exchange, Trotter forcefully launched into an exhortation as he called the president a "deceiver, a pledge-breaker and the most dishonorable man that has ever been President of the United States." The audience gave its speaker a standing ovation that lasted several minutes.[47]

On November 23, Faneuil Hall was packed with people eager to hear firsthand the "truth from Mr. Trotter." But before he spoke, the militant Rev. Montrose Thornton, who presided over the meeting, opened by declaring "to the whole world" that his race would "oppose" segregation to "the last of our whole might." "Jeff Davis could not have said any more if he had been in the White House," he continued. "Down with Woodrow Wilson as the leader of this great nation," screamed the preacher as the audience broke out in thunderous applause. Dr. Horace Bumstead spoke next and was greeted with a salute of handkerchiefs, a welcome gesture to the white speaker from a mostly black audience. Finally, the man of the hour, William Monroe Trotter, approached the podium as the audience exploded with excitement in prolonged applause that seemed to last forever. The black leader repeated the details of his meeting with the president and concluded his remarks in a defiant tone. "I have been taught in the Massachusetts schools and in one of her colleges," echoed the larger-than-life hero in the hall of freedom where William Lloyd Garrison and Wendell Phillips once stirred audiences, "that the President of the United States is not a king and is not to be approached with cowering spirit or any wavering." The audience roared with applause.[48]

If President Wilson's ill temperament during the November 16 meeting was influenced by the recent loss of his wife, Trotter's short fuse was perhaps ignited before the meeting took place as well. About a month before the NIERL delegation met with the president, Byron Gunner, along with the officers of the Washington branch, had made "inquiries" into the continued Jim Crow in federal departments. Shortly after the White House meeting, the *Guardian* printed the results of the investigation as they were presented to the president. Some of this was new, whereas other instances were either a continuation or an increase of Jim Crow from a year earlier.[49]

Black employees in the Bureau of Engraving and Printing were segregated "not only in dressing rooms but in working positions" and at "eating tables" as well. In the auditor's office of the Navy Department, an adjunct of Treasury, "toilets" were segregated, and blacks were forced to work together behind screens erected to keep them out of "view" of white clerks and visitors. Black men and women were segregated from whites on the sixth, seventh, and eighth floors in the office of auditor of the Post Office. Toilets were still segregated in the Main Treasury Building, described by the *Guardian* as the most "degrading" and "insulting" example of Jim Crow of all; and toilet segregation was enforced in the offices of auditor of the Interior, Post Office, War, and State departments. Even though there was just one black employee in the Marine Hospital Service building, the NIERL investigation found he also was required to use a toilet set aside for his use only. And in the Government Printing Office, black female employees were "herded" together at workstations and made to use separate toilets.[50]

During mass meetings and in the pages of black newspapers, the NIERL used the details of this latest investigation, along with the Wilson meeting, to rile people in protest. In January 1915 Trotter stumped through the Midwest, lambasting the hypocrisy of Wilson who had given insincere "assurances" to the delegation a year earlier that he would "investigate the segregation"—although there seems to have been no record giving details or even a synopsis of his western speeches.

Trotter used his sudden popularity to recruit members for the NIERL. It appears, however, that the NIERL never kept official membership numbers, much less the number of new members after the Trotter-Wilson meeting and the Midwest tour. The only references to membership growth appeared in a few commentaries, particularly in the *Guardian,* and they never mentioned how many new members had joined. Instead, they only vaguely pointed out that "new members" had been "recruited." Yet it does appear that some contributions began to trickle in to the coffers of the NIERL as a result of the publicized Trotter-Wilson meeting. The *Guardian* pages during this time are full of numerous contribution amounts, along with the names of the contributors, from all over the country.[51]

In addition, at the invitation of his militant comrade Ida Wells-Barnett, Trotter stopped in Chicago on his western tour to speak to her Negro Fellowship League (NFL). He was hugely popular with African Americans in the Windy City. Almost immediately after his speech, NFL members voted to establish a Chicago branch of the NIERL with Wells-Barnett as vice president. From that moment on, Wells-Barnett merged the activities of the NFL with the NIERL, often using NFL stationery to conduct business for the latter. Although technically the two remained autonomous organizations, her press releases rarely mentioned one without the other, and together they served as a powerful platform for her protest activities. Although it is unclear if any other NIERL branches were formed out west, the Chicago branch, under the guidance of Wells-Barnett, became a solid and active mechanism for battling racial injustice.[52]

Regardless of whether the NIERL grew in numbers, branches, and capital, however, one thing was certain: Trotter's coup d'état, for a moment, had made him the most controversial and notorious—and for some the most celebrated—black man in the country.

But as fate would have it, the potentially greatest Jim Crow protest movement America had ever seen, and the first significant collective effort on a national level since abolitionist days, would be drowned out prematurely by the clamor over what was quickly becoming a dangerous international war. Like the NAACP, the NIERL and its cause for justice at home could not compete with the daily attention given to the growing conflict abroad by the liberal press as well as the white mainstream media. On the eve of World War I, international matters had taken precedence over national problems.

Unlike the NAACP, which was positioning itself to fight Jim Crow in the courts, the NIERL was mostly a one-track protest organization with no legal department or ambitions, and thus it had no recourse when protest fell on deaf ears. The closest it came to a legal department was in the Chicago NIERL branch. Here, under the dynamic leadership of Wells-Barnett, it collectively battled Jim Crow legislation on the local, state, and national levels—often enlisting support from other groups such as the National Association of Colored Women.

Trotter sometimes gave the impression, particularly in his professional correspondence, that the NIERL was much larger and better organized than it actually was. Yet it was the sheer force of his personality that was huge and that reverberated all over the nation. But Trotter, a force in and of himself, was not enough. He desperately needed others to help make the earth-shattering impact he dreamed of, but they were not ready. The NIERL as a collective organization was and would continue to be relatively small. Moreover, the lack of a sufficient organizational base and financial department, despite the recent recruitment efforts, continued to weaken an already faltering NIERL. Many of its officers and members would eventually fall away and devote themselves to building the NAACP, already growing by leaps and bounds, into the largest organization for battling racial injustice in the twentieth century.

NOTES

1. November 1914 news clippings in William Monroe Trotter file, Boston Herald Traveler Library, Boston, MA [hereafter Trotter file]; *Guardian* excerpt with a brief description of Rev. Ricks, November 15, 1913, in Box 6, Moorfield Storey Papers, Manuscript Division, Library of Congress, Washington, DC [hereafter Storey Papers]; *Washington Star,* November 12, 1914.

2. Gunner obituary in *Crisis,* May 1922, 28; "Remarks of President Gunner," *Guardian,* November 28, 1914, Box 6, Storey Papers; David L. Lewis, *W.E.B. DuBois: Biography of a Race, 1868–1919* (New York: Henry Holt, 1993), 320; Evelyn Brooks Higginbotham, *Righteous Discontent: The Women's Movement in the Black Baptist Church, 1880–1920* (Cambridge: Harvard University Press, 1993), 101.

3. "Address Read to President by M. W. Spencer," and "For Best Interests of Both," *Guardian,* November 28, 1914, in Box 6, Storey Papers.

4. "Address of Mr. Walker," *Guardian,* November 28, 1914, Box 6, Storey Papers.

5. November 1914 news clippings in Trotter file; *Washington Herald,* November 16, 1914, quoted in Laurence J.W. Hayes, "The Negro Federal Government Worker, 1883–1938" (M.A. thesis, Howard University Graduate School, 1941), 44; Stephen Fox, *The Guardian of Boston: William Monroe Trotter* (New York: Atheneum, 1970), 180; Cary T. Grayson, *Woodrow Wilson: An Intimate Memoir* (Washington, DC: Potomac Books, 1960), 36.

6. James M. McPherson, *The Struggle for Equality* (Princeton: Princeton University Press, 1992), 343–344.

7. Christine Lunardini, "Standing Firm: William Monroe Trotter's Meetings With Woodrow Wilson, 1913–1914," *Journal of Negro History* 64 (Summer 1979): 255–263; *Crisis,* January 1915, 119–120; "Boston Still Stirred Up by Negro William Monroe Trotter," December 1967 article in Guardian of Boston Collection, Mugar Memorial Library, Boston University, Boston, MA; untitled news clipping in Trotter file; Arthur S. Link, *Wilson, the New Freedom* (Princeton: Princeton University Press, 1956), 463–465; Fox, 181; Lewis, 511.

8. Link, 463; Lewis, 511.

9. Lunardini, 255–256; *Crisis,* January 1915, 119. I have relied on four main sources while describing the second Trotter-Wilson meeting. Although much of the dialogue was taken from a printed transcript by Charles Swem, White House transcriber present during this meeting, and whose transcript was published in 1979 by Lunardini in *Journal of Negro History,* I have also incorporated details of the Trotter-Wilson meeting from *Guardian,* November 1914, *Crisis,* January 1915, and Stephen Fox's *The Guardian of Boston.* These latter two sources obtained their details from newspaper reports and printed interviews from the protestors present at the White House on November 12, 1914. I believe this will give the reader a more balanced perspective particularly since Swem's transcript, although

mostly accurate, contains a few errors and omissions. For example, Swem attributes remarks made by Ida-Wells Barnett during the first meeting to Trotter (see Chapter 5, note 66). In another case, he records a protestor's remarks, but omits the identity of the person making them. Furthermore, a crosscheck of Swem's transcript with the protestors' remarks and reports in *Crisis, Guardian,* and other newspapers, reveals variations from the Swem transcript as well, including the emotionally charged atmosphere surrounding the contentious White House meeting.

10. Lunardini, 257–258.

11. Ibid., 259.

12. Lunardini, 259; *Crisis,* January 1915, 119–120.

13. Lunardini, 259; *Crisis,* January 1915, 120.

14. Lunardini, 260; *Guardian,* November 21, 1914.

15. Lunardini, 260–261; *Crisis,* January 1915, 119–120; *Guardian,* November 21, 1914; Fox, 180–181.

16. Lunardini, 260–261; *Crisis,* January 1915, 120; *Guardian,* November 21, 1914; Fox, 181.

17. Lunardini, 261; *Crisis,* January 1915, 120; *Guardian,* November 21, 1914; Fox, 181.

18. Lunardini, 261; Fox, 181.

19. Lunardini, 261–262; Fox, 181.

20. Lunardini, 262; Fox, 181.

21. Ibid.

22. Ray Stannard Baker, *Following the Color Line: American Negro Citizenship in the Progressive Era* (New York: Harper Torchbooks, 1964), 136; Lunardini, 259.

23. Fox, 181. President Wilson's remorse at losing his temper during the Trotter meeting is taken from a later correspondence between Joseph Daniels and President Franklin Roosevelt, June 10, 1933, in which the former recounts a conversation he had with Wilson shortly after the meeting. See Fox, 182, and note 51.

24. Untitled news clipping in Trotter file.

25. Untitled newspaper excerpt in Trotter file; *Guardian* extract entitled "President Wilson Charges Insult to Cover Endorsement of Segregation," November 12, 1914, in Box 6, Storey Papers.

26. Oswald Garrison Villard to Archibald Grimke, November 11, 1913, Box 39-25, Archibald Grimke Papers, Moorland-Spingarn Research Center, Howard University, Washington, DC.

27. Lewis, 511. This is all the more amazing when considered in the context of remarks made recently by former president George Bush. He described to an interviewer that people will often come to the White House intending to "tell the President off," but by the time they actually enter the Oval Office and are seated before the chief executive their "knees are shaking" as a sense of awe and intimidation overwhelms them. "Save Our History: The White House: 200th Anniversary," A&E Television Networks, History Channel, January 26, 2001.

28. *New York Times,* November 13, 1914, quoted in Wolgemuth, 165, and note 19.

29. Commentary on *Savannah Tribune* article in *Guardian,* November 28, 1914, extract in Box 6, Storey Papers.

30. Pillsbury to Grimke, December 21, 1914, Nerney to Grimke, December 7, 1914, Box 39-25, Archibald Grimke Papers, Moorland-Spingarn Research Center, Howard University, Washington, DC.

31. Untitled *Guardian* extract, undated, in Box 6, Storey Papers.

32. Tumulty to Villard, November 18, 1914, quoted in Kellogg, 174. Also, Tumulty seems to have been sympathetic to the protestors' concerns in his private meetings with Villard and others, and on at least one occasion he made an attempt to bring one of the protest letters to the president's attention. After reading a protest letter addressed to the president from Robert Wood, Tumulty attached this note to his boss: "The secretary suggests that the President read the whole of the attached letter"; in Arthur S. Link, ed., *The Papers of Woodrow Wilson*, Vol. 28 (Princeton: Princeton University Press, 1966–1977), 115.

33. Tumulty to Villard, November 18, 1914, in Link, *Papers* 28: 115.

34. Press quotations in *Crisis,* January 1915, 120–127; *New York World,* November 13, 1914, quoted in Fox, 183; *Guardian* extract entitled "White Northern Press on Wilson-Trotter Incident," undated, in Box 6, Storey Papers; Lunardini, 263.

35. *Crisis,* January 1915, 120–127. Most newspaper comments on the Trotter-Wilson meeting are found in this source; others are found in various issues of *Guardian.*

36. Ibid.

37. Ibid.; Fox, 182; various newspaper excerpts quoted in *Guardian,* November 28, 1914, Box 6, Storey Papers.

38. *Crisis,* January 1915, 120–127, *Crisis,* November 1913, 333, and front page of *Guardian,* November 28, 1914, all in Box 6, Storey Papers.

39. *Guardian,* November 28, 1914, Box 6, Storey Papers.

40. James Ross to Wilson, November 12, 1914, Robert Moton to Wilson, November 16, 1914, Woodrow Wilson Papers, quoted in Ballew, 67–68. Moton seems to have been more accommodating to white prejudice and more critical of black equal rights advocates than even Washington was.

41. *Crisis,* January 1915, 120–127, *Crisis,* November 1913, 333, front page of *Guardian,* November 28, 1914, and excerpts in undated, untitled, all in Box 6, Storey Papers.

42. *Maryland Voice,* excerpt in *Guardian,* November 21, 1914, Box 6, Storey Papers.

43. *Washington Herald* quoted in "Jeers at Mention of Wilson Denied," reprinted from *Washington Evening Times,* November 16, 1914, in *Guardian,* November 28, 1914, Box 6, Storey Papers.

44. Meeting at Second Baptist Church in Washington, D.C., described in "Mass Meeting of D.C.," *Guardian,* November 28, 1914, Box 6, Storey Papers; "Negroes Jeer Wilson's Name," *Washington Herald,* November 16, 1914, Series 4, Box 231, Woodrow Wilson Papers, Manuscript Division, Library of Congress, Washington, D.C.

45. "Statement to the American People by Mass Meeting Under Independent Equal Rights League at District of Columbia," *Guardian,* November 28, 1914, Box 6, Storey Papers.

46. *Guardian* extracts entitled "Mass Meeting of D. of C.," "President Wilson Charges Insult to Cover Endorsement of Segregation," and "Washington Mu-So-Lit Club Endorsed Equal Rights League in Its Anti-Segregation Protest," November 28, 1914, all in Box 6, Storey Papers; Fox, 186.

47. "Trotter Tells of His Visit," *Boston Herald*, indecipherable date, extract in Trotter file; "Trotter Calls Wilson a Deceiver," November 28, 1914, reprint from *Boston Herald*, November 14, 1914, Box 6, Storey Papers.

48. November 23 Faneuil Hall mass meeting described in *Guardian* articles entitled "Great Welcome Home," undated, advertisement for Citizen's Anti-Segregation Meeting at Faneuil Hall, November 21, 1914, and "Faneuil Hall Meeting," November 28, 1914, Box 6, Storey Papers.

49. *Guardian* article with subtitle caption "Cases of Segregation," undated, Box 6, Storey Papers.

50. Ibid.; "Race Discrimination," *Boston Advertiser*, October 24, 1914, in Box 39-25, Archibald Grimke Papers, Moorland-Spingarn Research Center, Howard University, Washington, DC; Hayes, 38. This last source maintains that segregation under Wilson possibly started in the Navy Department, 39.

51. *Guardian* extract with subtitle caption "Cases of Segregation," undated, Box 6, Storey Papers.

52. Linda O. McMurray, *To Keep the Waters Troubled: The Life of Ida B. Wells* (New York: Oxford University Press, 1998), 302–303.

8

THE STRUGGLE MOVES ON

Was the protest of federal Jim Crow successful in accomplishing its objectives? The answer to this question is varied. By as early as October 1913, the *Springfield Republican* announced that segregation had been "halted," and in December John Lorance of the *Boston Advertiser* proclaimed that federal Jim Crow had "not only been effectively checked and therefore stopped, but it is rapidly being . . . wiped off the slate." The National Association for the Advancement of Colored People (NAACP) and the National Independent Political League (NIPL), eager to believe these reports, optimistically hailed the news as evidence that federal Jim Crow was being "undone." Freeman Murray hastily confirmed the Lorance report in the *Guardian*. And the NAACP went as far as to send President Wilson a letter on January 6, 1914, commending him for ending federal segregation.[1]

The victory celebration, however, was premature. In 1914 the NIERL and the NAACP uncovered more Jim Crow in several federal departments, which confirmed a sustained pattern of segregating, downgrading, and dismissing or terminating African American employees. By 1915 the NAACP was still grappling with how to handle the year-old civil service photograph policy that was quickly becoming a widespread requirement for federal job applicants and a trouble-free way to identify and exclude African Americans from federal employment. All of this led NAACP national director Charles Russell to complain that "segregation had greatly increased and could now be found anywhere." Around the same time, May Childs Nerney, in a letter to Grimke, expressed her frustration at the continued segregation in federal departments.[2] And in the December 1914 issue of the *Nation,* Villard attacked not only Wilson but the entire political system for failing to do anything about Jim Crow.[3] To make matters worse, by the time Wilson's appointments had been confirmed, only nine of thirty-one African Americans remained in office, and eight of those were Republican holdovers.[4] After more than a year and a half of intensive protest, Jim Crow not only remained in the federal government but was rapidly spreading and thereby severely limiting one of the most important avenues of black professional and economic mobility. With this said, was the protest a total failure?

In regard to affecting federal Jim Crow in any significant way, the answer to this question is probably yes. This is contrary to Kathleen Wolgemuth's optimistic conclusion that "Negro opposition" had been "victorious" in ending "segregation as a recognized system."[5] Although the protest never abolished federal Jim Crow, it did succeed in stopping some of the discrimination—at least temporarily—in a few departments.

The NAACP hailed its efforts as a victory in March 1914 after the new assistant treasury secretary, Charles S. Hamlin, issued an order forbidding racial discrimination in the new Bureau of Engraving and Printing building. Hamlin, ironically, had replaced the racist John Skelton Williams when the latter was appointed comptroller of treasury. Described as a "friend of the Negro," he eagerly assisted the NAACP in battling Jim Crow in parts of Treasury. Yet Hamlin was only one man in a Jim Crow administration. Moreover, as a progressive New Englander, he never shared the intimate friendship with his boss, the southern-born William Gibbs McAdoo, that his predecessor and McAdoo fellow southerner Williams had. Thus, Hamlin's influence and power were limited. And with such a high turnover rate among the top personnel at Treasury during the Wilson years, Hamlin, the lone racial justice liberal, soon moved on as well.[6]

In November 1913 William Monroe Trotter was convinced that an NIPL telegram protesting segregation in the Department of Commerce had caused the policy to be "acted upon." The *Guardian* declared in late 1914, more than likely erroneously, that the pro-segregationist auditor of the Post Office

Department, Charles Kram, was "undoing" racial segregation in his office as a result of the protests. And Archibald Grimke, in a vigorous fight during 1914, succeeded in getting a handful of black federal employees reinstated and promoted, and he persuasively argued against racist legislative proposals—some pertaining directly to segregation in the federal service—in front of House and Senate committees.[7]

Kram had been outspoken regarding his commitment to a segregated workforce even before the Wilson years. And although the protest succeeded in preventing racists from pushing federal Jim Crow as forcefully as they wished, Kram seems to have been undeterred. He not only segregated his lower-grade black employees, but he also removed practically every African American clerk from his office and had them downgraded and transferred.[8]

With only a few minor exceptions (and, as seen, even the impacts of these are in doubt), it appears little progress was made in altering the newly entrenched pattern of Jim Crow in the federal bureaucracy. In fact, by the conclusion of the Wilson years Jim Crow could be found not only in the federal departments but also in the Senate lunchroom in the United States Capitol building, the galleries of the U.S. Senate, and the restaurant and lunchroom of the Library of Congress.[9]

Yet the failure of the protest against federal Jim Crow had less to do with the dynamics of the protest and more to do with the times. In the early twentieth century most whites were still unsympathetic or indifferent to the protestors' concerns. Efforts to segregate African Americans in the civil service found them unresponsive at best. Although the protest was national in scope, it was never more than a small fraction of the population, consisting of blacks and liberal whites, that opposed federal Jim Crow in the first place. Besides the fact that the federal government had essentially been recaptured by the Confederacy, the North, displaying a striking indifference and often sympathy in regard to the racist policies of its southern neighbor and becoming increasingly Jim Crow itself, had offered little resistance. This led an exasperated Nerney to complain that Jim Crow has "the sympathy of the majority of unthinking people, even in the North."[10]

Besides this, the mainstream media had practically ignored the Wilson protest, and there were very few sympathetic members of Congress to champion the cause. From the outset, the protestors were fighting an uphill battle against a policy that had been widely accepted as a national institution by a large part of the white population and that would remain deeply entrenched in the South for more than fifty years. African Americans as well still lacked the resources and widespread support not only from whites but, most important, from indigenous members of the race who would have given their cause momentum. If, as Douglas Brinkley pointed out, blacks in the Deep South as late as the early 1950s had not quite abandoned the "go-along-to-get-along" ways to collectively fight Jim Crow, it is not hard to imagine the reluctance that must have prevailed fifty years earlier when accommodation held sway in African American life.[11]

THE DIALECTIC STRUGGLE OF RACIAL ADVANCEMENT

Although historians have placed much emphasis on the opposition between economic uplift/accommodation and agitation during the early twentieth century, the conflict between them comprised several currents that contained tensions and contradictions. These two views were not always incompatible with each other, ideologically or in practice, and were sometimes considered together by both radical and conservative leaders as viable approaches for advancing and protecting African Americans in a Jim Crow society. Radicals who saw protest as the best option almost always supported economic uplift but condemned accommodation, and conservatives, although believing the go-along-to-get-along approach was the safest policy for the time being, rarely endorsed—at least intentionally—the worst manifestations of Jim Crow. Moreover, some transferred their loyalties from one camp to another, and others straddled the fence between the conservatives and the radicals. Booker T. Washington would covertly challenge disfranchisement and publicly denounce lynching, peonage, and federal Jim Crow, whereas radicals such as W.E.B. DuBois and Trotter, along with the NAACP, would openly support or commend industrial education.

This is not an attempt to superficially blend very real differences in black thought in the early twentieth century or to downplay the factionalism that existed within strategies for racial uplift. It is only intended to briefly point out that black thought and methodology, as a response to an intensely antiblack racist order, were full of complexities that have been too often interpreted and blurred in the dichotomous contest between protest and accommodation. With this in mind, strategies and alternatives for black mobility are presented here instead as a dialectical process of racial advancement where opposing forces, internally and externally, push and pull against each other in a sort of tug-of-war—sharing some aspects of the opposition while rejecting others—until one side or something combining aspects of both or something altogether different emerges.

Besides the seeming contradictions and contrapositions within a strategy and a movement itself and among its participants and leaders and opponents, there is also the *historical* dialectic for racial advancement. In fact, perhaps nowhere in American history is the historical dialectical process so striking as in the movement—this continuous tension between progress and resistance—to advance African Americans.

Here we have a unique opportunity to see the dynamics of this struggle in progress and the emergence, particularly after the Wilson protest, of what would become the dominant approach among black leaders for racial advancement in the twentieth century.

In immediate post-emancipation America (although the dialectical process certainly began earlier), equal rights proponents, black and white, sought to guarantee the transition of African Americans into the democratic fabric by protecting and advancing black political and civil rights. Encountering severe resistance—such as the infamous Black Codes—and a national political establishment divided between white southern appeasement and black empowerment, not to mention differences among black equality advocates themselves as to the extent and type of reforms needed, Reconstruction precariously emerged as a noble effort to make democracy a reality for African Americans. With this process moving forward, white opposition soon forcefully reasserted itself through terror and intimidation and by local and state Jim Crow ordinances, statutes, laws, and practices. In short, the southern white power structure sought nothing less than to strip blacks of any semblance of equality with whites by any means necessary, thus intensely resisting the reconstruction of the former slaves into American citizens.

Although this had the effect of severely choking African American prospects, blacks resisted with tactical arguments on the most viable options for maintaining individual and collective power in an increasingly hostile environment. They continued to exercise the franchise and run for office whenever and wherever feasible. African American leaders argued eloquently—often from the floors of the white-dominated national and state legislatures—for education, economic opportunities, and political and civil rights. Some protested individually and collectively through sit-ins and boycotts and in more subtle ways, such as through attitudes and behavior that refused to give deference to whites; and others advocated armed self-defense and organized resistance to the terrorism of white mob violence.

Jim Crow practices and laws and antiblack violence could not stop African Americans from reaching for equality. By the turn of the twentieth century, however, the U.S. Supreme Court finally enshrined white supremacy–black inferiority in national law, thereby opening a Pandora's box of horrors as rank-and-file southerners added their own deadly twist of a ferocious physical and psychological terrorism for blacks who resisted, often masked in the pretext of white female rape. Moreover, a chorus of bourgeoisie white voices—professors, scientists, ministers, politicians, businessmen, entertainers, and advertisers—had created a "theodicy of whiteness," to borrow Kevin Gaines's suggestively burning moral indictment of white power during this time.[12] This made the utter degradation and exploitation of African Americans morally acceptable and sometimes even obligatory to preserve what had become a divinity of whiteness.

Out of this newly hazardous world arose Booker T. Washington who, rather than resist the devastation of black equality and personhood, advocated a tactical retreat for African Americans. With the consent and help of whites who had created and supported Jim Crow, he advised his race to relinquish its political and civil rights and build from within. Almost overnight he became the most visible and powerful black leader in America. Yet the black protest tradition was still an active force (a fact often eclipsed by the colossal shadow of Washington during this time), and almost from the moment of Washington's ascendancy, militant African Americans—although in unity with his advocacy for black economic development—bitterly opposed his acquiescence to Jim Crow.

Although much of the black leadership recognized and incorporated benefits implicit in the other position, as pointed out at the beginning of this section, most outwardly remained stalwarts for either agitation or economic uplift/accommodation, and the two sides consistently attacked each other in what amounted to a ten- or fifteen-year mudslinging campaign. This had much to do with the powerful figure of Washington, who attempted to control public discourse and squash opposition to and alternatives for racial advancement by using what seemed to be a supply of infinite resources at his disposal. Such exclusive command of dialogue and closing of the avenues of discourse bitterly provoked the defensive radicals, and instead of seeking a workable relationship with the other side—which was a possibility—they attacked Washington and magnified the flaws in his philosophy. This entrenched the Tuskegee camp even more and put it on the defensive as well. The result was a narrowly focused and often aggressive debate that restricted the main dialogue to clearly defined but narrow options. Thus both sides, in a sense, defined themselves in light of each other, and the debate between industrial training and higher education and between protest and accommodation took off full force during the first decade of the twentieth century.

By the end of the decade, in the midst of state-sanctioned repression and horrific violence and terror at the hands of white mobs, economic uplift and accommodation as the popular approach began to lose ground. No matter how much blacks desired to escape the humiliation and misery of the outside world and build from within, there was no way of avoiding contact with racist whites. Even a glance in the wrong direction or a misinterpreted facial expression could provoke a violent response from racist whites. With things getting worse day by day, organizations demanding black equality and an end to racial injustice were rising. Strategies were developing and being debated—legal and extralegal—to directly challenge Jim Crow. Even Washington sympathizers began to sound more militant in their columns and oratory.

Yet Washington was still the most popular black leader in America despite the fact that his power and influence were on the wane, and many African Americans still rallied behind his leadership. His equation that economic and moral uplift would eventually dissolve the fetters of race prejudice had not yet been empirically tested, although there was mounting evidence and fierce opinion that the more wealth blacks had accumulated or the more middle-class they seemed, the more whites detested them (later, in an article written shortly before his death, Washington himself inadvertently reinforced this view by emphasizing that whites in the Black Belt were amiable toward the "most ignorant" blacks). But as Gaines maintained, there was still the possibility in the minds of many leaders that a black middle class or something akin—educated, patriarchally structured, moral, and industrious blacks—would gain respectability from whites and pave the way for racial progress. Middle-class values could break down race prejudice and prove African Americans' worthiness through economic progress and individual and familial moral uplift instead of, in Washington's condemnation, the "artificial forcing" of black political and civil rights. This made democratic rights—indeed, human rights—conditional to one's class status or asset value at some future date, a point Gaines aptly stressed in describing the dominant theme and one of the principal weaknesses of uplift ideology.[13]

The confidence that material achievement and moral uplift would gain for blacks the respectability of whites was dealt a serious blow during Woodrow Wilson's first two years in office. Federal Jim Crow was demonstrably a watershed event in which the economic advancement argument was tested and failed to guarantee or protect black economic respectability or equality. Perhaps nowhere had thousands of African Americans achieved what they perceived as a respectable shared group status as they had in federal employment. By sheer merit and determination they had essentially integrated federal employment. And within their communities African Americans were middle-class and often associated with the professional class.

But most important, the ubiquitous presence of African Americans within the federal offices and departments meant they had, in most cases, outperformed the white competition on civil service exams. Here was a striking example of the uplift theory in action. Moreover, federal integration was a present-day fulfillment of Washington's future vision for assimilation and interracial cooperation, and as such it constituted an experiment as to whether it was enough to ensure African Americans' acceptance into the world of white respectability. It was not. The faith that black achievement, this middle-classing of blacks, would convince whites of their ability and humanity and dispel racist stereotypes now seemed unrealistic. Not only did the somewhat equalitarian federal government turn and attempt to crush its black aspirants during the Wilson years, but the relentless protest campaign during this time explicated powerful white resistance to black mobility where, theoretically, in the Washington scheme there should have been very little.

Thus, the protest of federal Jim Crow in 1913–1914 was part of a liminal moment when the economic uplift theory for racial advancement and acquiescence to white racism—with all its tensions, external and internal pressures, and contradictions—began to dialectically give way to a more militant and independent approach to black equality and respectability. Even Washington himself moved visibly beyond accommodation and attacked federal Jim Crow—indeed, the entire system of de jure segregation—and agreed with most of the tactics used in the protest without abandoning his belief in a "constructive" and gradual program for racial advancement while still giving kudos to white superiority. To be sure, economic uplift and white bourgeoisie ideas—including the dominant cultural racist vernacular, along with its class and gender bias—would seep into this new militancy, but no longer would racial advancement depend so much on white permissibility.

Taking control of their destiny, African Americans rose in protest and began to seize the power, individually and collectively, that had been denied them for so long. Signaling this changing attitude, Robert Bagnall, director of branches of the NAACP in the 1920s, wrote: "The old Negro had passed away—a new Negro is here. He is restless, discontented, eager, and ambitious." And this emerging militant attitude manifested in several ways through diverse organizations, outlets, beliefs, activities, and methodologies.[14] They included the ascendancy of a new avant-garde of militant black leadership and thought—including the emergence of black nationalism and, to a lesser degree, the radical left—and the gradual awakening to the potential of collective black power as a force for racial advancement; experimentation with the strategic use and threat of organized marching as a visible mass tactic for protesting racial injustice and achieving group objectives; growing episodes of direct physical confrontation and protest by African American groups and organizations, including blacks' growing willingness to physically resist the bloody riotous terror of white mobs; and the reconstruction of the black image on *black terms* through the cultural achievements and contributions of the Harlem Renaissance and by rescuing the black past from Anglo- and Euro-centric historians in such groundbreaking revisionist black studies and publications as the *Journal of Negro History.*

Perhaps the most enduring manifestation of the militant African American was the rising NAACP and its shift to aggressive litigation for battling racial injustice after the Wilson years. Critics have often faulted the equal rights organization for not directly challenging the American political and economic system as did, for example, the radical left. And its choice battleground in the courts is seen as an abandonment of more aggressive pressure-group tactics and protest. But the NAACP's strategy was nothing short of a radical challenge to the powerfully dominant American doctrine of whiteness. Using the white man's own legal apparatus that institutionalized white supremacy and turning de jure racism on its head, the NAACP would ingeniously attack the system of Jim Crow case by case, law by law, statute by statute until its edifice began to crumble. Moreover, the NAACP's legal approach was nontraditional and considered by some as even unethical, since it used (and crystallized) a "test case" litigation strategy that included staging confrontations that broke the law, such as sit-ins, to create facts and leverage for its cases to challenge racist laws. Prior to the NAACP, with the exception of a few cases such as *Plessy v. Ferguson,* this strategy was almost unheard of.

Although at odds with Marcus Garvey and the Black Nationalist Movement in the 1920s and critical of the radical left, the equal rights organization included leaders and members who sympathized with, and sometimes participated in, these more unconventional efforts to uplift African Americans. In fact, even some of the founders of the NAACP—including William English Walling, Mary White Ovington, and Dr. Henry Moskowitz—were, at least ideologically, on the left; and W.E.B. DuBois, who kept leaning to the left until he finally became a Marxist, also committed himself to unifying and promoting the interests of the African diaspora—sentiments Garvey spent a great deal of time promoting in America. And although it is generally believed that no united organization arose out of the philosophically diverse 1916 Amenia Conference (the first interracial conference of radicals and conservatives to address the problems facing African Americans), many conservatives—including soon-to-be NAACP field secretary James Weldon Johnson—facing a vacuum in leadership after the death of Booker T. Washington in 1915, now joined ranks with the moderates and radicals who began to flow into the growing NAACP. Even the NAACP's old enemy, the *New York Age,* essentially called on African Americans to join the NAACP and for protest organizations to merge with the one group capable of being "on the job all the time."[15]

During the Wilson years, the NAACP experienced a massive growth from 329 members in 1912 to over 100,000 by 1921. And this does not reflect the countless number of sympathizers, particularly African Americans in the South who could not join or endorse the NAACP without fear of violent reprisal—an obstacle to mass southern participation that would plague the association until World War II.

Although it is not clear what measurable impact Wilsonian Jim Crow and the protest had on the NAACP's swelling membership and growing popularity, it does appear to have influenced the formation and growth of numerous branches in towns, cities, and college campuses all over the country. Social historian Kenneth Kusmer, for example, has said that "the impetus for the founding of the Cleveland NAACP" in 1914 "came less from local incidents than from segregation policies of the federal government under the administration of Woodrow Wilson." And the NAACP's successful recruitment campaign during the New Freedom years based its appeal largely on the Jim Crow actions of the Wilson administration, particularly federal Jim Crow and the onslaught of proposed racist legislation in Washington.[16]

Finally, the activist spirit mushroomed as African Americans, responding to the growing racial hostility and exclusion of the Wilson years—including the resurgence of the Ku Klux Klan—formed new associations and augmented the membership roles of older ones. Besides the NAACP and Marcus Garvey's United Negro Improvement Association, a wave of new members swelled the ranks of national organizations such as the National Association of Colored Women, the National Urban League, and the National Association of Postal Employees. The latter, formed by black postal workers in 1913, was a collective response to the racial exclusionary policies of white postal unions and became one of the most powerful unions representing African American federal employees.[17]

The racism of the Progressive Era seems to have sparked the formation of another minority organization as well. The Anti-Defamation League was organized in Chicago during late fall 1913 to "eradicate the defamation of the Jewish people by appeals to the press, legislation, vigilance work and an educational movement." Although the *Guardian* went perhaps too far by implying that American Jews had taken a cue from blacks in the Wilson protest to "agitate" against race discrimination, the avalanche of prejudice toward minority groups during the early Wilson years—including the anti-immigrant sentiment in Washington and the country at large—and the spreading anti-Semitism in America persuaded many Jews that organization and agitation were needed for defense and protection in an increasingly hostile world.[18]

BEYOND THE WILSON YEARS:
THE DECLINING STATUS OF BLACK FEDERAL EMPLOYEES

Toward the end of his life, Oswald Villard wrote in his memoirs that "the colored people were left much worse off than when Wilson took office, for the precedent had been set."[19] After the Wilson years, protestors—mostly through Trotter, his dwindling political organization, and the NAACP—unremittingly challenged the new precedent of Jim Crow in the federal government. They confronted both Presidents Harding and Coolidge and found both men unsympathetic to the policy but lacking the strong leadership necessary to control their federal departments. The former, in fact, had made a fleeting promise during the 1920 campaign to James Weldon Johnson, executive director of the NAACP, that he would abolish federal Jim Crow by executive order. The latter in 1926 assured Trotter and the NAACP that he would stamp out Jim Crow in federal departments. Although no presidential action was taken, protestors continued to hold mass meetings, fire off petitions and protest letters to government officials, and lobby political leaders for help in reversing the negative pattern in the executive branch; and black and liberal white journalists kept up a steady stream of scathing editorials regarding the antiblack policies of the federal government.[20]

Although the *Republican Campaign Textbooks* of 1916, 1920, and 1924 hauled the Democrats over the coals for promoting federal Jim Crow and for their abysmal record on black federal appointments, not to mention blaming the party for every racial injustice since Reconstruction, the criticisms appear to have been political ploys to lure blacks back into their ranks rather than representing any sincere concern for racial injustice. Simply put, Republicans were just as guilty of Jim Crow as the Democrats.

As pointed out in Chapter 1, conditions drastically worsened for African Americans during the fourteen-year reign of Republican power that lasted from 1896 to 1910. The party that had once symbolized freedom did little to challenge the spread of de jure racism in the South during this time and often gave the movement its nod of approval, if not its endorsement. And although the Wilson years established the negative precedent of federal Jim Crow—a vital point that William Bradbury Jr., in his monumental 1952 dissertation "Racial Discrimination in the Federal Service," says can hardly be exaggerated—black federal employees continued to suffer "overt manifestations of discriminations based on color" under the next three Republican administrations. Federal appointments continued to decline, and black civil service employees were en masse demoted and terminated, barred from advancement, and segregated from whites in practically all federal departments and buildings for decades to come—including workstations, cafeterias, elevators, restrooms, and locker rooms. The separate but equal doctrine or, in reality, separate but unequal doctrine, after penetrating almost every facet of American life, had finally made its sweep complete with its arrival in the federal government during the Wilson administration.[21]

Although the number of black federal workers increased during the Wilson years as a result of the war and the expanded role of the federal government, it is estimated that their proportional numbers declined from nearly 6 percent of the total civil service in 1910 to about 4.9 percent in 1918, sinking almost to their original 4.4 percent when the Civil Service Act was first signed in 1883.[22] Taking a broader view, it appears that the proportionate employment of black federal workers in competitive positions had increased by only 1.4 percent in the fifty-five-year period from 1883 to 1938.[23]

In addition, a Department of Labor investigation conducted in mid-1920 found that wages in most federal jobs—especially in the lowest-paying positions, which accounted for the bulk of the federal service—fell far below both the cost of living and the scale of wages in the private sector. The House Committee of Labor estimated that over 50,000 of these employees received less than three dollars a day.[24] "The brunt of this low wage was, of course," said Laurence Hayes, "carried on the shoulders of Negro Federal Government workers" whose annual salaries in the District of Columbia were on average far lower than those of their white counterparts.[25] Most African Americans—stripped of federal appointments and removed, demoted, or blocked from the higher-ranked positions in the civil service during the Wilson years—had by 1928 fallen predominantly into the lowest-paying positions, according to a Department of Labor press release.[26]

Around the same time, a private study of black employment in Washington, D.C., found that the thousands of black federal clerks who had worked there before the Wilson years had been "reduced" to about 300 by the early 1930s. Further, William Bradbury Jr. explained that "although four out of every five positions in the executive branch were now subject to civil service controls, the practice of hiring only whites for work above the custodial level remained general throughout the 'twenties." A few years after World War II, the Fair Employment Practice Committee (FEPC) discovered that prior to the war, over 90 percent of black federal employees were working in custodial occupations compared with an overall 10 percent for all government employees. Many other observers from 1914 and beyond emphasized as well the consistent downgrading, freezing or reduction of salaries, and dismissal of African Americans working in the federal government.[27]

CHANGING THE PATTERN: ORGANIZED PRESSURE AND EXECUTIVE ORDER 8802

On June 25, 1941, President Franklin Delano Roosevelt (FDR) issued Executive Order 8802, essentially banning racial discrimination in the mounting defense industries and in all government employment, including federal departments. This order established the FEPC, an agency responsible for investigating and remedying complaints of discrimination and directly accountable to the president. A few months later Professor Arthur Davis, in a militant address during the formal opening of Virginia Union University, told his mostly African American audience that this recent executive order was "the most revolutionary legislation yet passed in America" and lauded FDR for battling against "reactionary elements" to make it a reality.[28]

Hailed as the first executive order concerning African Americans since the Emancipation Proclamation, with the stroke of a pen the New Deal president disrupted the almost thirty-year-old pattern of federal Jim Crow that had been established during the Wilson years. But more significant, for the first time in history a president had officially put the power of his office against Jim Crow—a compelling signal to Americans that the days of sanctioned racial discrimination were on the decline. Even one of 8802's bitterest opponents, Governor Frank Dixon of Alabama, saw the writing on the wall when he described the order as an absurd reform "dedicated to the abolition of segregation."[29]

The elevation of FDR to hero status by Professor Davis and others in the immediate 8802 aftermath, not to mention Roosevelt mudslinging from southern leaders, overshadowed the fact that this ban on federal Jim Crow was actually the result of years of African American protest and recent pressure-group tactics. Far from being a visionary leader of change in regard to federal Jim Crow, President Roosevelt tried to sidestep the issue for as long as he could, refusing to disrupt the pattern of discrimination in federal employment. But African American groups and newspapers wielded the threat of mass protest so persuasively that FDR finally caved in to their demands.

Since the Wilson years, the NAACP had been challenging—with varied success—the removal, downgrading, and dismissal of African American civil servants, mostly on a case-by-case basis, through appeals and protests to local, state, and national officials. By the early 1940s, as complaints of discrimination and requests for help flooded into national and branch offices daily, coupled with the escalating discrimination and exclusion of African Americans in the booming defense industry, the NAACP became overwhelmed.[30] Under the leadership of A. Philip Randolph, the "energetic" and well-known leader of the Brotherhood of Sleeping Car Porters, the NAACP and the National Urban League (NUL) came together and amassed their strength to fight racial discrimination in the U.S. government. After several tense meetings between the alliance and the chief executive, his Cabinet, and government officials yielded no results, African Americans—weary of seeking help from a government that was largely the problem and growing increasingly bitter—looked to mass direct action to demand change.[31]

The architect of this mass direct action was A. Philip Randolph. In January 1941 he proposed the strategic March on Washington (MOW), in which an unprecedented 10,000 or more African Americans would march on the capital for an end to racial discrimination in federal employment, including national defense jobs (NAACP executive secretary Walter White stunned FDR when he exaggerated the potential number as 100,000). With local branch leadership and financial support from the NAACP, NUL, and black unions; extensive publicity from the black press; potential mass support from a disconcerted black community; and an unyielding Randolph in control of the MOW, African Americans waved a powerful symbol of mass discontent that threatened to erupt at the president's front door. As the countdown to the march neared its July 1 date and a resolute Randolph refused pleas from a nervous White House to call off the march, President Roosevelt hastily issued the executive order with only a week remaining.[32]

To be sure, there was a backlash of virulent opposition to 8802, particularly in the South where federal buildings and government employers—along with private defense industries doing business with the government, such as southern shipyards—were now prohibited from discriminating against African Americans. Making things even more complex for southerners, federal money for local and state projects now had strings attached that required certain quotas be met to ensure that African Americans were hired. But the South's response was simply to ignore the order and, if that failed, to violently oppose it. Even progress in eradicating the entrenched pattern of Jim Crow in federal departments at Washington was slow.[33]

But progress did come in Washington and the South. Much like the decision to integrate schools in the *Brown* case over a dozen years later, 8802 was met with stiff resistance or just plain ambivalence. It would take years of continual pressure by the NAACP and Randolph—indeed, by the African American community—resulting in more vigorous executive orders and efforts, to break down federal Jim Crow, including military segregation. But 8802 and the FEPC spelled the beginning of the end of the entire system of Jim Crow. Ironically, one of the last strongholds of resistance to Jim Crow to fall during the Wilson years, the federal government, was where the first symbolic victory against systematic racism in the United States would occur in 1941 and where the enormous potential of mass direct action would be realized. Moreover, it was here, at the federal level, where strategic mass protest for black equality would evolve from the collective yet mostly traditional methods used in the Wilson protest—such as petitions, mass meetings, conferences, appeals, and similar methods—to the use of mass direct action as a powerful political and social pressure-group tactic.

THE LEADERS AFTER THE PROTEST

What became of the leaders in the Wilson protest? In July 1914 Oswald Villard gave up the chairmanship of the NAACP to the militant Joel Spingarn. Although he continued serving the organization in various capacities for several more years, Villard's interest in helping African Americans secure their political and civil rights could not compete with what would become an all-consuming obsession with opposing war, unleashed by America's involvement in World War I. "The trauma of these bitter years," explained Stephan Thernstrom, "fixed Villard's anti-war convictions so deeply that nothing—not even Hitler—could shake them."[34]

Villard came to vehemently loathe Wilson, a man he had once devotedly admired, for involving the country in the senseless mass slaughter of human lives. Furthermore, he believed fervently, wrote Thernstrom, that the president had "sacrificed American democracy at the shrine of Big Business and the militarists." Editor of the *Nation* in the 1920s and early 1930s and contributing editor until 1940, the ardent pacifist pursued his convictions with a religious zeal until he was pushed off the scene altogether, becoming a "has been" in Villard's own words, with America's enthusiastic entry into World War II.[35]

In December 1914 May Childs Nerney, frustrated over the never-ending internal squabbles in the NAACP and hot-tempered when things did not go her way, resigned as executive secretary. She seems to have disappeared from the scene as suddenly as she had entered it, but she resurfaced in 1928 as the coordinator responsible for categorizing the millions of disorganized and neglected papers of Thomas Edison—another puzzle for her amazing talents. Inspired by the man whose papers were committed to her care, she wrote a book on Edison's life subtitled *A Modern Olympian*, a fitting description for her own efforts during the early years of the NAACP.[36]

Ida Wells-Barnett, unlike Nerney, was conspicuous during her entire career. During the Wilson protest, she withdrew from serving in any kind of advisory capacity to the NAACP because the organization had compounded its mistake of excluding her on the original formation committee years earlier by not inviting her to national meetings. Nevertheless, the driven Wells-Barnett, like Trotter, was a force in and of herself, needing little but the passion that burned deep inside her. Relentlessly, the tiny crusader pushed for black equality and suffrage and protested racial injustice through her control of both the Negro Fellowship League and the Chicago branch of Trotter's National Equal Rights League.[37]

Wells-Barnett continued to protest against black lynchings, often traveling to the place where they occurred to investigate the events surrounding each case. "More than any other single individual," said Clark Cook, "Ida B. Wells' efforts were responsible for the worldwide condemnation of lynching that forced the federal government to intercede and take action." She wrote extensively on the race riots in East St. Louis (1917), Chicago (1919), and Arkansas (1922). In 1930 Wells-Barnett became one of the first African American women to run for public office in the United States as she led a failed campaign for the Illinois state legislature. One year later, weary from a life of championing the oppressed, Wells-Barnett quietly passed away.[38]

W.E.B. DuBois, perhaps the most controversial and towering black figure of the first half of the twentieth century and certainly the most written about, aggressively protested against the caste system throughout his long life. He continued to edit *Crisis*, which by the end of 1914 had reached a monthly circulation of 33,000.[39] In 1919 DuBois led the Pan-African Congress in Paris to focus world opinion on the condition of black people everywhere, the resolutions from which were presented at the Paris Peace Conference; and he succeeded in personally meeting with members of Wilson's inner circle and others.[40]

Unlike the confrontational Trotter, DuBois challenged the notion of black inferiority and addressed the plight of black Americans mostly through scholarship, being more suited for writing fiery prose than for active leadership. The black scholar eventually broke from the NAACP in 1934, influenced in part by the controversy surrounding his support for "voluntary segregation" to foster independent black enterprises and in part by his socialist leanings in *Crisis*. His journey, moreover, had become intensely intellectual. Exasperated over the dominance of racial prejudice in American life and convinced of the inherent weaknesses of capitalism during the Great Depression, DuBois eventually came to believe the American political and economic system was largely the problem and saw Marxism as the potential liberator from the bondage of human degradation. He joined the American Communist Party in the late 1950s and soon moved to Ghana, Africa, where he became a citizen and spent the last days of his life.[41]

The story of William Monroe Trotter after the Wilson protest campaign could not have been scripted any better. It combines the Steinbeckian triumph of the human spirit with inevitable tragedy in a precarious world. "In a sense, his life was a long arc of failures," said Lerone Bennett Jr., "yet, in some respects, it was a splendid triumph." Trotter and his faltering organization, always on the brink of financial collapse, continued to protest against federal Jim Crow in government departments for years. After being assaulted and arrested in Boston while protesting *Birth of a Nation,* he led a failed campaign to have the film banned in other cities and for years continued to appeal to leaders, including Wilson, to have the film removed "from [the] American stage."[42]

In 1918 Trotter's wife and confidante in the struggle for black equality, Deenie, died, a loss he felt deeply for the rest of his life. In the pangs of depression, the equal rights advocate sailed to France to bring the plight of black Americans before the world and to get a racial equality clause adopted at the Versailles Conference. Denied a passport by the American government, Trotter learned French and went to New York disguised as a cook in search of a ship going to Europe. The brilliant Harvard graduate scrounged his way aboard the USS *Yarmouth* and peeled potatoes in the ship's kitchen while crossing the Atlantic. Alone in Paris and with virtually no resources, the tattered crusader was turned away from official participation in the conference but still managed to get petitions and news releases into the French and American press and also to meet with some of the leading delegates. Keeping in touch with other radicals at home, including Ida Wells-Barnett, Trotter consistently sent appeals and protests on behalf of "14,000,000" black Americans, attached with numerous names of "race petitioners" from America, to delegates in France and to President Wilson who was staying at "Maison Blanche, 11, Place des Etats Unis, Paris." Nevertheless, Trotter was unsuccessful in getting his plank in the Versailles Peace Treaty.[43]

Once back in the states, Trotter continued to badger the president. In "An Open Appeal to President Wilson," the leader pointed out the president's hypocrisy in promoting democracy and freedom abroad while remaining silent about the "oppression" of black Americans at home. "Act now, Mr. President, so that in these United State[s] as by your edict in Poland, 'all shall enjoy the same civil and political rights' and 'all racial minorities shall enjoy the same treatment and security in law and in fact as all others.'"[44]

A few years later, in 1920, the bold protestor confronted a series of racial injustices, including a sit-in at a segregated barbershop in Philadelphia. Trotter's fight to desegregate Boston City Hospital in 1928 led to the admittance of African American women to its nursing program less than one year later. He protested and caused the removal of a "Colored Only" sign from a large insurance company in Roxbury, he pressured a white secretarial school into accepting a black applicant, and he secured the removal of offensive textbooks with racist themes from the Cambridge schools. But to the chagrin of a growing number of black Bostonians, Trotter actively opposed the establishment of black schools, a black YMCA, black churches, and the expansion and relocation of a black hospital. "Once segregated," Trotter wholeheartedly believed, with much justification, "there is no end to the exclusion and injury just for color."[45]

Despite the success of Trotter's tour to organize western branches for the NIERL in 1915, by 1921 the organization had become nothing more than a small group of his personal followers. The *Guardian* eventually faltered as well, losing readership and support. The shining Phi Beta Kappa from Harvard was replaced by a "shabby" vendor "walking around the streets" of Boston selling his newspaper just to make ends meet. Trotter became depressed and discouraged in the 1920s by the continued racial injustice in America. He saw his utopian Harvard fall victim to racial discrimination in 1923 as President A. Lawrence Lowell prohibited blacks from residing in freshman dormitories, a policy that was finally reversed with Trotter's help after he protested in the *Guardian* and the *New York Times*. Like his ancestors, who had condemned colonization schemes as an unmerited stigma of inferiority for blacks and who saw America with all its potential as their homeland, the Boston patriot rejected extreme Garveyism with its emphasis on returning to Africa because he passionately believed the struggle for blacks in America must be one that sought inclusiveness in its noble institutions. Besides, like his ancestors, Trotter believed separatism would fail to challenge the notion of black inferiority in the minds of many whites and thus was really a form of escape that failed to confront white society with its sickness. The battle for him had always been for the dignity of his race. Moreover, there was a tinge to his zeal, perhaps even a subconscious motivation, that seems to have had a need to devour the white competition since as early as childhood and to prove himself—indeed, to prove African Americans—superior to Anglo-Saxons.[46]

Finally, Trotter's life was a never-ending crusade that charged again and again the impregnable fortress of racial prejudice in America until his spirit had been utterly broken. Mostly isolated and alone, save for a few close friends and his sister, Maude Trotter Steward, a penniless Trotter fell to his death from the roof of his Boston apartment in 1934. Some believed the "man fifty years ahead of his time" had committed suicide.[47]

NOTES

1. Untitled clipping, *Springfield Republican*, October 15, 1913, in Box C-432, NAACP Papers, Manuscript Division, Library of Congress, Washington, DC; Rolfe Colbleigh to Grimke, March 18, 1914, John Lorance, "Segregation Is Being Undone," *Boston Advertiser*, December

10, 1913, in Box 39-25, Archibald Grimke Papers, Moorland-Spingarn Research Center, Howard University, Washington, DC; "Murray Confirms Report of Undoing Segregation," *Guardian,* undated, Box 6, Moorfield Storey Papers, Manuscript Division, Library of Congress, Washington, DC; NAACP to Wilson, January 6, 1914, quoted in Kathleen Wolgemuth, "Woodrow Wilson and Federal Segregation," *Journal of Negro History* 44 (April 1959): 171.

2. Charles Russell quoted in Archibald Grimke to May Childs Nerney, November 13, 1914, Box C-432, NAACP Papers, Manuscript Division, Library of Congress, Washington, DC; Rolfe Colbleigh to Archibald Grimke, March 18, 1914, R. McCants Andrews to DuBois, November 14, 1914, and Nerney to Grimke, December 18, 1914, all in Box 39-25, Archibald Grimke Papers, Moorland-Spingarn Research Center, Howard University, Washington, DC.

3. "The Race Problem: Its Dangers and Opportunities," *Nation* 99 (December 24, 1914): 738–740.

4. Leslie S. Fishel Jr. and Benjamin Quarles, *The Negro American: A Documentary History* (Glenview, IL: Scott, Foresman, 1967), 390.

5. Wolgemuth, "Woodrow Wilson and Federal Segregation," 171.

6. Nerney to Grimke, March 7, 1914, Rolfe Colbleigh to Grimke, March 18, 1914, Box 39-25, Archibald Grimke Papers, Manuscript Division, Library of Congress, Washington, DC; Nerney to Charles Hamlin, March 7, 1914, Box C-403, NAACP Papers, Manuscript Division, Library of Congress, Washington, DC; John J. Broesamle, *William Gibbs McAdoo: A Passion for Change, 1863–1917* (Port Washington, NY: Kennikat, 1973), 80–81.

7. Department of Commerce . . . "acted upon": Trotter to Murray, November 21, 1913, Box 74-1, Freeman Murray Papers, Moorland-Spingarn Research Center, Howard University, Washington, DC; untitled *Guardian* article, indecipherable date, Box 6, Moorfield Storey Papers, Manuscript Division, Library of Congress, Washington, DC; Morton Sosna, "The South in the Saddle: Racial Politics During the Wilson Years," *Wisconsin Magazine of History* 54 (Autumn 1970), 39–49.

8. *Republican Campaign Textbook, 1916,* 378.

9. Charles Flint Kellogg, *NAACP: A History of the National Association for the Advancement of Colored People,* vol. 1, *1909–1920* (Baltimore: Johns Hopkins University Press, 1967), 181–182.

10. Nerney to Mr. W. L. Stoddard, November 12, 1913, Box C-403, NAACP Papers, Manuscript Division, Library of Congress, Washington, DC.

11. Douglas Brinkley, *Rosa Parks* (New York: Penguin Putnam, 2000), 99.

12. Kevin Gaines, *Uplifting the Race: Black Leadership, Politics, and Culture in the Twentieth Century* (Chapel Hill: University of North Carolina Press, 1996), 3.

13. Ibid., xiv, 3, 14.

14. Robert Bagnall, "Negroes in the New Abolition Movement," in Herbert Aptheker, ed., *A Documentary History of the Negro People in the United States, 1910–1932,* vol. 2 (Secaucus, NJ: Citadel, 1973), 498.

15. William J. Moses, ed., *Classical Black Nationalism: From the American Revolution to Marcus Garvey* (New York: New York University Press, 1996), 30–31; Aptheker, *A Documentary History,* 378; Kellogg, 133, 294.

16. Kenneth Kusmer, *A Ghetto Takes Shape: Black Cleveland, 1870–1930* (Urbana: University of Illinois Press, 1976), 260 note 38.

17. Laurence J.W. Hayes, "The Negro Federal Government Worker, 1883–1938" (M.A. thesis, Howard University Graduate School, 1941), 79–80.

18. *Guardian* article entitled "Jews Organize to Agitate Against Discrimination," undated, Box 6, Moorfield Storey Papers, Manuscript Division, Library of Congress, Washington, DC. Interestingly, during the 1930s and early 1940s it was the black press and publications in America that continually warned of the growing and dangerous tide of anti-Semitism and Jewish persecution sweeping across Germany. See Lunabelle Wedlock, "The Reaction of Negro Publications and Organizations to German Anti-Semitism," *Howard University Studies in the Social Sciences* 3 (Washington, DC: Graduate School of Howard University, 1942).

19. Oswald Villard, *Fighting Years: Memoirs of a Liberal Editor* (New York: Harcourt, Brace, 1939), 241.

20. August Meier and Elliott Rudwick, eds., *Along the Color Line: Explorations in the Black Experience* (Urbana: University of Illinois Press, 1976), 178–184; newspaper article entitled "Nevel H. Thomas Makes Vigorous Protest to Coolidge Against Segregation in Interior Department," August 21, 1926, Box 39-38, Archibald Grimke Papers, Moorland-Spingarn Research Center, Howard University, Washington, DC. Warren Harding was probably sincere in his attitude toward African Americans. In his acceptance speech, he told an audience gathered on the grounds of his home in Marion, Ohio, that he believed the "Negro citizens of America should be guaranteed the enjoyment of all their rights, that they have earned their full measure of citizenship bestowed, that their sacrifices in blood on the battlefield of the Republic have entitled them to all of freedom and opportunity, all of sympathy and aid that the American spirit of fairness and justice demands." *Republican Campaign Textbook,* 1920, 50, quoted in Hayes, 62.

21. William C. Bradbury Jr., "Racial Discrimination in the Federal Service: A Study in the Sociology of Administration" (Ph.D. diss., Columbia University, 1952) 27–28, 59–61.

22. Paul Van Riper, *History of the United States Civil Service* (Evanston, IL: Row, Peterson, 1958), 242; Thomas N. Roberts, "The Negro in Government War Agencies," *Journal of Negro Education* 12 (Summer 1943): 367; Leon A. Ransom, "Combating Discrimination in the Employment of Negroes in War Industries and Government Agencies," *Journal of Negro Education* 12 (Summer 1943): 408.

23. Roberts, 367; Ransom, 408.

24. Mary Conyngton, "The Government's Wage Policy for the Last Quarter Century," U.S. Bureau of Labor Statistics, *Monthly Labor Review* 10 (June 1920): 19–35; House Committee on Labor, Minimum Wage Bill for Federal Employees, 67th Congress, 1st Session, May 6, 1921, quoted in Sterling Spero, *The Labor Movement in a Government Industry: A Study of Employee Organization in the Postal Service* (New York: George H. Doran, 1924), 33.

25. Hayes, 64; Conyngton, 21.

26. Department of Labor Press Release 3052, September 8, 1928, quoted in Hayes, 66; William F. Nowlin, *The Negro in American National Politics* (Boston: Stratford, 1931), 136.

27. Lorenzo J. Greene and Myra Colson Callis, *The Employment of Negroes in the District of Columbia* (Washington, DC: Association for the Study of Negro Life, 1931), 59; FEPC findings quoted in Ransom, 414; also Bradbury, 27–28; Nowlin, 119–120.

28. John A. Davis and Cornelius L. Golightly, "Negro Employment in the Federal Government," *Phylon* 6 (December 1945): 339; Herbert Garfinkel, *When Negroes March: The March on Washington Movement in the Organizational Politics for FEPC* (Glencoe, IL: Free Press, 1959), 16, 60–61; Arthur P. Davis, "The Negro Student and World Revolution," *Journal of Negro Education* 12 (Winter 1943): 12.

29. Governor Frank Dixon quoted in Garfinkel, 41; also Davis, 12; Adam Fairclough, *Better Day Coming: Blacks and Equality, 1890–2000* (New York: Penguin Putnam, 2001), 186.

30. Kellogg, 165–182; NAACP 28th Annual Report for 1937, 20–21; NAACP 29th Annual Report for 1938, 16; NAACP 30th Annual Report for 1939, 15–16; NAACP Annual Report for 1940, 7–8; NAACP Annual Report for 1941, 3–4.

31. NAACP Civil Service Case Files leading up to FDR's Executive Order 8802, C-228, NAACP Papers, Manuscript Division, Library of Congress, Washington, DC; Garfinkel, 34, 37–38, 60–61.

32. Garfinkel, 38–39, 54, 61.

33. Fairclough, 186–188; Bradbury, 27–28, 61, 71, 247–248, 250.

34. Henry Blumenthal, "Woodrow Wilson and the Race Question," *Journal of Negro History* 48 (January 1963): 20; Stephan Thernstrom, "Oswald Garrison Villard and the Politics of Pacifism," *Harvard Library Bulletin* 14 (Winter 1960): 130.

35. Thernstrom, 130.

36. May Childs Nerney, *Thomas Edison: A Modern Olympian* (New York: H. Smith and R. Hass, 1934).

37. Linda O. McMurray, *To Keep the Waters Troubled: The Life of Ida B. Wells* (New York: Oxford University Press, 1998), 302–304.

38. Ibid., 314, 326–327, 335–336; Clark Cook, "Ida B. Wells: A Biographical Tribute," http://www.cris.com/~Azulao/tribute.html, accessed January 20, 2001.

39. David L. Lewis, *W.E.B. DuBois: Biography of a Race, 1868–1919* (New York: Henry Holt, 1993), 474.

40. Ibid., 576.

41. Thomas C. Holt, "The Political Uses of Alienation: W.E.B. DuBois on Politics, Race and Culture," *American Quarterly* 42 (1990): 307–310.

42. Lerone Bennett Jr., *Before the Mayflower: A History of the Negro in America, 1619–1964* (Baltimore: Penguin, 1970), 285; Robert C. Hayden, "William Monroe Trotter: A One Man Protestor for Civil Rights," *Trotter Institute Review* 2 (Winter 1988): 9–10; William A. Edwards, "William Monroe Trotter: A Twentieth Century Abolitionist," *Trotter Institute Review* 2 (Winter 1988): 16–17; "William Monroe Trotter: 'For Every Right With All Thy Might,'" *Boston Globe,* February 11, 1973, in William Monroe Trotter File, Boston Herald Traveler Library, Boston, MA; "Boston Still Stirred Up by Negro William Trotter," newspaper article, December 1967, in Guardian of Boston Collection, Mugar Memorial Library, Boston University, Boston, MA.

43. Numerous correspondences from Trotter while in France, Trotter File, Woodrow Wilson Papers, Seeley G. Mudd Library, Princeton University, Princeton, NJ.

44. Ibid. The strain of racism that tainted the Paris Peace Conference laid the basis for the later struggles of oppressed peoples in countries such as Vietnam and South Africa.

45. Hayden, 9–10; Edwards, 16–17; Trotter quoted in Stephen Fox, *The Guardian of Boston: William Monroe Trotter* (New York: Atheneum, 1970), 264.

46. Werner Sollors, Caldwell Titcomb, and Thomas A. Underwood, eds., *Blacks at Harvard: A Documentary History of African-American Experience at Harvard and Radcliffe* (New York: New York University Press, 1993), 195, 209–210; Hayden, 9–10; Edwards, 16–17; Benjamin Quarles, *Black Abolitionists* (New York: Da Capo, 1991), 3–8.

47. Hayden, 9–10; Edwards, 16–17.

ORIGINAL MANUSCRIPTS AND COLLECTIONS

Atlanta University, Robert W. Woodruff Library, Atlanta, GA
>   George A. Towns Papers

Boston Herald Traveler Library, Boston, MA
>   William Monroe Trotter File

Boston University, Mugar Memorial Library, Boston, MA
>   Guardian Microfilm
>   Guardian of Boston Collection

Harvard University, Houghton Library, Cambridge, MA
>   Oswald Villard Papers; most of the material looked at in this collection and used in this book can be found in secondary sources.

Harvard University, Widener Library, Cambridge, MA

Howard University, Moorland-Spingarn Research Center, Washington, DC
>   Thomas H.R. Clarke Papers
>   Archibald Grimke Papers
>   Freeman Murray Papers
>   Joel E. Spingarn Papers

Library of Congress, Manuscript Division, Washington, DC
>   Ray Stannard Baker Papers
>   Charlotte Hopkins Papers
>   NAACP Microfilm
>   NAACP Papers
>   Records of the National Association of Colored Women
>   Moorfield Storey Papers. In addition to providing insight into the NAACP's role in the protest, the Storey papers contain perhaps the only public collection of *Guardian* clippings pertaining to the protest for the years 1913–1914. Unfortunately, beause of their extremely fragile condition, they may not be available to the public until the Library of Congress has had a chance to photocopy or transfer them to microfilm.
>   Woodrow Wilson Papers

National Archives II, College Park, MD
>   General Records of the Department of Treasury

Princeton University, Seeley G. Mudd Library, Princeton, NJ
>   Woodrow Wilson Papers

University of Illinois at Urbana-Champaign, University Archives
>   John A. Fairlie Papers

University of Virginia, Special Collections, Charlottesville, VA
  John Skelton Williams Papers

Although in published volumes listed in the "Published Sources" of this bibliography, other original correspondence used in this book includes:
  W.E.B. DuBois Papers
  Booker T. Washington Papers
  Papers of Woodrow Wilson

PUBLISHED SOURCES

BOOKS

Adams, Cyrus. *The Republican Party and the Afro-American: A Book of Facts and Figures.* Washington, DC: Republican National Committee, 1912.

Aptheker, Herbert, ed. *A Documentary History of the Negro People in the United States, 1910–1932,* vol. 2. New York: Citadel, 1990.

———. *The Correspondences of W.E.B. DuBois,* vol. 1, *Selections, 1877–1934.* Amherst: University of Massachusetts Press, 1973.

Auchincloss, Louis. *Woodrow Wilson.* New York: Penguin Putnam, 2000.

Bailey, Thomas A. *Woodrow Wilson and the Great Betrayal.* Chicago: Quadrangle Books, 1963.

Baker, Ray Stannard. *Following the Color Line: American Negro Citizenship in the Progressive Era.* New York: Harper Torchbooks, 1964.

———. *Woodrow Wilson, Life and Letters: Youth, 1856–1890.* New York: Doubleday, Page, 1927.

Barkin, Elazar. *The Retreat of Scientific Racism.* Cambridge, UK: Cambridge University Press, 1992.

Bennett, Lerone, Jr. *Before the Mayflower: A History of the Negro in America, 1619–1964.* Baltimore: Penguin, 1970.

Blum, John M. *Woodrow Wilson and the Politics of Morality.* Boston: Little, Brown, 1956.

Bragdon, Henry W. *Woodrow Wilson: The Academic Years.* Cambridge: Belknap Press of Harvard University, 1967.

Brinkley, Douglas. *Rosa Parks.* New York: Penguin Putnam, 2000.

Broderick, Francis L., and August Meier. *Negro Protest Thought in the Twentieth Century.* New York: The Bobbs-Merrill Company, Inc., 1965.

Broesamle, John J. *William Gibbs McAdoo: A Passion for Change, 1863–1917.* New York: Kennikat, 1973.

Brown, Katherine L. *Woodrow Wilson on the Constitution: Son of the Staunton Manse.* Staunton, VA: Woodrow Wilson Birthplace Foundation, 1988.

Bruce, Dickson D., Jr. *Archibald Grimke: Portrait of a Black Independent.* Baton Rouge: Louisiana State University Press, 1993.

Campbell, Ballard C., ed. *The Human Tradition in the Gilded Age and the Progressive Era.* Wilmington, DE: Scholarly Resources, 2000.

Casdorph, Paul D. *Republicans, Negroes, and Progressives in the South, 1912–1916.* University: University of Alabama Press, 1981.

Cell, John W. *The Highest Stage of White Supremacy: The Origins of Segregation in South Africa and the American South.* Cambridge, UK: Cambridge University Press, 1982.

Clemants, Kendrick. *Woodrow Wilson: World Statesman.* Boston: Twayne, 1987.

Cody, Archibald. *The Race Question From the White Chief: A Story of the Life and Times of James K. Vardaman.* Vicksburg: Mississippi Printing, 1944.

Cook, Clark. "Ida B. Wells: A Biographical Tribute." http://www.cris.com/~Azulao/tribute.html. January 20, 2001.

Cooper, John Milton, Jr. *Pivotal Decades: The United States, 1900–1920.* New York: Norton, 1990.

Cooper, John Milton, Jr., and Charles E. Neu, eds. *The Wilson Era: Essays in Honor of Arthur S. Link.* Arlington Heights, IL: Harlan Davidson, 1991.

Cronon, E. David, ed. *The Cabinet Diaries of Josephus Daniels, 1913–1921.* Lincoln: University of Nebraska Press, 1963.

DuBois, W.E.B. *The Souls of Black Folk.* Grand Rapids, MI: Candace, 1996.

———. *Black Reconstruction in America, 1860–1880.* New York: Simon and Schuster, 1995.

Fairclough, Adam. *Better Day Coming: Blacks and Equality, 1890–2000.* New York: Penguin Putnam, 2001.

Fishel, Leslie S., Jr., and Benjamin Quarles. *The Negro American: A Documentary History.* Glenview, IL: Scott, Foresman, 1967.

Fox, Stephen. *The Guardian of Boston: William Monroe Trotter.* New York: Atheneum, 1970.

Franklin, John Hope. *From Slavery to Freedom: A History of Negro Americans.* New York: Alfred A. Knopf, 1967.

Frazier, E. Franklin. *Black Bourgeoisie.* New York: Simon and Schuster, 1997.

———. *The Negro Church in America.* Liverpool: University of Liverpool, 1963.

Frazier, Walter J., R. Frank Saunders Jr., and Jon L. Wakelyn, eds. *The Web of Southern Social Relations: Women, Family, and Education.* Athens: University of Georgia Press, 1985.

Gaines, Kevin. *Uplifting the Race: Black Leadership, Politics, and Culture in the Twentieth Century.* Chapel Hill: University of North Carolina Press, 1996.

Garfinkel, Herbert. *When Negroes March: The March on Washington Movement in the Organizational Politics for FEPC.* Glencoe, IL: Free Press, 1959.

George, Alexander L., and Juliette L. George. *Woodrow Wilson and Colonel House: A Personality Study.* New York: Dover, 1964.

Glenn, A. L. *History of the National Alliance of Postal Employees, 1913–1955.* Cleveland: NAPE, 1956.

Gordon, Ann D., ed. *African American Women and the Vote, 1837–1965.* Amherst: University of Massachusetts Press, 1997.

Gordon-Reed, Annette. *Thomas Jefferson and Sally Hemings: An American Controversy.* Charlottesville: University of Virginia Press, 1997.

Grayson, Cary T. *Woodrow Wilson: An Intimate Memoir.* Washington, DC: Potomac Books, 1960.

Green, Constance McLaughlin. *Washington: Capital City, 1879–1950.* Princeton: Princeton University Press, 1963.

Greene, Lorenzo J., and Myra Colson Callis. *The Employment of Negroes in the District of Columbia.* Washington, DC: Association for the Study of Negro Life, 1931.

Greene, Lorenzo J., and Carter G. Woodson. *The Negro Wage Earner.* Washington, DC: Association for the Study of Negro Life, 1931.

Grimke, Francis. "Christianity and Race Prejudice." Two Discourses Delivered in the Fifteenth Street Presbyterian Church, Washington DC, May 29, June 5, 1913. Widener Library, Harvard University, Cambridge, MA.

Hale, Grace Elizabeth. *Making Whiteness: The Culture of Segregation in the South, 1890–1940*. New York: Pantheon, 1998.

Harlan, Louis R. *Booker T. Washington: The Making of a Black Leader, 1856–1901*. Oxford: Oxford University Press, 1972.

Harlan, Louis R., and Raymond W. Smock, eds. *The Booker T. Washington Papers*, vol. 12, *1912–1914*. Urbana: University of Illinois Press, 1982.

Heckscher, August. *Woodrow Wilson: A Biography*. New York: Macmillan Publishing Co., 1991.

Higginbotham, Evelyn Brooks. *Righteous Discontent: The Women's Movement in the Black Baptist Church, 1880–1920*. Cambridge: Harvard University Press, 1993.

Holmes, William F. *The White Chief: James Kimble Vardaman*. Baton Rouge: Louisiana State University Press, 1970.

Jones, Beverly Washington. *Quest for Equality: The Life and Writings of Mary Church Terrell, 1863–1954*. New York: Carlson, 1990.

Jones, Jacqueline. *Labor of Love, Labor of Sorrow: Black Women, Work, and the Family, From Slavery to the Present*. New York: Vintage, 1985.

Kellogg, Charles Flint. *NAACP: A History of the National Association for the Advancement of Colored People*, vol. 1, *1909–1920*. Baltimore: Johns Hopkins University Press, 1967.

King, Coretta Scott. *My Life With Martin Luther King Jr.* New York: Penguin, 1994.

Kousser, J. Morgan. *The Shaping of Southern Politics: Suffrage Restriction and the Establishment of the One-Party South, 1890–1910*. New Haven: Yale University Press, 1974.

Kusmer, Kenneth. *A Ghetto Takes Shape: Black Cleveland, 1870–1930*. Urbana: University of Illinois Press, 1976.

Lewis, David L. *W.E.B. DuBois: Biography of a Race, 1868–1919*. New York: Henry Holt, 1993.

Link, Arthur S. *Woodrow Wilson and the Progressive Era, 1910–1917*. New York: Harper and Row, 1954.

———. *Wilson: The Road to the White House*. Princeton: Princeton University Press, 1947.

———. *Wilson: The New Freedom*. Princeton: Princeton University Press, 1956.

———, ed. *The Papers of Woodrow Wilson*. 63 vols. Princeton: Princeton University Press, 1966–1977.

Logan, Rayford. *The Negro in American Thought and Life: The Nadir, 1877–1901*. New York, Dial Press, 1954.

———. *The Negro in the United States*. Princeton, NJ: D. Van Nostrand Company, Inc., 1957.

McCray, Carrie Allen. *Freedom's Child: The Life of a Confederate General's Black Daughter*. Chapel Hill, NC: Algonquin, 1998.

McLaughlin, Jack. *Jefferson and Monticello*. New York: Henry Holt, 1988.

McMurray, Linda O. *To Keep the Waters Troubled: The Life of Ida B. Wells*. New York: Oxford University Press, 1998.

McPherson, James M. *The Struggle for Equality*. Princeton: Princeton University Press, 1992.

———. *The Abolitionist Legacy: From Reconstruction to the NAACP*. Princeton: Princeton University Press, 1975.

Meier, August. *Negro Thought in America, 1880–1915: Racial Ideologies in the Age of Booker T. Washington.* Ann Arbor: University of Michigan Press, 1963.

Meier, August, and Elliott Rudwick, eds. *Along the Color Line: Explorations in the Black Experience.* Urbana: University of Illinois Press, 1976.

Middleton, Phillip, and David Pilgrim. "On-line Jim Crow Museum of Racist Memorabilia." http://www.ferris.edu, accessed March 23, 2002.

Miller, Kelly. *Race Adjustment: Essays on the Negro in America.* New York: Arno, 1968.

Moon, Henry Lee. *Balance of Power: The Negro Vote.* New York: Doubleday, 1948.

Moses, William J., ed. *Classical Black Nationalism: From the American Revolution to Marcus Garvey.* New York: New York University Press, 1996.

NAACP Annual Reports, 1912, 1913, 1914, 1937, 1938, 1939, 1940, 1941. New York: NAACP.

Nazel, Joe. *Ida B. Wells.* Los Angeles: Holloway House, 1995.

Newby, I. A. *Jim Crow's Defense: Anti-Negro Thought in America, 1900–1930.* Baton Rouge: Louisiana State University Press, 1965.

Nowlin, William F. *The Negro in American National Politics.* Boston: Stratford, 1931.

Onuf, Peter S., ed. *Jeffersonian Legacies.* Charlottesville: University Press of Virginia, 1993.

Quarles, Benjamin. *Black Abolitionists.* New York: Da Capo, 1991.

Roper, Daniel C. *The United States Post Office.* New York: Funk and Wagnalls, 1917.

Ross, B. Joyce. *J. E. Spingarn and the Rise of the NAACP, 1911–1939.* New York: Atheneum, 1972.

Salem, Dorothy. *To Better Our World: Black Women and Organized Reform, 1890–1920.* New York: Carlson, 1990.

"Save Our History: The White House: 200th Anniversary." A&E Television Networks, History Channel. January 26, 2001.

Smith, J. Clay, Jr. *Emancipation: The Making of a Black Lawyer, 1844–1944.* Philadelphia: University of Pennsylvania Press, 1993.

Sollors, Werner, Caldwell Titcomb, and Thomas A. Underwood, eds. *Blacks at Harvard: A Documentary History of African-American Experience at Harvard and Radcliffe.* New York: New York University Press, 1993.

Spero, Sterling. *The Labor Movement in a Government Industry: A Study of Employee Organization in the Postal Service.* New York: George H. Doran, 1924.

Spero, Sterling, and Abram Harris. *The Black Worker: The Negro and the Labor Movement.* New York: Columbia University Press, 1931.

St. James, Warren D. *The National Association for the Advancement of Colored People: A Case Study in Pressure Groups.* New York: Exposition, 1958.

Thompson, Eric Trice. *The Changing South and the Presbyterian Church.* Richmond, VA: John Knox, 1950.

Van Riper, Paul. *History of the United States Civil Service.* Evanston, IL: Row, Peterson, 1958.

Villard, Oswald. *Fighting Years: Memoirs of a Liberal Editor.* New York: Harcourt, Brace, and Company, 1939.

Waldron, J. M., and J. D. Harkless. *The Political Situation in a Nut-Shell: Some Un-Colored Truths for Colored Voters.* Washington, DC: Trades Allied Printing Council, 1912.

Washington, Booker T. *Up From Slavery.* New York: Oxford University Press, 1995.

Wells, Rolla. *Report of the Treasurer of the Democratic National Committee. Presidential Campaign of 1912.* New York: Democratic National Committee, 1913.

Who's Who in America, 1914–15. Chicago: A. N. Marquis, 1915.

Williamson, Joel. *A Rage for Order: Black-White Relations in the American South Since Emancipation.* Oxford: Oxford University Press, 1976.

Wilson, Edith Bolling. *Selected Literary and Political Papers and Addresses of Woodrow Wilson, Volume 2.* New York: Grosset and Dunlap, 1927.

Wilson, Woodrow. *Division and Reunion, 1829–1889.* Gloucester, MA: Peter Smith, 1974.

———. *The State.* Washington, DC: Heath, 1918.

———. *A History of the American People, Volume 5.* New York: Harper and Brothers, 1902.

———. *George Washington.* New York: Harper and Brothers, 1897.

———. *Mere Literature and Other Essays.* New York: Houghton, Mifflin, 1896.

———. *The New Freedom: A Call for the Emancipation of the Generous Energies of a People.* New York: Doubleday, Page, & Company, 1913.

Wood, Virgil A., ed. Introduction. *Holy Bible: African American Jubilee Edition.* New York: American Bible Society, 1999.

Woodward, C. Vann. *The Strange Career of Jim Crow.* New York: Oxford University Press, 1974.

———. *The Origins of the New South, 1877–1913.* Baton Rouge: Louisiana State University Press, 1971.

Zanuck, Darryl, prod. *Wilson.* Hollywood, CA: 20th Century Fox, 1944.

JOURNALS AND MAGAZINES

Bennett, Lerone, Jr. "Thomas Jefferson's Negro Grandchildren." *Ebony* 10 (November 1954): 78–80.

Blakely, Allison. "Black U.S. Consuls and Diplomats and Black Leadership, 1880–1920." *UMOJA: A Scholarly Journal of Black Studies* 1 (November 1977): 1–16.

Bloomfield, Maxwell. "*The Leopard's Spots:* A Study in Popular Racism." *American Quarterly* 16 (Fall 1964): 389–401.

Blumenthal, Henry. "Woodrow Wilson and the Race Question." *Journal of Negro History* 48 (January 1963): 1–21.

Brewer, James H. "The War Against Jim Crow in the Land of Goshen." *Negro History Bulletin* 24 (December 1960): 53–57.

Broderick, Francis L. "DuBois and the Democratic Party, 1908–1916." *Negro History Bulletin* 21 (November 1957): 41–44.

Cable, George Washington. "The Freedman's Case in Equity." *Century Magazine* 29 (January 1885): 417–425.

Carter, Everett. "Cultural History Written With Lightening: The Significance of the *Birth of a Nation.*" *American Quarterly* 12 (Fall 1960): 347–357.

Colbleigh, Rolfe. "Turning the Negro Back." *Congregationalist and Christian World* (September 18, 1913): 1.

Crowe, Charles. "Racial Violence and Social Reform—Origins of the Atlanta Riot of 1906." *Journal of Negro History* 53 (July 1968): 234–256.

Current Literature 53 (1912): 611.

Davis, Arthur P. "The Negro Student and World Revolution." *Journal of Negro Education* 12 (Winter 1943): 7–13.

Davis, John A., and Cornelius L. Golightly. "Negro Employment in the Federal Government." *Phylon: The Atlanta University Review* 6 (December 1945): 337–347.

Desantis, Vincent P. "The Republican Party and the Southern Negro, 1877–1897." *Journal of Negro History* 45 (April 1960): 71–87.

Dorrah, David Lewis. "President Taft and the Solid South." *Nineteenth Century* 72 (November 1912): 1015–1029.

Dummett, Clifton O. "Prevention Began Early: Charles Edwin Bentley, DDS, 1859–1929." *Journal of the National Medical Association* 75 (1983): 1235–1236.

Edwards, William A. "William Monroe Trotter: A Twentieth Century Abolitionist." *Trotter Institute Review* 2 (Winter 1988): 13–18.

Feldman, Egal. "The Social Gospel and the Jews." *American Jewish Historical Quarterly* 58 (March 1969): 312–325.

Glazier, Kenneth M. "W.E.B. DuBois' Impressions of Woodrow Wilson." *Journal of Negro History* 58 (October 1973): 452–459.

Grantham, Dewey W., Jr. "The Progressive Movement and the Negro." *South Atlantic Quarterly* 54 (October 1955): 461–477.

Hallberg, Gerald N. "Bellingham, Washington's Anti-Hindu Riot." *Journal of the West* 12 (January 1973): 163–175.

Harrison, William. "William Monroe Trotter—Fighter." *Phylon: The Atlanta University Review* 7 (July 1946): 237–245.

Harvard College Class of 1895, 7th Class Report: Secretary's Report. Boston: Harvard College, 1925.

Hayden, Robert C. "William Monroe Trotter: A One Man Protestor for Civil Rights." *Trotter Institute Review* 2 (Winter 1988): 7–10.

Holt, Thomas C. "The Political Uses of Alienation: W.E.B. DuBois on Politics, Race and Culture." *American Quarterly* 42 (1990): 301–323.

La Follette, Belle Case. "The Color Line." *La Follette's Weekly* (August 1913): 6–7.

Lerner, Gerda. "Early Community Work of Black Club Women." *Journal of Negro History* 59 (April 1974): 158–167.

Link, Arthur S. "The Negro as a Factor in the Campaign of 1912." *Journal of Negro History* 32 (January 1947): 81–99.

Lunardini, Christine. "Standing Firm: William Monroe Trotter's Meetings With Woodrow Wilson, 1913–1914." *Journal of Negro History* 64 (Summer 1979): 244–264.

Meier, August. "The Negro and the Democratic Party, 1875–1915." *Phylon: The Atlanta University Review* 17 (1963): 173–191.

———. "Booker T. Washington and the Rise of the NAACP." *Crisis,* February 1959, 115–130.

———. "Booker T. Washington and the Negro Press." *Journal of Negro History* 38 (January 1953): 67–90.

Meier, August, and Elliott Rudwick. "The Boycott Movement Against Jim Crow Streetcars in the South, 1900–1906." *Journal of American History* 55 (March 1969): 756–775.

———. "The Rise of Segregation in the Federal Bureaucracy, 1900–1930." *Phylon: The Atlanta University Review* 28 (1967): 178–184.

"Mr. Burleson and the Negro." *New Republic* 19 (May 31, 1919): 1–2.

Osborn, George C. "Woodrow Wilson Appoints a Negro Judge." *Journal of Southern History* 24 (1958): 481–493.

Patterson, Thomas G. "American Businessmen and Consular Service Reform, 1890s to 1906." *Business History Review* 40 (Spring 1966): 77–97.

Putthammer, Charles, and Ruth Worthy. "William Monroe Trotter, 1872–1934." *Journal of Negro History* 43 (October 1958): 298–316.

Ransom, Leon A. "Combating Discrimination in the Employment of Negroes in War Industries and Government Agencies." *Journal of Negro Education* 12 (Summer 1943): 405–415.

Reid, Ira De A. "Negro Movements and Messiahs, 1900–1949." *Phylon: The Atlanta University Reveiw* 10 (1949): 362–369.

Roberts, Thomas N. "The Negro in Government War Agencies." *Journal of Negro Education* 12 (Summer 1943): 367–375.

Scheiner, Seth M. "President Roosevelt and the Negro, 1901–1908." *Journal of Negro History* 47 (July 1962): 169–182.

Scott, Anne Firor. "Most Invisible of All: Black Women's Voluntary Associations." *Journal of Southern History* 56 (February 1990): 3–13.

Sosna, Morton. "The South in the Saddle: Racial Politics During the Wilson Years." *Wisconsin Magazine of History* 54 (Autumn 1970): 30–49.

"The Southern Situation." *American Missionary* 43 (January 1889): 1.

Thernstrom, Stephan. "Oswald Garrison Villard and the Politics of Pacifism." *Harvard Library Bulletin* 14 (Winter 1960): 126–152.

Thornbrough, Emma Lou. "American Negro Newspapers, 1880–1914." *Business History Review* 40 (Winter 1966): 469–486.

Villard, Oswald. "The Race Problem: Its Dangers and Opportunities." *Nation* 99 (December 24, 1914): 738–740.

Warren, Samuel E. "The Development of Negro Labor: An Adventure in Teaching Certain Aspects of American Labor History." *Journal of Negro History* 25 (January 1940): 45–59.

Wedlock, Lunabelle. "The Reaction of Negro Publications and Organizations to German Anti-Semitism," *The Howard University Studies in the Social Sciences* 3 (Washington, DC: The Graduate School of Howard University, 1942).

Weiss, Nancy J. "The Negro and the New Freedom: Fighting Wilsonian Segregation." *Political Science Quarterly* 84 (March 1969): 61–79.

Welliver, Judson C. "The Triumph of the South." *Munsey's Magazine* 49 (1913): 738–740.

"White Supremacy at Princeton." *Negro Digest* (January 1943): 60–61.

Wilson, Woodrow. "The Reconstruction of the Southern States." *Atlantic Monthly* 87 (1901): 1–6.

Wolgemuth, Kathleen L. "Woodrow Wilson and Federal Segregation." *Journal of Negro History* 44 (April 1959): 158–173.

———. "Woodrow Wilson's Appointment Policy and the Negro." *Journal of Southern History* 24 (November 1958): 457–471.

GOVERNMENT AND POLITICAL PUBLICATIONS/PAMPHLETS

Biographical Directory of the United States Congress, 1774–1989. Washington, DC: U.S. Government Printing Office, 1989.

Congressional Information Service Index to Presidential Executive Orders and Proclamations, April 30, 1789 to March 4, 1921, George Washington to Woodrow Wilson. Washington, DC: Congressional Information Service, 1987.

Congressional Quarterly's Guide to the U.S. Supreme Court. Washington, DC: Congressional Quarterly, Inc., 1979.

Conyngton, Mary. "The Government's Wage Policy for the Last Quarter Century." U.S. Bureau of Labor Statistics, *Monthly Labor Review* 10 (June 1920): 19–35.

Crummell, Alexander. *A Defence of the Negro Race in America From the Assaults and Charges of Rev. J. L. Tucker, D.D., in His Paper Before the "Church Congress" of 1882, on "The Relations of the Church to the Colored Race."* Washington, DC: Judd and Detweiler, 1883. Pamphlet on Microfilm no. 18176E, Humanities and Social Sciences Division, Library of Congress, Washington, DC.

Department Circular no. 9, *Circular Instructions of the Treasury Department, William G. McAdoo.* Washington, DC: Government Printing Office, 1915.

Department of Commerce, Bureau of the Census, 1910. Release no. 8-4499, "Negroes in the U.S." Department of Labor Press Release 3052.

"From Slavery to Freedom: African American Pamphlet Collection, 1824–1909." Online, American Memory, Library of Congress, Washington, DC, http://memory.loc.gov/cgi-bin/query/r?ammem/rbaapc, accessed March 17, 2002.

Historical Statistics of the United States: Colonial Times to 1957. Washington, DC: U.S. Bureau of the Census, 1960.

Republican Campaign Textbooks, 1910, 1912, 1916, 1920, 1924. Washington, DC: Republican National Committee.

Republican Textbook for the Congressional Campaign, 1910. Washington, DC: Republican National Committee.

Smith, Darrell Hevenor. *The United States Civil Service Commission: Its History, Activities, and Organization.* Service Monographs of the United States Government, no. 49. Baltimore: Johns Hopkins University Press, 1928.

Thompson, J. A. *Progressivism.* London: British Association for American Studies, Pamphlet 2, 1979.

United States Official Postal Guide 6 (July 1913).

NEWSPAPERS

Akron (OH) *Beacon Journal.* April 4, 1998.

Bath County (VA) *Enterprise News and Herald,* September 20, 1912.

Boston Advertiser. December 10, 1913; October 24, 1914.

Boston Globe. February 11, 1973.

Boston Herald. November 14, 1914.

Boston Record. November 10, 12, 1913.

Chicago Defender. September 27, 1913.

Christian Science Monitor. December 9, 1913.

Cincinnati Union. April 19, 1934.

Crisis. September, November 1912; June–December 1913; January, March–December 1914; January 1915; February 1916; May 1922; July 1932; April 1939. These original issues are accessible and in excellent condition at Harvard University's Widener Library. Also, several undated yet insightful newspaper commentaries regarding Trotter's second meeting with the president appeared in *Crisis* and are used in this book. They are as follows: *New York Express, New Republic, Boston Traveler and Evening Herald, New Haven Register, Rochester Post Express*, New York *Evening Post, Springfield Republican, Des Moines Register Leader, New York Daily Eagle, Syracuse Herald, Meriden* (CT) *Journal, Beaumont* (TX) *Enterprise, Macon* (GA) *Telegraph, New Orleans Times Picayune, Shreveport Sunday Caucasian, Savannah Morning News, El Paso Times, Lexington* (KY) *Herald*, Louisville *Courier-Journal, Birmingham Reporter*, Washington *Bee*, and *Richmond St. Luke Herald*.

Guardian. June 7, October 24, November 11, 13, 15, 22, 28, December 10, 1913; November 12, 21, 28, 1914. In addition, many of the *Guardian* articles used in this book have indecipherable dates. Like the commentaries in *Crisis* regarding Trotter's second meeting with the president, the *Guardian* printed several as well, although the issues I looked at have far fewer examples. This newspaper focused mostly on the response of the white southern press. They are as follows: *Beaumont* (TX) *Enterprise, Macon* (GA) *Telegraph, Shreveport Sunday Caucasian, Savannah Morning News, El Paso Times*, and Louisville *Courier-Journal*.

Louisville *Courier-Journal*. September 20, 1913.

New York Age. September 11, 1913.

New York *Evening Post*. September 9, November 17, 1913.

New York Globe. June 26, 1913.

New York Times. May 4, August 18, 1913; November 13, 1914.

New York World. November 13, 1914.

Philadelphia *Public Ledger*. October 22, 1913.

Richmond *Times-Dispatch*. November 6, 1912.

Washington Herald. May 15, November 16, 1913; December 16, 1914.

Washington Post. March 24, November 9, 1913.

Washington Star. December 9, 1913.

UNPUBLISHED SOURCES

Ballew, Charles LeBron. "Woodrow Wilson and the Negro." M.A. thesis, University of Maryland, 1965.

Bradbury, William C., Jr. "Racial Discrimination in the Federal Service: A Study in the Sociology of Administration." Ph.D. diss., Columbia University, 1952.

Cash, Floris Loretta Barnett. "Womanhood and Protest: The Club Movement Among Black Women, 1892–1922." Ph.D. diss., State University of New York, Stony Brook, 1986.

Hayes, Laurence J.W. "The Negro Federal Government Worker, 1883–1938." M.A. thesis, Howard University Graduate School, 1941.

Will and Codicil of Thomas Jefferson, March 16 and 17, 1826, MSS 514, Thomas Jefferson Collection, University of Virginia, Charlottesville, VA.

Worthy, Ruth. "A Negro in Our History: William Monroe Trotter, 1872–1934." M.A. thesis, Columbia University, 1952.

INDEX

Page numbers in italics indicate illustrations

AAC. *See* Afro-American Council
Addams, Jane, 157
Advertiser (Montgomery) (newspaper), 25
Advocate (Piedmont) (newspaper), 135
African Zion Church, 31
Afro-American Council (AAC), 25
Afro-American League, 25
Agriculture Department, 18
Alabama, 97
Alley Campaign, 64
Alley Improvement Association, 64
Amenia Conference, 204
American Bar Association, 98
American Colonization Association, 135
American Communist Party, 211
A.M.E. Zion Church (Boston), 130–31, 145
Anglo-Saxon superiority, 78, 80
Anti-Defamation League, 205
Antilynching legislation, 25
Appointees, 16; Wilson's, 55–56
Architects Office (Treasury Department), 19, 155
Armenians, genocide of, 88–89(n50)
Army, blacks in, 23
Arthur, Chester, 10, 14
Asbury M.E. Church, 188–89
Asbury, Nettie J., 93
Associated Press, 144; on NAACP segregation report, 157–58
Aswell, J. B., 40
Atlanta, 15, 26
Atlanta Baptist College, 79
Atlantic City, 98
Auchincloss, Louis, 81
Auditors Division, 18, 155

Bagnall, Robert, 203
Baker, Ray Stannard, 65, 87(n31)
Ballew, Charles, 77
Baltimore, 96, 102, 105
Barber, J. Max, 33

Barry, William, 136
Beneficent Congregational Church (Providence), 99
Bennet, Lerone, Jr., 212
Bentley, Charles, 118, 147(n2)
Berea College, 185
Bethlehem African Methodist Episcopal Church (Baltimore), 105
Birth of a Nation (film), 39–40, 76, 128, 212
"Black Belt" district, 16, 202
Black Codes, 80, 200
Black consciousness, 121
Black Nationalist Movement, 204
The Black Worker (Spero and Harris), 3, 16
Blumenthal, Henry, 75, 83
Boston, 161; desegregation activity in, 212–13; mass protest meetings in, 96, 98, 99–100, 145, 189
Boston City Hospital, 212–13
Boston Record (newspaper), 143, 144
Boston Riot, 130–31
Boston School Committee, 7
Boston Suffrage League, 25, 130
Boston Transcript (newspaper), 64
Boston Traveler and Evening Herald (newspaper), 183
Boycotts, 4–5, 28–29, 142
Bradbury, William, Jr., "Racial Discrimination in the Federal Service," 206–7
Brawley, Benjamin, 111
Breckinridge, Desha, 185
Brinkley, Douglas, 199
Brinsmade, Chapin, 168
Brooks, Walter H., 107
Brotherhood of Sleeping Car Porters, 209
Brown, Samuel A., 99
Brownsville (Texas), riot in, 23, 33
Bruce, Roscoe Conkling, 94–95
Buffalo *Informer* (newspaper), 186
Bull Moose Party, 33
Bumstead, Horace, 146, 189

Bureau of Engraving and Printing, 18, 64, 197; lunchroom protests at, 65–66; segregation in, 158, 163–64, 190

Burgess, John, 74

Burleson, Albert, 18–19, 44, 54, 66, 100, 107, 139, *Pl. 3;* NIPL and, 138, 143

Burnings, 24, 25

Burroughs, Nanny, 27, 28, 65, 166

Bryan, William Jennings, 33, 103

Cable, George Washington, 75

California, northern, 96, 100

Calvinists, 122–23

Cambridge Lyceum, 100

Cannibalism, by white mob, 24–25

Cardozo, Frank, 105

Carnegie, Andrew, 74

Cell, John, 13, 74

Chase, Calvin, 55

Chelsea (Mass.), 146

Chicago, 16, 101, 190–91, 211

Chicago Evening Post (newspaper), 91, 95

Chief Clerk's Office (Treasury Department), 155

Chillicothe, 122–23

Chinese, 79, 169

Christianity, 116(n61); social role of, 109–11; Wilson's, 111–12

Churches, 27, 80, 97, 135; meetings in, 4, 97, 98, 99, 101–2, 104, 109, 145, 187–89

Cincinnati, 97–98, 122

City Post Office (Washington, D.C.), 138, 163

City Post Office Annex (Washington, D.C.), 18, 138

Civic organizations, in Washington, D.C., 165–66

Civil rights, 6, 127, 200

Civil Service Act, 10, 11, 12, 14, 207. *See also* U. S. Civil Service Commission

Civil service, 22, 36, 53(n106), 197, 198; employment in, 16–17, 206–7; equal employment in, 14, 202–3

Civil service examinations, 2, 11, 14

Civil Service Law, 11

The Clansman (Dixon), 39, 40

Clapp, Edwin Moses, 98, 154–55, *Pl. 7*

Clarke, Thomas, 162

Cleveland, 101

Cleveland, Grover, 22, 48–49(n41), 121, 160, 176

Cobb, Frank, 183

Cobleigh, Rolfe, 56, 98

Collective organization, 7

Colleges, funding for, 169

Collier's Weekly (newspaper), 95

Colored Women's League of Washington, D.C., 166

Columbus (Ohio), 98

Columbus Avenue A.M.E. Zion Church (Boston), 130–31, 145

Commerce Department, 18

Commission of Southern Universities, 78

Committee of Fifty and More, 108–9

Committee of Forty, 120

Community Church of New York City, 99

Congregational Church, 110

Congregationalist and Christian World (journal), 56, 72–73, 110

Connecticut, 135

Cook, Clark, 211

Coolidge, Calvin, 206

Cope, Edward Drinker, 74

Corruption, in federal hiring practices, 167–68

Crawford, George W., 98

Crisis (journal), 33, 72, 55, 104, 211; DuBois' contributions to, 128, 129, 170; on Wilson's racism, 78, 186

Curley, James M., 133

Current Literature, 166

Curtis, James, 55

Daniels, Josephus, 13, 44

Davenport, Charles, 74

Davis, Arthur, 208

Dead Letter Office, 158, 159

Dean, W. H., 109

Debs, Eugene, 33

Deep South, 199; NAACP in, 96–97

Defender (Chicago) (newspaper), 58, 155

Defense industry, 209

Democratic Caucus, 155

Democratic Fair Play Association (DFPA), 35, 41, 44, 55, 89(n51), 107; membership and goals of, 36–38; James Vardaman and, 42–43

Democratic National Committee, 35

Democratic party, 34; blacks and, 3–4, 20–23, 33, 179; 1912 election, 10, 30–31, 48(n36); segregation and, 12–13

Denver, 100

Department of Labor, 207

Detroit, 101

DFPA. *See* Democratic Fair Play Association

Discrimination, 55, 65, 73, 165, 178, 197, 205, 213; banning, 208–10; boycotts against, 28–29; civil service, 15, 18, 170; by

federal government, 66, 183; Railway Mail Service, 144–45; U.S. Civil Service Commission and, 43, 167
Disempowerment, 28
Disenfranchisement, 1–2; by Republican Party, 30–31
District of Columbia. *See* Washington, D.C.
District of Columbia School Board, 166
Division and Reunion (Wilson), 76–77
Dixon, Frank, 208
Dixon, Thomas, Jr., 22, 70(n26), 140; *The Clansman,* 39, 40; *The Leopard's Spots,* 39
Donahue, Frank J., 136
Dorroh, David Lewis, 121
Douglass, Frederick, 7, 99
DuBois, W. E. B., 7, 14, 15, 26, 33, 35, 43, 55, 56, 61, 66, 72, 82, 111, 118, 120, 127, 161, 170, 199, 204, 211, *Pl. 6;* historical scholarship of, 127–28; and NAACP, 58, 59, 69–70(n25), 104; *The Souls of Black Folk,* 129; and Booker T. Washington, 126, 128
Dunne, Edward F., 146
Dunning, William, 74
Durant, E. F., 23

East St. Louis, 211
Ebeneezer Church, 109
Economic uplift, 82, 127, 199, 201, 202–3
Economics: 79–80
Edison, Thomas, 210
Education, 169; of blacks, 14, 85(n15), 87(n31); NAACP promotion of, 58, 59, 92–93
Eichler, Rabbi, 99, 110
Eighth Report of the Civil Service Commission, 11
Election campaign, 1912: 20–21, 30–31, 34–35, 48(n36), 51(n72), 69(n22), 81, 83, 88–89(n47), 150(n50)
Eliot, Charles, 43, 167
Elites, 39, 78, 119
El Paso Times (newspaper), 185
Emancipation, celebration of, 7
Employees: discrimination against, 17, 144–45, 170; federal politics and, 162–63; segregation information on, 161–62
Employment, 2, 14, 15; discrimination in, 65, 208–9; federal, 2, 3, 11, 12, 47(n30), 48–49(n41), 206–7
Enterprise (Beaumont)(newspaper), 184
Episcopal Church, 110
Equality, 4, 7, 14, 25, 26–27, 32, 127, 154–55, 170, 200, 201, 215(n20)

Ethnic groups: prejudice against, 78–79
Eugenics, 75
Europeans, southern, 169
Examining Division, 18, 63
Executive branch, 2, 11–12
"Executive Committee of the Illinois Commission on Half Century Anniversary of Freedom," 146
Executive Order 8802, 208, 209–10
Executive orders: FDR's, 208, 209–10; Wilson's, 156

Fair Employment Practice Committee (FEPC), 207, 209
Falconer, Jacob, 100
Faneuil Hall, 99–100, 189
Federal contracts, antidiscrimination laws and, 209–10
Federal Jim Crow, 1; challenging, 4, 5–6, 189–90; economic advancement and, 202–3; executive department and, 11–12; investigations of, 156–57, 196–97; support for, 64, 70(n26), 198–99; William Trotter's actions against, 130, 137–38
Federation of Citizens Association, 165
Felton, Rebecca, 38–39
FEPC. *See* Fair Employment Practice Committee
Ferguson, G. O., 74
Ferguson, Leroy, 126
Fifteenth Amendment, 26, 59
Fifteenth Street Presbyterian Church (Washington, D.C.), 110
First Baptist Church (Tacoma), 100
Fitzgerald, John F. (Honey Fitz), 100, 137
Foraker, Joseph Benson, 23, 98, 154
Fortune, T. Thomas, 25
Foss, Eugene, 31, 98, 136
Fossett, Elizabeth Ann, 123
Fossett, Joseph, 123
Fourth Annual Report (NAACP), 104, 108–9
Fourth Auditor Division (Treasury Department), 138
Fourteenth Amendment, 59
Fox, Stephen P., 123
Frazier, E. Franklin, 29
Freedmen's Bureau, 128
Freeman (Indianapolis) (newspaper), 91
Furniss, Henry W., 55

Gaines, Kevin, 111, 201, 202
Galton, Francis, 75
Gardner, Augustus Peabody, 98

Garrison, Bessie, 110
Garrison, Francis Jackson, 34, 94
Garrison, William Lloyd, 7, 60, 69(n24), 99, 125
Garvey, Marcus, 118, 204, 205, 213
Gavit, John P., 43
Genocide, against Armenians, 88–89(n50)
Georgia Equal Rights Convention, 26
Ghana, 211
Gladstone, William E., 80
Glenn, A. L., 3
Government Printing Office, 18, 19, 61
Graves, Letitia A., 28
Great Depression, 211
Greensboro Herald, 91
Grimke, Archibald, 104, 107, 160, 164, 170, 198, Pl. 11; on civil service hiring, 167–68; informants to, 162, 163, 165; "Why Disfranchisment Is Bad," 161
Grimke, Francis, 110, 111, 112
Guardian (Boston), 126, 130, 132, 134, 142, 143, 162, 185, 186, 188, 213; on federal Jim Crow, 190, 196
Gunner, Byron, 112, 136, 176, 189
Gunner, Cicely, 95, 176

Haiti, minister to, 55, 103, 133
Hale, Grace Elizabeth, 28, 75
Hallinan, Charles, 91, 95, 101
Hamlin, Charles S., 197
Hampton (industrial school), 93, 127
Harding, Warren G., 206, 215(n20)
Harlan, John Marshall, 185
Harper, louis, 14
Harper's Weekly, 81, 95
Harris, Abram, The Black Worker, 3, 16
Harrop, Roy M., 36, 37
Hart, Albert Bushnell, 85–86(n17)
Harvard University, 43, 124, 128, 160, 213
Harvey, George, 81
Hayes, Laurence, 17, 207
Hayes, Rutherford B., 21
Haynes, T. L., 165–66
Heckscher, August, 78
Hemings, Burwell, 123
Hemings, Eston, 123
Hemings, John, 123
Hemings, Madison, 123
Hemings, Mary, 123
Hemings, Sally, 123
Hendricks, Thomas, 22
Herald (Richmond St. Luke)(newspaper), 135, 186

Herbert, Hilary A., 22
Hershaw, Lafayette, 109, 162
Higgenbotham, Evelyn Brooks, 28, 111, 140
Hill, Leslie Pinckney, 93
Hillsdale Citizens Association, 146
Hiring practices, corrupt, 167–68
Historical dialectic process, racial advancement and, 199–200
A History of the American People (Wilson), 79, 80
Holmes, John Haynes, 99, 107
Holmes, William F., 41
Hopkins, Charlotte, 36, 63–64, 65, 66, 165
Horner, R. R., 146
Hose, Sam, 24, 25
House Committee on Labor, 207
House of Representatives, 2, 10
Houston, 15
Howard University, 102
Hyde Park, 121, 161

Illiteracy, and letter writing campaign, 91–92
Immigrants, immigration: non-white, 78–79; restrictions on, 169
Indianapolis, 101
Indian Hindus, 78–79
Industrial education, 93
Interdenominational Ministers' Union of Greater Boston, 189
Interior Department, 18, 56
Intermarriage, 60, 69(n24), 169
Internal Revenue Service, 18

Jackson, Robert R., 14
Jacksonville, 15
Japanese, 79, 169
Jefferson, Thomas, 123
Jews, discrimination against, 99, 205, 215(n18)
Jobs, federal, 2, 206–7
Johnson, Henry Lincoln, 16
Johnson, James Weldon, 204, 206
Journal of Negro History, 204
Judiciary, 56, 74
Justice, Wilson's view of, 81–82

Kansas City, 101
Kellogg, Charles Flint, 59
Kelly, Florence, 99
Kentucky, 185
King, Coretta Scott, 97
Kram, Charles, 158, 198

Ku Klux Klan (KKK), 39, 80, 205
Kusmer, Kenneth, 205

Labor Department, 18
Labor unions, 3, 43
La Follette, Bella C., 65
LaFollette, Robert M., 154
La Follette's Weekly Magazine, 21, 65, 95
Lane, Franklin, 66
Leadership, 201; black women's, 26–28,
   50(n57); Ida Wells-Barnett on, 141–42
The Leopard's Spots (Dixon), 39
"A Letter to President Wilson on Federal Race
   Discrimination," 66
Letter writing campaigns: NAACP and, 90–92,
   95, 96, 97–98, 100, 113(n5), 132–33;
   NIPL and, 136–37
Lewis, David Levering, 26, 182
Lexington Herald (newspaper), 92, 185
Liberia, minister to, 55, 56
Library of Congress, 198
Lincoln, Abraham, 7
Link, Arthur, 10, 65
Little Rock, 143
Livingston College, 145
Lodge, Henry Cabot, 150(n50)
Logan, Rayford, 28, 121
Lorance, John, 144, 196
Louisville Courier-Journal (newspaper), 185
Lowell, A. Lawrence, 213
Lower class, 29
Lunchrooms, 158–59; segregated, 65–66, 163–
   64, 198

McAdoo, William Gibbs, 18, 20, 34, 40, 44,
   58, 69(n22), 100, 138, 152–53(n79), 170,
   197, *Pl. 4;* NAACP and, 66, 164; protest
   speeches against, 102, 105; and segregation,
   57, 107–8, 139, 140, 156
McCombs, William, 34, 69(n22)
Macon Telegraph (newspaper), 184
McPherson, James M., 61, 94
McVeagh, Franklin, 57
Madagascar, 56
Madden, Martin, 16
March on Washington (MOW), 209
Marine Hospital Service building, 18, 19, 190
Marketing, of black stereotypes, 75
Marriage, interracial, 2, 60, 76, 169
Marriage laws, 2, 60, 169
Martin, Ernest D., 36
Martin, Granville, 131

Mason, M.C.B., 97–98
Massachusetts, 35, 135. *See also* Boston
Mass meetings, 4; NAACP, 96–101, 104–5,
   107; NIERL, 186–89; NIPL, 135, 145–46
M.E. Church, and Women's Home Missionary
   Society, 110
Meier, August, 64
Mere Literature and Other Essays (Wilson), 80
Metropolitan African Methodist Episcopal
   Church (Washington, D.C.), 104
Middle class, black, 14–15, 17, 29, 202
Middleton, Phillip, 75
Milgrim, David, 75
Milholland, John E., 58
Militancy, 202
Ministers, 186. *See also* Churches
Minorities, prejudice against, 78–79
Miscegenation, 2, 76, 86(n26)
Miscellaneous Division, 18, 63
Mississippi, 41
Mississippi Constitutional Convention, 13
Mobile, 15
Mob rule, white, 24–25, 200, 203–4
Montgomery, 4, 15
Monticello, 123
Moore, Fred R., 34
Morality, 74, 75, 201
Morehouse, Henry L., 79
Morehouse College, 79
Moskowitz, Henry, 204
Moton, Robert, 186
Mound Bayou (Miss.), 135
MOW. *See* March on Washington
Murray, Freeman, 129–30, 132, 133, 136,
   146, 196
Murraye, R. A., 66
Mu-So-Lit Club, 189
Mutilations, 24

NAACP. *See* National Association for the
   Advancement of Colored People
NACW. *See* National Association of Colored
   Women
Nail, John, 91
Nation, 210
National Afro-American Council, 58
National Alliance of Postal Employees, 3, 14
National Association for the Advancement of
   Colored People (NAACP), 5, 26, 29, 31,
   49(n54), 56, 58, 69–70(n25), 82, 154,
   160, 168, 192, 196, 197, 203, 204; AP
   report on, 157–58; Committee of Fifty and

More, 108–9; education promotion by, 92–93; and employment discrimination, 208–9; and federal Jim Crow, 62–63; investigations by, 162, 163, 164–65; letter writing campaign of, 90–92, 95, 113(n5), 132–33; mass meetings, 96–102, 104–5, 107; membership in, 59–60, 205; and NIPL, 120, 135, 145; protests by, 66–67, 72; on segregation as subordination, 61–62; *Segregation in the Government Department at Washington,* 156–57; and William Trotter, 118, 120–21, 131–32; and Booker T. Washington, 93–94; and Ida Wells-Barnett, 210–11; women in, 27–28, 50(n57); and World War I, 169, 170–71

National Association of Colored Women (NACW), 27, 28, 29, 58–59, 65, 142, 145, 146, 166, 169, 205

National Association of Postal Employees, 205

National Citizens' Rights Association, 25

National Civil Service Commission (NCSC), 167

National Civil Service Reform League (NCSRL), 36

National Colored Democratic League (NCDL), 31

National Council of Congregational Churches, 110

National Equal Rights League, 91, 211

National Federation of Post Office Clerks, in Seattle, 162–63

National Independent Equal Rights League (NIERL), 213; failure of, 191–92; mass meetings of, 186–89; meeting with Wilson, 175–80, 181–82; and Negro Fellowship League, 190–91; press response to, 182–86

National Independent Political League (NIPL), 5, 9–10, 26, 29, 31, 32, 49(n54), 94, 112, 113(n5), 130, 143, 162, 196; mass meetings of, 145–46; meeting with Wilson, 136–37, 138–40, 141–42; and NAACP, 120, 132; petition crusade of, 133–36, 175; William Trotter and, 117–18, 126

Nationalism, black, 203

National Negro Business League, 127

National Negro Press Association, 95

National Negro Wilson League, 30

"National petition Against Jim Crow and Color Segregation by the Federal Government," 134, 137

National Race Commission, 82

National Training School for Women and Girls, 166

National Urban League (NUL), 105, 209

National Woman American Suffrage Association, 101

Navy Department, 18, 19, 155, 190

NCDL. *See* National Colored Democratic League

NCSC. *See* National Civil Service Commission

NCSRL. *See* National Civil Service Reform League

Negro American Political League, 117–18, 120

Negro Fellowship League (NFL), 190–91, 211

Nelson, J. A., 100

Nerney, May Childs, 103, 161, 183, 197, 198, 210; and Charlotte Hopkins, 63–64; investigations by, 156–57, 158, 164–65; NAACP and, 58, 62, 63, 95, 104; *Segregation in the Government Departments at Washington,* 156–59, 160, 172(n10)

NESL. *See* New England Suffrage League

New England Suffrage League (NESL), 25–26, 58

New Freedom, 3, 30, 89(n49)

New Haven, 96, 98

New Haven Register, 72, 183

New Iberia, 176

New Jersey, 35, 81, 101, 135

New Orleans Times Picayune (newspaper), 184

New Republic (newspaper), 183

Newspapers, 91, 97, 142; and NAACP segregation report, 157–60, 172(n10); NILP petition and, 135, 143; response to NIERL-Trotter meeting, 182–86. *See also by name*

New York (state), 101, 135

New York Age (newspaper), 34, 64, 91, 130, 204

New York City, 35, 96, 99

New York Evening Post (newspaper), 94, 95, 155, 159, 184

New York Express (newspaper), 183

New York Herald (newspaper), 143

New York Times (newspaper), 55, 64, 92, 94, 182

New York World (newspaper), 183

NFL. *See* Negro Fellowship League

Niagara Movement, 26, 29, 58, 127, 130

NIERL. *See* National Independent Equal Rights League

Nineteenth Street Baptist Church (Washington, D.C.), 145

NIPL. *See* National Independent Political League

North American Review, 95

North Carolina, 135

Northeastern Federation of Women's Clubs, 95, 176

Northeast Washington Citizen's Association, 146–47
Northwest, Indian Hindus in, 78–79
NUL. *See* National Urban League

Odd Fellows Journal, 134
Odd Fellows Lodge, 99
Officeholders, 2, 55
Ogden, 100
Ohio, 101. *See also* Cincinnati; Columbus
"An Open Appeal to President Wilson" (Trotter), 212
Ovington, Mary White, 144, 204

Page, Thomas Nelson, 74
Palmetto (Ga.), 24
Pan-African Congress, 211
Panama Canal Service, 168
Paris Peace Conference, 129, 211, 212
Park Street Church (Boston), 98
Patillo, John, 30
Patronage, Wilsons' lack of, 12, 35, 55
Patterson, A. E., 22
Pennsylvania, 101
Pension Bureau, 159
Peters, Andrew, 135, 136
Petitions: NAACP, 96, *106;* NIPL, 133–35, 175
Philadelphia Bulletin (newspaper), 183
Philippine School Service, 168
Phillips, Wendell, 7, 99
Phobia, racial, 38–41
Photographs, job applications and, 167–68, 197
Pillsbury, Albert, 98, 183
Planet (Richmond) (newspaper), 135
Plantation life, romance of, 77
Plessy v. Ferguson, 1, 25, 185
Political machines, Democratic, 21
Portland (Maine), 96, 98, 100
Postal clerks, discrimination against, 54–55
Post Office, Postal Department, 20; employment in, 14, 15, 18–19; workplace segregation in, 11, 17–18, 54–55, 63, 108, 138, 139, 156, 158–59, 190, 197–98
Post Office Building, 18
Prejudices, 110; Woodrow Wilson's, 72–73, 78–79
Presbyterian Church, 122
Presbyterian Church of the South, 79
Priest, Oscar de, 111
Princeton University, black exclusion from, 77–78

Progressive Era, 7, 29, 74, 110, 111; racism in, 6, 39, 53(n109), 205
"Prohibition of Use of Towels by More Than One Person," 156
Protestant Episcopal Church (Richmond), 74
Protests, 7, 65; against Jim Crow, 4, 49(n47); letter writing campaigns as, 90–92, 95, 96, 97–98, 100, 113(n5), 132–33
Providence, 96, 99
Puttkammer, Charles, 126, 130

Quincy (Ill.), 101

Racial advancement, 199–200
"Racial Discrimination in the Federal Service" (Bradbury), 206–7
Racial superiority, whites and, 73, 74–75, 76–77, 80, 200–201
Racism, 2, 5, 85–86(nn17, 26), 88–89(n50), 201–2, 203–4; phobia against blacks and, 38–40; Progressive Era, 6, 53(n109), 205; southern, 13, 75–77, 88(n36); James Vardaman's, 41–43; of Treasury Department officials, 57–58; Wilson's, 78–79, 80–81, 84–85(nn9, 12)
Railway Mail Association, 43
Railway Mail Service (RMS), 14, 15, 18, 22; discrimination in, 144–45; segregation in, 19, 44, 54–55, 143
Randolph, A. Philip, 208–9
Randolph, Edmund, 57
Ransom, Reverdy, 127
Rape, fear of, 40
Rauschenbusch, Walter, 109
Reconstruction, 2, 77, 79, 85–86(n17), 200; historical revision of, 127–28
Redfield, William, 66, 144
Register Leader (Des Moines) (newspaper), 184
Registry Division (Treasury Department), 18, 158
Reid, Ira De A., 6
Religion, 116(n61); role of, 109–11; and support of Wilson, 111–12
Republican Party, 150(n50), 206; blacks and, 21–22, 122; disenfranchisement and, 30–31
Restrooms, segregated, 19, 56–57, 139, 155, 190
Retrogressionism, 73; Joseph Tucker and, 74–75
Richmond, 4–5, 74
Ricks, E. E., 175, 176
Riots, 211; Atlanta, 26; Boston, 130–31; Brownsville, 23; after Washington's speech, 128

RMS. *See* Railway Mail Service
Rogers, John, 135
Room 629, 108
Roosevelt, Franklin D., 208, 209
Roosevelt, Theodore, 10, 36; federal Jim Crow of, 11–12; and 1912 election campaign, 20, 22, 30; and Twenty-fifth Infantry, 23, 33
Root, Elihu, 94
Ross, James, 186
Roxbury (Mass.), 213
Rudwick, Elliot, 64
Russell, Charles Edward, 101, 197

St. Louis, 14, 101
St. Mark's Guild, 99
Salaries, 15, 207
Salem, Dorothy, 27
Salisbury (N.C.), NIPL money for, 145–46
San Francisco, 79
Sanitation, 18, 20
Santo Domingo, ministers to, 103, 160
Saturday Evening Post, 95
Savannah Morning News (newspaper), 185
Savannah Tribune (newspaper), 96, 182
Sayre, Jessie W., 65
Schools, 25
Seattle, 28, 100, 162–63
Second Baptist Church (Washington, D.C.), 187
Segregation, 1, 2, 18, 71(n44), 143, 198–99, 208, 211; AP report on, 157–58; Democratic Fair Play Association, 36–38; employee opposition to, 161–62; federal employment, 11, 17, 45(n11); McAdoo's views of, 107–8; NAACP membership and, 59–60; NAACP response to, 62–63, 66–67; postal employees, 54–55; press opposition to, 185–86; promotion of, 35–36, 43; protests against, 4, 49(n47), 138–39, 144–46, 212–13; southern Democrats and, 12–13; as subordination, 61–62; in universities, 77–78; Wilsons' views on, 73, 88(n46), 103, 133–34, 183; workplace, 19–20, 40–41, 44, 155, 163–64, 190, 197–98; in Treasury Department, 56–58, 63–64
Segregation in the Government Departments at Washington (Nerney), 156–58, 172(n10)
Self-determination, 29, 58
Senate, 10, 198; black equality and, 154–55
Separate but equal policy, 61
Separatism, 213
Services, segregated, 20
Settlement houses, 59

Sexual imagery, racial phobia and, 40–41, 43
Seymor, W. W., 100
Shaler, Nathaniel, 74
"Shall the Negro Rule" (Vardaman), 41, *42*
Shipyards, southern, 209
Shreveport Sunday Caucasian (newspaper), 184
Sinclair, William, 136, 145
Sit-ins, at Bureau of Engraving and Printing, 65
Slavery, slaves, 77, 122, 123
Smith, Hoke, 13, 38, 83, 88–89(n47), 121, 169
Smith, Laura, 4
Smith, Madison R., 55
Smith-Lever Bill, 169
Social activism, 27, 127, 143
Social class, 29
Social gospel movement, 109–10
Social relations, interracial, 65
Soldiers, and Brownsville riot, 23
Sosna, Morton, 3
The Souls of Black Folk (DuBois), 129
South, 1, 24, 57, 59, 79, 87(n31), 88(nn36, 47); federal contracts and, 209–10; press response to Trotter in, 184–86; racism in, 13, 75–77, 80–81, 206; segregation in, 198–99; and Wilson's election, 9–10
Southern University Commission on Race Problems, 88(n36)
Spencer, Maurice, 129–30, 136, 145, 176, 187
Spero, Sterling, *The Black Worker,* 3, 16
Spingarn, Arthur, 110
Spingarn, Joel, 58, 110, 131, 132, 210; and protest meetings, 99, 101, 102
Spokane, 100
Spooner, John, 23
Springfield Republican (newspaper), 184, 196
State Department, 18
Stephens, Alexander H., 144, 145
Stereotypes, racial, 75, 76, 82–83
Steward, Maude Trotter, 213
Storey, Moorfield, 36, 58, 66, 99, 132, 157, 167
Stratton, John Roach, 74
Street cars, segregation on, 4, 169
Students, NAACP and, 102
Subordination, segregation as, 61–62
Suffrage, 13, 59, 151(n65); women's, 169–70
Supervisors, black, 16
Supply Division (Post Office Department), 138
Swain, B. W., 99

Tacoma, 96, 100
Taft, William Howard, 10, 36, 59; and 1912 election campaign, 20, 22, 30, 33

Talladega (Ala.), 97
Tammany Hall, 33
Tennessee, transportation segregation in, 4, 140–41
Tennessee Supreme Court, 141
Terrell, Mary Church, 29, 58, 166
Terrell, Robert, 23, 56, 111
Thacher, Thomas, 135, 136, 146
Thernstrom, Stephan, 210
Third Annual Report (NAACP), 93
Thornton, B. T., 127
Thornton, Montrose, 189
Tillman, Pitchfork Ben, 13, 38, 83
Todd, Laurence, 168
Toilets. See Restrooms
Topeka, 96, 100–101
Tourgee, Albion W., 25
Trains, segregation on, 4
Transportation, in Tennessee, 4, 26, 140–41
Treasury Department: departmental Jim Crow
    in, 17, 18; discrimination in, 145, 170;
    racism in, 57–58; segregation in, 11, 19, 20,
    40–41, 56–58, 63–64, 73, 102, 138, 139,
    144, 155–56, 158, 159, 163, 190
Trolleys, boycotts of, 4
Trotter, Geraldine (Deenie), 142, 212
Trotter, James, 122
Trotter, Letitia, 122
Trotter, Virginia Issacs, 122
Trotter, William Monroe, 5–6, 25, 43, 54, 91,
    92, 101, 111, 112, 145, 161, 183, 197,
    199, Pl. 5; activism of, 128–29, 130–31,
    144, 212–13; career of, 121–22; in Chicago,
    190–91; and federal Jim Crow, 129–30,
    137–38; leadership of, 29, 118–19; lineage
    of, 123–24; and NAACP, 120–21, 131–33;
    and Niagara Movement, 26, 76; and NIERL
    meeting, 178–80, 181–82, 184–86; and
    NIPL, 117–18, 135–36; notoriety of, 186–
    87, 190; "An Open Appeal to President
    Wilson," 212; speeches of, 187–88, 189,
    190–91; and Booker T. Washington, 124–
    25; and Woodrow Wilson, 31–32, 73, 119–
    20, 136–37, 138–40, 143, 176–77
Tucker, Joseph Louis, 74–75
Tumulty, Joseph, 76, 133, 177, 181, 183,
    194(n31)
Turkey, Armenian genocide in, 88–89(n50)
Tuskegee Institute, 93, 127, 161, 201
Twelfth Baptist Church (Boston), 189
Twenty-fifth Infantry, 23, 33
Tyler, Ralph, 16, 162

Union (Cincinnati) (newspaper), 162
Union College, 102
Unitarian Church, 110
Unitary Conference of Middle States and Canada,
    146
United Negro Democracy of New Jersey, 32
United Negro Improvement Association, 205
U.S. Civil Service Commission (USCSC), 10–
    11, 43; and hiring practices, 167–68. See
    also Civil service; Civil service examinations
U.S. Congress, 1–2, 10, 13, 154–55, 198
U.S. Supreme Court, 1, 74, 200
United Negro Improvement Association, 118
Uplift organizations, 29
USCSC. See U.S. Civil Service Commission

Vardaman, James, 13, 23, 38, 42–43, 81, 83,
    85(n15), 121, 169; "Shall the Negro Rule,"
    41
Versailles Conference. See Paris Peace Conference
Villard, Oswald Garrison, 30, 32, 34, 40, 43,
    66, 67, 125–26, 132, 157, 183, 206, 210,
    Pl. 9; at Faneuil Hall meeting, 99–100;
    leadership of, 60–61, 93; and NAACP, 58,
    69–70(n25); and Nerney's report, 160, 164;
    and 1912 campaign, 35, 69(n22); and
    Booker T. Washington, 94–95; and
    Woodrow Wilson, 73, 82, 102–4, 105,
    140, 184
Violence, against blacks, 13, 15, 24–25, 88–
    89(n50), 200, 203–4
Virginia, 35, 135. See also Richmond
Vocational training, 92–93
Voluntary organizations, 26–27

Wages, 15, 207
Wald, Lillian D., 157
Waldron, J. Milton, 31, 64, 82, 112, 160; and
    1912 campaign, 34–35
Walker, Thomas, 136, 176, 187
Walling, William English, 120, 204
Walsh, David, 136
Walters, Alexander, 31, 33, 145–46, 152–
    53(n79)
War Department, 18, 190
Warren, Francis H., 118
Washington, Booker T., 23, 26, 49(n54), 73,
    92, 113–14(n19), 126–27, 128, 134, 142,
    161, 184, 187, 199, 201, 202, Pl. 8; and
    NAACP, 93–94; Trotter's opposition to,
    124–25, 130
Washington, George, Wilson's biography of, 77

Washington, D.C., 2, 18, 35, 56, 64, 135, 173(n34), 207; church meetings in, 104, 109, 145; civic organization meeting in, 165–66; mass protest meetings, in, 102, 187; NAACP in, 94–95, 96, 160

Washington Bee (newspaper), 168

Washington Evening Times (newspaper), 187

Washington Post (newspaper), 143

Washington Star (newspaper), 162

Waterson, Henry, 185

Watson, Tom, 38, 83, 88–89(n47), 121

Wells-Barnett, Ida, 4, 25, 120, 166, 175, 190, 210–11, 212, *Pl. 10;* activism of, 140–41, 145, 191; leadership of, 27, 28, 29; and Wilson, 141–42

White, Walter, 209

White Railway Workers Union, 89(n51)

White supremacy, 73–74, 80, 176, 200–201; and Democratic Fair Play Association, 35–36; and racial phobia, 38–40

"Why Disfranchisement Is Bad" (Grimke), 161

Wilberforce (Ohio), 146

Williamson, Joel, 38

Williams, John Skelton, 56–57, 144, 145, 155, *Pl. 4*

Wilmeth, James, 56, 108, 170

Wilson, Butler, 101

Wilson, Edith, 76

Wilson, Ellen, 36, 70–71(n37), 166, 177, *Pl. 2;* workplace reform and, 64–65

Wilson, Emmet, 41

Wilson, Jessie Woodrow, 122

Wilson, Joseph Ruggles, 79

Wilson, Margaret, 165–66

Wilson, Mary, 27, 58, 109; speaking tour of, 101–2

Wilson, Woodrow, 2, 36, *Pl. 1;* and *Birth of a Nation,* 39–40; black support for, 3–4, 12, 23, 30–33, 48(n36), 51(n79), 81; Christianity of, 111–12; *Division and Reunion,* 76–77; election campaign, 9–10, 20–21, 34–35, 51(n72), 69(n12); *A History of the American People,* 79, 80; on justice, 81–82; *Mere Literature and Other Essays,* 80; NIERL meeting and, 175–80; NIPL meeting, 136–37, 138–40, 141–42, 143; opposition to, 187–88; prejudices of, 72–73; racial views of, 75, 78, 82–83, 84–85(nn9, 12), 88(nn36, 46), 90(n51); William Monroe Trotter and, 5–6, 119–20, 176–77; on segregation, 20, 61, 70(n26), 133–34, 155–56, 183; and racial violence, 88–89(n50); and Villard, 102–4

Wolgemuth, Kathleen, 6, 110, 113(n5), 197

Women, 111; employment of, 70–71(n37); and equal rights organizations, 26–27; in NAACP leadership, 27–28, 50(n57); suffrage for, 169–70; workplace discrimination against, 64–65

Women's Baptist Convention, 59

Women's clubs, 101–2

Women's Home Missionary Society (M.E. Church), 110

Woodson, Lewis, 122

Woodrow, Thomas, 122–23

Woodward, C. Vann, 13

Woolley, Celia Parker, 110

Woolley, Robert, 56, 57, 58, 108, 139, 156, 170

Working conditions: dangerous, 18, 20; reform of, 64–65

Workplace, 108; segregation in, 19–20, 37–38, 40–41, 43, 44, 63, 155, 163–64

World War I, 168–69, 170–71, 210

Yazoo (Miss.), 15

Young Men's Hebrew Association (Chelsea, Mass.), 146

Zion Church, 99

Printed in the United States
69803LV00006B/217-222